Bahar Başer is Associate Professor at the Centre for Trust, Peace and Social Relations. She is also an associate research fellow at the Security Institute for Governance and Leadership in Africa (SIGLA), Stellenbosch University, South Africa and a visiting fellow at Tampere Peace Research Institute (TAPRI), Tampere University, Finland. She is the author of "Diasporas and Homeland Conflicts: A Comparative Perspective (Routledge, 2015) and she has numerous articles on ethnic and migration studies with a specific focus on Middle Eastern diasporas. She has a PhD from the European University Institute, Florence, Italy.

Paul T. Levin is the founding Director of the Stockholm University Institute for Turkish Studies (SUITS) and Director of the Consortium for European Symposia on Turkey (CEST). He is an Associate Researcher at the Swedish Institute for International Affairs, a Research Fellow at the Swedish Research Institute in Istanbul, and a member of the International Advisory Board of the journal *Turkish Studies*. The author of *Turkey and the European Union: Christian and Secular Images of Islam* (2011) and numerous articles on Turkish affairs and international politics, Paul is a Docent in International Relations and received his Ph.D from the School of International Relations at the University of Southern California, USA. He lives in Stockholm, Sweden.

'Turkey is the largest source country of immigration in Europe and Sweden is the most inclusive one in terms of immigrants' rights. There are many analyses that compare either countries of origin or destination societies, but few have studied comprehensively how these two contexts interact. Başer and Levin's book provides a fascinating portrait of a deeply heterogeneous category of immigrants and their pathways towards integration in a society that has embraced multiculturalism and equality of opportunity and rights more than others, but that has still struggled with overcoming patterns of social segregation. This is a balanced and insightful book that shatters clichés and raises awareness of the challenges of integration for both immigrants and native populations.'

Rainer Bauböck, Professor of Social and Political Theory, European University Institute, Florence

'This volume offers a richness of perspectives on a heterogeneous migrant diaspora from a homeland in social and political upheaval and their history and present in a country experiencing a confounding transformation of its once exceptional politics of integration.'

Carl-Ulrik Schierup, Professor, Director of The Institute for Research on Migration, Ethnicity and Society (REMESO), Linköping University, Sweden

'Migration and integration are part of life itself. A reality best explained when seen from different angles. This book does not offer any simple answers, but it gives us valuable facts, background and exciting stories about a migration that has formed Sweden and its new inhabitants.'

Jens Orback, Former Minister of Integration and secretary General of the Olof Palme International Centre

MIGRATION FROM TURKEY TO SWEDEN

Integration, Belonging and Transnational Community

Edited by
BAHAR BAŞER
AND
PAUL T. LEVIN

I.B. TAURIS
LONDON • NEW YORK • OXFORD • NEW DELHI • SYDNEY

I.B. TAURIS
Bloomsbury Publishing Plc
50 Bedford Square, London, WC1B 3DP, UK
1385 Broadway, New York, NY 10018, USA
29 Earlsfort Terrace, Dublin 2, Ireland

BLOOMSBURY, I.B. TAURIS and the I.B. Tauris logo
are trademarks of Bloomsbury Publishing Plc

First published in Great Britain 2017
Paperback edition first published 2021

A catalogue record for this book is available from the British Library.

A full CIP record is available from the Library of Congress

ISBN: HB: 978-1-7845-3869-9
PB: 978-0-7556-4353-0
ePDF: 978-1-7867-3245-3
eBook: 978-1-7867-2245-4

Series: Library of Modern Turkey, Volume 32

Typeset in Stone Serif by OKS Prepress Services, Chennai, India

To find out more about our authors and books visit
www.bloomsbury.com and sign up for our newsletters.

For my beloved sister Burçe Başer – BB
For my children A, I. and J. – PTL

CONTENTS

LIST OF ILLUSTRATIONS

Graphs

Figures

Tables

NOTES ON CONTRIBUTORS

Idris Ahmedi is a lecturer at the Department of Security, Strategy and Leadership, Swedish Defence University. Prior to this, he was a senior lecturer at the Department of Political Science, Stockholm University. He has also been a visiting scholar at the Department of Government, Georgetown University. His research interests span a wide range of topics including international politics, American foreign policy towards the Middle East, and Kurdish politics.

Altuğ Akın is Associate Professor and Rector's academic advisor at the Izmir University of Economics, Turkey. Akın's research focus is mainly about broadly defined communication/media practices that extend beyond national borders and scales. In this context, Turkish media experience – particularly in relation to Europe and the Middle East – constitutes the core of his research activities. He completed his doctoral studies in audio-visual communication at the Autonomous University of Barcelona (UAB), Spain; and masters' studies in journalism at the Stockholm University and in information systems at the Royal Institute of Technology (KTH), Sweden. Parallel to his academic career, Akın has contributed to several media outlets, including Swedish Public Service Radio (SR) and the BBC World Service Turkish Section, where he worked as a journalist. He currently teaches at the Department of Media and Communication at Izmir University of Economics, practises freelance journalism, and translates literature from Spanish to Turkish.

Yasemin Akiş Kalaylıoğlu is Research Assistant in the Department of Sociology at the Middle East Technical University. Previously she has attended Stockholm University, Oxford University and the University of California, Berkeley, as a Visiting Academic for her doctoral studies. She has recently completed her PhD Dissertation which focuses on Documented Iranian Migrants in Ankara, Turkey, in terms of their 'Different Capital Accumulations and Status Passages'. She has published in the fields of international migration, gender and refugee studies.

Memet Aktürk-Drake is an affiliated researcher at Vrije Universiteit Brussel and Stockholm University, Sweden. He is a linguist with a PhD in bilingualism from Stockholm University. His main research interest has been the effects of language contact on Turkish. He has also written on historical and contemporary language diversity in Turkey, especially in Istanbul. His work has been published in international peer-reviewed journals such as *Turkic Languages*, *Lingua* and the *International Journal of Bilingualism*.

Bahar Başer is a research fellow at the Centre for Trust, Peace and Social Relations, Coventry University. She is an associate research fellow at the Security Institute for Governance and Leadership in Africa (SIGLA), Faculty of Military Science at Stellenbosch University in South Africa, funded by the National Research Foundation. She completed her PhD in Social and Political Sciences at the European University Institute in Florence, Italy. Başer's research interests include ethno-national conflicts and political violence, conflict resolution, third party mediation, migration and diaspora studies. Başer is the author of *Diasporas and Homeland Conflicts* (2015) and has various publications in peer-reviewed academic journals such as *Terrorism and Political Violence*; *Studies in Conflict and Terrorism*; *Ethnopolitics* and *Middle Eastern Journal of Culture and Communication*.

Mahir Kalaylıoğlu is Research Assistant at the Middle East Technical University, Department of Sociology. He has recently finished his PhD dissertation, which studies the political discourse of Turkey's ruling party, the Justice and Development Party, from a discourse analytical perspective. His research interests include political sociology, post-structuralism, discourse theory and psychoanalysis. He has been a visiting researcher at Stockholm University and the University of Essex, Department of Government, as part of his doctoral studies.

Paul T. Levin is the founding Director of the Stockholm University Institute for Turkish Studies (SUITS). He has published in the fields of international relations, Turkish studies, and public administration and is the author of *Turkey and the European Union: Christian and Secular Images of Islam* (2011). Before assuming his current position, he served as Program Director for Governance and Management Training, and taught International Relations at the Department of Economic History, both at Stockholm University, and was a recurring guest lecturer at Oxford University's Programmes in Leadership and Public Policy. A frequent commentator on Turkish affairs in Swedish and international media, he has been invited to give lectures in Turkey, China, the USA, Iran, Poland and elsewhere. He received his PhD from the School of International Relations at the University of Southern California in 2007, after earning an MA in Political Science also at USC.

Aryo Makko is a Postdoctoral Researcher and Lecturer at Stockholm University and a Visiting Scholar in the Cold War Studies Program at Harvard's Davis Center for Russian and Eurasian Studies. He has co-edited *The Assyrian Heritage: Threads of Continuity and Influence* (2012) and published articles in journals such as the *Journal of Cold War Studies*, *Scandinavian Journal of History*, and *Diplomacy & Statecraft*, among others.

Öncel Naldemirci received his PhD in sociology from the University of Gothenburg in 2013. His interests include migration, aging, sociology of emotions, health and care. He has done fieldwork with Turkish migrants in Sweden for his thesis, 'Caring (in) Diaspora: Aging and caring experiences of older Turkish migrants in a Swedish context'. He is currently a research fellow in the Department of Sociology and Work Science, University of Gothenburg and his recent work focuses on the models of person-centred care.

Mari Toivanen is an Academy of Finland Postdoctoral Researcher (2015–18) at the University of Turku, Finland. She completed a post-doctoral researcher exchange at EHESS (School for Advanced Studies in Social Sciences) in Paris in 2015–16. Her prior research focused on the second generation of Kurdish background in Finland, whereas her current research project deals with the political and civic participation of Kurdish diaspora communities towards the Kurdish regions in the Middle East. She has written scientific articles concerning political activism, diaspora participation, Kurdish diaspora and identity. Her research interests also cover broader themes such as multiculturalism, nationalism and belonging. She holds a PhD degree in Social Sciences from the University of Turku.

Constanza Vera-Larrucea is currently an Ahlström & Terserus post-doctorate fellow at the Political Science department in Stockholm University. She defended her dissertation 'Citizenship by citizens' in the same institution. Her research interests are citizenship, international migration and ethnic relations, dual citizens, descendants of immigrants and the Turkish diaspora. Her work, based on the experiences of descendants of Turks in Europe, has been published in journals such as the *Journal of International Migration and Integration* and edited volumes, among others, Crul & Mollenkopf (eds) *The Changing Face of World Cities: Young Adult Children of Immigrants in Europe and the United States* (2012).

Charles Westin is Professor of Migration and Ethnicity Studies at the Department of Social Anthropology, Stockholm University. He is the Chair of The Expo Foundation, a non-profit organisation researching anti-democratic, right-wing extremist and racist tendencies in society. His recent book is *On the Move: Experiences of Handling Forced Migration with Examples from Africa, Australia and Europe* (with S. Hassanen, 2013). He recently edited *Identity Processes and Dynamics in Multi-ethnic Europe* (with J. Bastos, J. Dahinden & P. Gois, 2010) and *The Integration of Descendants from Turkey in Stockholm: The Ties Study in Sweden* (2015).

CHAPTER 1

THE 50TH ANNIVERSARY OF THE BEGINNING OF MIGRATION FROM TURKEY TO SWEDEN: LESSONS CONCERNING INTEGRATION, COHESION, AND INCLUSION

Paul T. Levin and Bahar Başer

The idea behind this edited volume is to evaluate trajectories of migration from Turkey to Sweden on the 50th anniversary of the start of this migration. Although the official agreements for labour migration between Turkey and Sweden were signed in 1967 (and though travel between Asia Minor and Scandinavia dates back to the time of the Vikings and Byzantines), Turkish diaspora organisations in Sweden as well as other relevant actors have taken 1965 as the year that migration to Sweden from Turkey started in earnest and organised a range of festivities during the year of 2015 accordingly. Hence, 2015 became an occasion for both state officials and migrants themselves to celebrate and discuss the experiences of Turkish migrants in Sweden and reflect upon the future. Turkish state

institutions organised seminars on the topic and participated in celebrations arranged in Sweden. The Turkish
national TV channel, TRT's religious Diyanet channel,
produced and aired 'Stockholm Train', a documentary
that included interviews with Turkish migrants and their
experiences in Sweden. A number of migrant associations
in Sweden created a joint committee to coordinate the
celebrations and set up a website dedicated to the 50th
anniversary, filled with stories and advertisements for
events. There have also been festivities in the small Central
Anatolian town of Kulu, near Konya, from where most of
the ethnic Turkish migrants in Sweden originate. Similar
celebrations have also been organised in Germany and the
Netherlands, European countries where a large number of
Turkish and Kurdish migrants reside.

Marking this date, the aim of this volume is to provide
an overview of Turkish migrants' experiences in Sweden
over the last 50 years, to present their stories and
perspectives, and to identify challenges and opportunities with respect to the question of integration. In so
doing, we also hope that this volume will make a broader
contribution to our understanding of the integration of
immigrants in northern and western Europe, a topic that
is both politically charged and of great significance to
contemporary European societies. In Sweden, as elsewhere in Europe, this topic is subject to lively discussion
and debate at the time of writing, fuelled both by a rise
in support for anti-immigration parties and by outrage
over the tragic fate of refugees from the war in Syria.
In this book, we build on the public conversation as well
as existing research regarding the experience of Turkish
immigrants in Sweden, while introducing a fresh scholarly
contribution to the current debates on migration to
Sweden, emigration from Turkey as well as the situation of
migrants in Europe in general. Looking back at the

achievements of migrants and Swedish institutions over the course of the past 50 years also gives us an excellent opportunity to evaluate Swedish policies concerning immigration and integration, which may reveal insights that can guide us towards policy lessons for the future.

The History of Migration from Turkey to Sweden

Immigration from Turkey to Sweden began in the mid-1960s with the recruitment of workers to satisfy the needs of the expanding Swedish industrial economy. At that time, the preferred destinations for Turkish migrants for labour migration were countries such as Germany, France and the Netherlands, which had signed labour agreements with the Turkish state. However, many also found their way to Sweden through individual networks. Most of these labour migrants from Kulu were characteristically of peasant origin, with a low educational background. The second biggest group was from Cihanbeyli, a neighbouring town to Kulu. There were also other migrants from different parts of Turkey, including Istanbul, who were high-skilled compared to those from Central Anatolia. These workers were not considered 'guest workers' as in the case of Germany, therefore the usual guest scheme did not apply to them in Sweden.[1] Along with significant numbers of labour migrants from Finland and Southern European countries like Greece and Italy, Turkish migration continued until 1973, when Swedish labour unions, during the economic downturn that followed the oil crisis, introduced stringent restrictions on labour migration.

The profile of migrants from Turkey shifted with the arrival of asylum-seekers (mostly Assyrians and Kurds) who came to Sweden after the 1971 military intervention. In the 1970s and afterwards, family reunification also became a way to migrate to Sweden. Yet another wave of migration began after the military coup in 1980 and on this occasion the asylum-seekers were mostly, albeit not exclusively, of Kurdish origin. A sense of the diversity of this group and of the reasons for leaving Turkey can be gleaned from Table 1.1, which is adapted from a large recent study, The Integration of the European Second Generation (TIES), which will be discussed further below as well as in later chapters.

Today, migrants from Turkey no longer constitute one of the larger migrant groups in Sweden. According to Statistics Sweden, there were 46,373 Swedish residents in December 2015 who were born in Turkey.[2] However, if we include the children and grandchildren of the first generation immigrants from Turkey, we can safely say that the number of Swedes with their origins in Turkey far exceeds 100,000. Pinning down the exact number of 'Swedish Turks' is challenging because of naturalisation rates and uncertainty about how to count the second and third generations.

Table 1.1 Second generation Turks in Sweden, fathers' reason to migrate (per cent)[3]

Reason to migrate	Reported ethnicity of father		
	Ethnic Turks	Kurds	Assyrians
Family reunification	45.1	28.7	11.5
Work	40.7	37.3	15.6
Studies	2.0	6.1	0
Asylum/refugee	0	22.4	56.6
Other reasons	9.5	2.7	13
Doesn't know	2.7	2.7	3.3
Total	100	100	100

An Understudied Topic

Turkish migration to Europe has been a popular topic for researchers from various fields for decades. However, attention has usually been focused on the large number of Turkish migrants who reside in Germany, whereas other countries were understudied in the literature. Until very recently, our scholarly understanding of the migrants from Turkey in Sweden was based on a smaller number of empirical studies conducted by pioneering authors such as Alpay[4], Lundberg and Svanberg,[5] Lundberg,[6] Erder,[7] Akpinar,[8] Jorgensen[9] and Westin.[10] Most of the authors were based in Sweden or Turkey, and their studies – often published in the format of PhD or MA Theses – were typically only available in Swedish or Turkish. In the English-language literature, Sweden was long overlooked as a host country. Only more recently have we begun to see studies on the Turkish or Kurdish communities in Sweden published in English. Several of the contributing authors to the current volume have published such theses and reports: Naldemirci,[11] Akın,[12] and Larrucea,[13] while co-editor Başer is the author of a recent monograph on the Turkish and Kurdish diasporas in Sweden and Germany.[14] Most of these publications are based on predominantly qualitative research that provides valuable insight into the Turkish community in Sweden but lack statistical data and the generalisability of their results consequently varies.

There are now also exceptions to the above-mentioned dearth of quantitative studies. Vedder and Virta[15] modelled the psychological adaptation of Turkish migrants in Sweden and the Netherlands, looking at whether stronger competence in one's ethnic language or the host country majority language best predicts adaptation. Bayram et al.[16] measured the integration of

Turkish immigrants in Sweden, looking at their perceptions of ethnic identity, media consumption habits, and transnational ties to Turkey. Both of these studies found that Turks in Sweden maintain a comparatively strong Turkish ethnic identity and ethnic language competence. Interestingly, Vedder and Virta found that this also appeared to be a recipe for psychological adaptation, whereas stronger competence in Swedish did not predict adaptation. Two larger recent international quantitative studies have also featured Turkish-origin immigrants in Sweden: ICSEY (International Comparative Studies of Ethnocultural Youth) and the above-mentioned TIES. The latter project is a broad comparative study based on surveys conducted in several large European cities, and it has generated a smaller number of important publications on the Swedish case. The most notable of these is the Swedish TIES volume edited by Charles Westin[17] and published in 2015, on the 50th anniversary of the beginning of Turkish migration to Sweden. The TIES study generated similar results to Bayram et al. and Vedder and Virta when it comes to the comparatively strong self-identification of their respondents as Turks, but adds several layers of complexity to our understanding of identity and sense of belonging. In fact, the TIES project and Westin's anthology, which are wholly quantitative, raised a number of questions regarding integration, identification and institutions that demand further study, and several of the chapters in the current volume therefore take the TIES study as their starting point.

A significant drawback of many of these quantitative studies is that they focused on 'Turkish migrants', including Kurdish and Assyrian groups without fully acknowledging the heterogeneity of this community or paying attention to the often very different experiences of these groups, which emigrated from Turkey for very different reasons and arrived in Sweden under varied conditions. (As Westin argues in Chapter 2, this critique also applies to the TIES study, even though it did include questions about respondents' Turkish, Kurdish, or Syriac ethnic identities.) Our general conclusion from reading the existing literature was therefore that there are gaps to be filled and that this topic deserved further attention. For that reason, we gathered a group of scholars at a workshop at the Stockholm University Institute for Turkish Studies on 9 October 2015, and the current edited volume is the outcome of that process.

What is so Special about Turks in Sweden?

As we have just argued, compared to the burgeoning academic literature on other Turkey-originated migrant communities in various European countries, the overall number of studies focusing on Sweden is still relatively low, especially if we limit ourselves to English-language publications. This is surprising in light of the fact that Sweden harbours a highly interesting amalgam of ethnic and religious groups from Turkey that is unique in a number of ways. For one thing, almost 40 per cent (and a majority of the ethnic Turks)[18] of them originate from a single small town: the above-mentioned district of Kulu in Konya, central Anatolia. Rarely in Europe do we find this high degree of concentration of Turkish immigrants in terms of their place of origin.[19] This pattern of labour migration matters: the social and political attitudes, sense-of-belonging and diasporic activism of the 'Kulu-Turks' in Sweden have arguably been very much affected by a shared and nostalgic idea of the small town as well as by their traditional and often conservative background. The 'Kulu connection' as they call it, also became an important focal point for relations between the Swedish state and the Turkish migrant community. There is a park in Kulu named after the late Swedish Prime Minister, Olof Palme, and Sweden recently opened an honorary consulate there where returnees to Kulu can vote in Swedish elections. Hence, the case of migration from Turkey to Sweden promises to give us special insight into popular issues today such as return migration, transnational ties or external voting and citizenship rights.

Paradoxically, the composition of immigrants of Turkish origin in Sweden is also distinctive in terms of the breadth of geographic origins compared to the diaspora in other European countries. Hence, apart from the large number from the central Anatolian town of Kulu, TIES data shows that the immigrants from Turkey in Sweden trace their origins from places as diverse as Mardin and Diyarbakır in the south-east, the north-western cities of Istanbul, Sakarya, and Bolu, as well as other Anatolian cities like Ankara and Nevşehir. The ethnic composition is also unusually diverse, with large numbers of self-identified ethnic Turks, Assyrians/Syriacs, and Kurds, respectively. Among the latter, an unusually high proportion speaks the small and distinctive Kurdish dialect/language of Zaza. In terms of religion, Assyrians are almost exclusively Christian, but among Kurds and Turks we also find an uncharacteristically high proportion of Alevis alongside the Sunni Muslim majority (and of course also many who are secular or atheists).

Sweden is also a special case when it comes to the Kurdish diaspora. As was suggested in Table 1.1 regarding the reason for emigration, the Kurds are divided between labour migrants (mainly from Kulu), and political refugees (from Diyarbakır, Ankara, and Istanbul, many of them having had to flee around the time of the coup in 1980). It is a simplification but one not without merit to say that the latter group of refugees tended to be leftist in political orientation and many of them continued their political activism in Sweden, whereas a large proportion of the Kurds coming from Kulu tend to be more conservative Muslims. The politically mobilised parts of the Kurdish diaspora, thanks to the opportunities provided by the Swedish state, managed to revitalise the Kurdish language (in particular the main dialect spoken in Turkey: Kurmanji) at a time when it was forbidden in Turkey, and more generally contribute to the preservation of Kurdish culture. In Kurdish studies, the diaspora activism of the Kurds in Sweden is recognised as so significant that it has been given its own name: 'Isvec Ekolu' (the Swedish School), a distinctive approach that placed great importance on keeping language and culture alive.

For its part, the Assyrian/Syriac community in Sweden has a symbolic importance to the rest of this diaspora outside of Sweden. Due to forced deportations or 'voluntary exile', many Assyrians left Turkey and chose Sweden as their new home. It is said that there are currently more Assyrians living in Sweden than there are in Turkey. They are active in Swedish political circles, and elements in both the Kurdish and Assyrian groups have been highly successful when it comes to integration into the Swedish public sphere, with a number of high-profile athletes, artists, columnists and politicians.

In light of the fact that the case of Sweden as a host country clearly provides researchers with an abundance of topics that should be of interest to audiences beyond Sweden, the relative dearth of English-language publications is surprising. Moreover, apart from being interesting in itself, the uniqueness of the Turkish-origin diaspora in Sweden also means that studies of, for instance, Turks in Germany or the Netherlands will not necessary 'travel' to the Swedish context, which makes it all the more important to explore the Swedish case in its own right. The assertion that the Swedish case is somewhat of an outlier in many areas is also supported by comparative studies like TIES.

While several chapters in this book make significant use of the TIES study, we also intend to push beyond the limitations imposed by the quantitative data sets in the TIES and ICSEY studies, probing deeper into the subjective experiences of immigrants and looking closer at institutions such as immigrant organisations and media, linguistic practices, and complex identity formation practices among the different ethnic groups in question. In so doing, we hope to complement the existing English-language literature on this case and to contribute to broader debates on immigration and integration in Sweden and beyond concerning such questions as the desirability of multiculturalism versus assimilation, the meaning of integration, and what counts as successful integration. In light of today's refugee crisis and the rise of the European far right, it seems pertinent to consider the lessons we can draw from the Turkish case example on these important topics.

This volume combines analyses of the diverse ethnic groups that emigrated from Turkey in one book. We believe that each group deserves to be analysed individually, rather than being grouped under the category of 'Turkish migrants.' While the authors in this book are cognisant of their shared migration experiences, we have chosen to consider each group's experiences in order to avoid recreating existing homeland hierarchies. The qualitative approaches in the book complement the predominantly quantitative nature of much of the existing English-language literature on this topic, enabling us to explore the lived and subjective experiences of immigrants to an extent that the large quantitative studies have not, and examining some of the questions regarding social integration/isolation that they raised.

The Broader Swedish Context:
Rising Immigration Figures

In the 19th century, Swedes seeking to escape poverty emigrated in significant numbers, often to the New World. Between 1870 and 1970, Sweden experienced a period of sustained growth, political stability, and the emergence of a welfare state that eliminated many of the factors behind the emigration phenomenon, and ever since World War II Sweden has instead been a country of immigration. Today, according to Statistics Sweden, immigration by far surpasses natural net birth/death rates as the main source of Swedish population growth, and around 22 per cent of the Swedish population is now of foreign descent (born abroad or with both parents born abroad).

Average immigration rates in the 1990s were slightly above 50,000 people per annum and increased to nearly 80,000 in the first decade of the new millennium.[20] After accounting for emigration rates, the net immigration figures for these decades were approximately 20,000 and 40,000 respectively. The Syrian refugee crisis made 2015 a record-breaking year in terms of immigration numbers and asylum seekers in Sweden. Never before had so many people sought asylum in Sweden: nearly 140,000 people entered the country during 2015 (a net immigration rate of over 78,000). Graph 1.1 shows immigration and emigration rates from 1875–2015. In it, the transformation of Sweden from a country of net emigration in the 1800s to the country of net immigration that Sweden is today is clearly visible. We can also see the relatively dramatic spike in immigrant arrivals in 2015, as well as

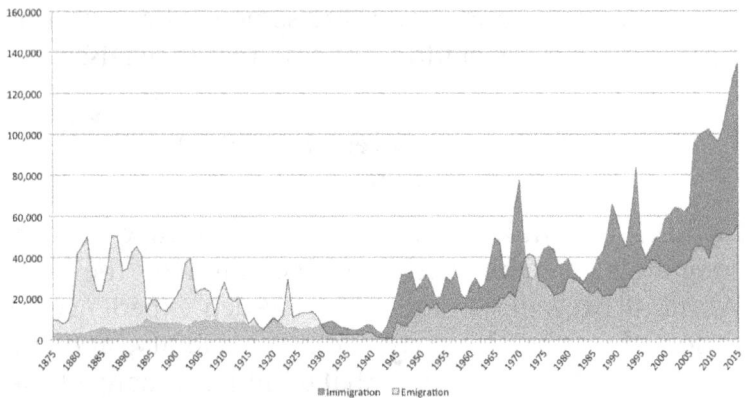

| | | | | | | | | | | | | | | | | | | | | | | | | | | | |

Graph 1.1   Immigration and Emigration in Sweden 1875–2015.

the fact that this spike came after two decades of already relatively high net immigration.

With an aging population, the Swedish economy and welfare state needs population growth, hence immigration arguably benefits the country in the long run. However, the very large influx of people in 2014 and 2015 placed tremendous additional stress on a system for managing asylum seekers that was already straining to cope with high volumes.

As one of only a handful of countries in the EU that welcomed Syrians seeking asylum in Europe in 2014 and 2015, Sweden was rapidly being overwhelmed. By the fall of 2015, municipalities began signalling that the situation was becoming untenable. One Social Democratic mayor famously cried on Swedish public radio when describing the municipality's failure to cope with the large number of refugees they were receiving and the pressure on her employees.[21] In November 2015, the Swedish Migration Agency declared that they were no longer able to provide housing for all newly arrived asylum seekers.[22] Shortly thereafter, in the middle of the

Swedish winter, a small number of municipalities would begin temporarily sheltering asylum seekers in outdoor tent camps because they had no other place to offer. Finally, on 24 November 2015, another Swedish politician was in tears: a very emotional Green Party spokesperson and Deputy Prime Minister, Dr Åsa Romson, declared that the Swedish open-doors policy of welcoming all asylum seekers had come to an end.[23] In order to limit immigration to the minimum required by the EU, the Social Democratic-led coalition government declared that they would introduce a series of measures, including ID controls at the borders, temporary residence permits, and restrictions on family reunification. Romson described it as a 'terrible decision', and the Prime Minister described it as a temporary emergency measure intended to 'give some breathing space' to an overstretched system of processing asylum requests on the national and municipal levels.[24]

A debate about the purported failures of Swedish society to successfully integrate the newcomers had already emerged in mainstream media, triggered in part by the electoral success of the anti-immigrant Sweden Democrats in the parliamentary elections of 2010, when they first entered the legislature, and their subsequent doubling in size in the 2014 elections. Events such as the May 2013 riots in suburban areas of Stockholm, triggered by the tragic police shooting of a 68-year-old man armed with a large knife in Husby, contributed to a sense that all was not well with Swedish immigration and integration policy.[25] Chapter 2 examines this debate further, but all the chapters in this volume combine to provide a multidimensional and nuanced look at both the successes and short-comings of official multiculturalism and integration efforts in Sweden.

Turkish Diaspora Management meets Swedish Integration Debates

The Swedish political landscape has been dramatically transformed in the past few years when it comes to the public discourse on immigration. As we noted above, the profile of migrants from Turkey also changed over the course of the 50 years that we examined, and the second generation brought a whole new dynamic to the homeland-diaspora nexus. At the same time, Turkey has adapted to the idea that the 'Turks abroad' were permanently gone and the country itself has also been radically transformed during the nearly decade-and-a-half long period of AKP rule. This has generated both a need and a desire to formulate new policies that go beyond traditional emigration policies that mainly regulate how to transfer pensions from one country to another or how to send remittances back home. We have described how the political scene has changed in Sweden, and throughout the rest of the book the contributing authors will shed light on changes affecting the Turkey-originated communities who live in Sweden by focusing on different generations and ethnic mobilisations. We find it useful to also mention here how Turkish state policies have changed.

Turkey-originated groups constitute a sizeable community in Sweden, but compared to countries such as Germany, the visibility of 'ethnic' Turks (by which we simply mean those who self-identify as Swedish Turks) in the public sphere has been relatively low. The Kurdish and Assyrian communities have long been much more active than Turkish communities in terms of joining political parties, bringing homeland politics to the Swedish political arena and acting on them constantly seeking transnational support. The ethnic Turkish community was also organised but without a clear political agenda, and it had not managed to bring its issues to the attention of Swedish media or decision makers as much as the Kurds or Assyrians have been able to do. Only recently can one observe that Turkish organisations in Sweden are trying to carve out some political space for themselves to make their voice heard. Arguably, this is an overdue development and is not accidental. This new aspiration of becoming a mobilised diaspora coincides with the Turkish state's attempts to reach out to its diaspora after 50 years.

Since the beginning of the 1960s, Turkey has been gradually formulating policies aimed at facilitating Turkish immigrants' lives abroad but at the same time tapping from this community as much as possible via remittances, skill transfers and other means. These emigration policies were transformed into diaspora engagement policies during the last decade. The governing party, the Justice and Development Party (better known by its Turkish acronym, the AKP), has cultivated policies to activate the government-friendly diaspora communities abroad and use them as bridges between the homeland and the host country. Since 2004, chapters of a new umbrella organisation for the Turkish diaspora in Europe, the AKP-linked Union of European Turkish Democrats (UETD), have mushroomed all around Europe, including in Sweden. In 2010, a new government agency, The Agency for Turks Abroad (also known by its Turkish acronym: YTB), was created under the auspices of the Prime Ministry and now has representatives in some 20 countries across the world, including Sweden. These initiatives were aimed at mobilising and making use of the diaspora as an instrument of public diplomacy but have also served to shore up (electoral etc.) support among the diaspora for the AKP and/or Turkish government and its policies.

The Turkish Presidency of Religious Affairs, or Diyanet, has always trained and certified imams for Turkish mosques, that is, those frequented by Turks both in Turkey and abroad. Diyanet-licenced imams are then sent to countries like Sweden in order to serve the diaspora community for a limited period of time. Like imams in Turkey, they typically begin their service by reading the *khutba* (or *'hutbe'* in Turkish), a short sermon given before the Friday prayer. While written by local committees since 2007, the *khutba* is carefully regulated and controlled by the Diyanet. According to the agency's directives, the *khutba* should, among other things, strengthen religiosity and national unity as well as counteract separatist and harmful tendencies among Turks.[26] With respect to the Turkish diaspora, the emphasis on national unity means that the Diyanet tries '[t]o contribute to Turks living abroad not to lose their self-identity and be in harmony with the society they are living in without being assimilated.'[27] Hence, apart from the purely religious functions, one of the key tasks of Diyanet and the imams it sends is diaspora management and their actions thereby affect integration policy in host countries like Sweden.

The actors mentioned above – Diyanet, YTB, and UETD – have not only engaged with the first generation Turkish emigrants, but have also formulated programs and activities to rekindle the sense-of-belonging to Turkey among second- and third-generation Turkish youth. Up until very recently, these policies mostly targeted Turkish immigrant groups in Germany and France, which left countries with small Turkish populations to remain at the peripheries of the Turkish state's attention and interest. The policies of the last ten years however, have targeted each and every country where Turks reside and have had a much more comprehensive approach. Therefore, in Sweden, too, one can observe changing dynamics among the Turkish diaspora organisations and between them and the Turkish state.

Perhaps the most dramatic change is that the conflict dynamics in Turkish politics have also become more visible in relations between the different ethno-national groups from Turkey now residing in Sweden. Earlier studies have pointed to a higher degree of segregation between the Turkish and Kurdish communities in Sweden than in Germany, for instance, but relations between the two have rarely turned violent. However, a series of developments since the summer of 2015 suggests that the intensified conflict in Turkey coupled with the recent mobilisation of nationalist and conservative sentiments among Turks in Sweden might have already transformed these relations for the worse. There were violent clashes between nationalist Turkish demonstrators and supporters of the Kurdish PKK in central Stockholm in September 2015, the detonation of explosive devices at three different Turkish and Kurdish community centres around the same time, and additional clashes in a suburb of Stockholm in February 2016 that were followed by a shooting which nearly killed the deputy leader of PJAK in Sweden, an Iranian Kurdish party that is closely aligned with the PKK.

Moreover, the increasing presence of the Turkish government and the growing clout of conservative, nationalist, and/or Islamist actors within the Turkish diaspora community in Sweden have changed both the character of some of the diaspora organisations and how they are perceived by mainstream Swedish society. On April 9, 2016, the deputy head of the largest Turkish migrant association in Sweden, Turkiska Riksförbundet (TR, see Chapter 7 for more on this and other organis-ations), gave a speech during a rally at Sergels Torg in central Stockholm, clips from which went viral and was widely condemned. At the rally in question, which was organised by TR in support of Azerbaijan during the resurgence of fighting over the disputed province of Nagorno-Karabakh, the official repeatedly called for the death of 'Armenian dogs' to the cheers of the small audience. The official later gave a tearful apology on Swedish national TV, but was forced to resign and an entirely new leadership was elected.[28] Following the scandal, TR was expelled from ABF, the influential Workers' Educational Association, and a government investigation into whether TR should continue to receive state funding for its activities is currently under way.[29]

Finally, in a separate scandal that erupted later that same April, Mehmet Kaplan, a leading Green Party politician and one of the most prominent Swedes of Turkish descent and Muslim faith, was forced to resign from his post as minister of Housing and Urban Development following a series of revelations that cast doubt on whether he fully embraced the democratic and progressive values of his party. Several Swedish news outlets had published pictures that showed Kaplan socialising with conservative, nationalist, and/or extremist individuals and groups in a range of contexts. The most serious criticism followed revelations that he had attended an *iftar* dinner along with the head of the Swedish branch of the Grey Wolves (Ülkü Ocakları İsveç). The organisation is the militant youth branch of the ultranationalist Turkish party, the MHP, which is represented in the Turkish parliament, but it is also infamous for being associated with extrajudicial executions and attacks on Kurds and leftists in Turkey in previous decades. Additional photos then surfaced, showing Kaplan participating in events organised by the conservative Islamist organisation Milli Görüş and repeatedly socialising with individuals close to the AKP, the conservative and increasingly Islamist ruling party in Turkey, during trips to Turkey as well as in Sweden. The final straw came with the release of a video of a meeting in which Kaplan appeared to relativise the Holocaust, and after this Kaplan announced that he was resigning his ministerial post.[30] The scandal triggered a serious broader crisis in the Green Party, where the democratic and progressive credentials of other Muslim politicians were questioned along with the general abilities of the leadership of the party. One of the party's two spokespersons (the above-mentioned Deputy Prime Minister, Åsa Romson) was forced to resign during a tumultuous period of soul-searching. For the first time since perhaps the 1980s (when it was briefly suspected that the PKK might be behind the assassination of Olof Palme), developments within the diaspora communities from Turkey made a visible imprint on the media and public discourse of mainstream Swedish society.[31]

In some ways, the Kaplan scandal and the existential questions it triggered within the Green Party can serve as symbols of a broader uncertainty that has surfaced in Swedish society. In a reflection of Swedish immigration and integration policy, the Greens have pursued a policy of embracing members from ethnic and religious minority groups, including leading Swedish Muslim activists like Kaplan and Yasri Khan, Chairman and along with Kaplan co-founder of Swedish Muslims for Peace and Justice. Sweden has long pursued one of the most open and generous immigration policies in Europe, and officially embraced multiculturalism as an approach to integration (see Chapter 2 for a more extensive discussion of the evolution of Swedish integration policy). As we noted above, this relative openness meant that the Europe-wide migration crisis of 2015 was felt particularly hard in Sweden, and the dramatic influx of refugees from

Syria and Afghanistan further fuelled an emerging debate about how to manage the challenge of finding shared values in a society with a long-established multicultural approach to the question of integration. There were suddenly open debates in the media about alleged sexual assaults by male immigrants at music concerts and in mixed public bathhouses. Some of the responses by the authorities – an alleged cover-up by the police of assaults at concerts and proposals to abolish mixed bathhouses, a cherished Swedish institution – evoked anger and further stoked rising xenophobic and Islamophobic sentiments.[32] Suddenly progressives, not just in the Green Party but also in Swedish society as a whole, appeared to be in a position where they had to choose between feminism and a multicultural openness to other cultures and traditions, especially conservative Islam. For their part, devout Swedish Muslims wondered if they were welcome in Swedish politics when not just Kaplan was forced out but also his above-mentioned colleague, Yasri Khan, who abandoned his candidature for a senior post in the Green Party after Swedish media seized on a video of him refusing to shake the hand of a female reporter from Swedish television.

The official multicultural approach to integration in Sweden, today amended but not abandoned, has been successful in many ways. In Chapter 2, Charles Westin notes that Sweden ranks at the very top in indexes like MIPEX, which measures integration policy and legislative framework. Memet Aktürk-Drake notes (in Chapter 5) that in addition to the high MIPEX score, Sweden also scores high on measures such as the Multiculturalism Policy Index, so multiculturalism does not appear to be counteracting integration. MIPEX focuses on policy and legislation, not outcome, but Westin notes that the Turkish community in Sweden also fares well compared to Turks in many other European countries in major international studies like TIES, when looking at outcome variables like education etc. Memet Aktürk-Drake, too, shows that multicultural policies such as free mother-tongue instruction for all students with a different language in the home have not negatively affected students' competence in the majority language. Indeed, the Turkish diaspora in Sweden distinguishes itself from the Turkish diaspora in other European countries by its higher competence in the majority language (Swedish) relative to their heritage language (Turkish). If there is a problem, he notes, it is that the children of Turkish immigrants in Sweden appear to be losing their Turkish language competence, not their Swedish.

Chapter 8 provides further evidence that the multicultural tendencies in Swedish integration policy have been good for the diaspora communities. Başer, Idris Ahmedi and Mari Toivanen show that funding for Kurdish associations, libraries and publishing houses has been a significant boon to the Kurdish community and the broader stateless Kurdish movement. Moreover, the example of the Turkish youth association TUF discussed in Chapter 7 shows how diaspora organisations can transcend the limitations of 'ethnic' organisations and empower their members in their interactions with and integration into majority Swedish society. In one sense, the multicultural approach by Swedish institutions has helped Kurds, Turks and Assyrians in Sweden to develop complex identities that include Swedishness as well as distinct ethnic identities.

At the same time, the state policy of financially and institutionally supporting diaspora communities who organise along ethno-national lines has also created a situation in which ethnic groups are incentivised to protect their distinctiveness and separateness, and this has clearly raised obstacles in the way of integration. In Chapter 7, the chairman of one Turkish association interviewed expresses deep pessimism about diaspora organisations, many of which effectively function as coffee houses for men who feel alienated from the rest of society: 'You know, we say that their actual goal is to make us mix with Swedish people, but we do the contrary.' Likewise, in his survey of developments within the Swedish Syriac/Assyrian diaspora community (Chapter 9), Aryo Makko argues that 'the multicultural policies of the Swedish state' have served to allow members of the diaspora to 'develop a strong Assyrian identity rather than tight bonds with Swedes'.

In different ways, several of the chapters report a similar finding, namely, that people with Kurdish, Assyrian, or Turkish background in Sweden rarely feel like Swedes and that they rarely identify with Sweden or with Swedes. But an equally intriguing collective result of the research conducted by the various authors in this volume is that these questions about belonging and identity are exceedingly complex and that simple answers are untenable. The complexities are addressed in detail by Vera-Larrucea in Chapter 4. While many of her respondents (and participants in the TIES survey) claim that they feel 'Turkish' etc. rather than 'Swedish', they simultaneously report feeling much more 'at home' in Sweden than in Turkey, and their strongest identification is with Stockholm (the Swedish city in which they live), not Turkey or any Turkish city. To add to the complexity, Aryo Makko's interviews and document analysis presents him with the conclusion that Swedish Assyrians are generally very well integrated in the sense of *participating* in Swedish society, including political and economic institutions, but that they do not generally feel a strong *emotional identification* with Sweden or 'native' Swedes. Something similar might be said of the Kurdish diaspora. A highly visible and active elite within this group has been successful in influencing public perception of their cause and in garnering high-level political support for it as well as financial and institutional support for the development of Kurdish culture in Sweden. At the same time, ethnic nationalist Kurdish organisations in Sweden like the PKK have been strengthened over the course of recent decades and, as we argued above, ethno-national polarisation between Turks and Kurds appears to have been strengthened rather than weakened. Some of this polarisation is undoubtedly the result of political developments in Turkey, but Swedish policy has failed to prevent what from a Swedish perspective is hardly a desired outcome when it comes to societal integration.

However, it is also clear from several of the chapters in the volume that the shortcomings regarding the integration of people from Turkey living in Sweden (most of these shortcomings still being on a far smaller scale than in many other EU countries that also host significant Turkish communities) are not just or even mainly an outcome of Swedish multicultural policies. In Chapter 2, Charles Westin discusses the growth of racism in Sweden, first in the 1990s and then again today, as seen most dramatically in the recent electoral successes of the anti-immigrant party, the Sweden Democrats. Needless to say, it is difficult for an immigrant to integrate into Swedish majority society or to emotionally identify with Swedes if such integration is typically not welcomed by the latter, and Westin notes that a majority of Muslims in the TIES study reported having personally experienced discrimination and/or harassment. According to Aryo Makko, the retreat and increasing isolation of the Assyrian/Syriani community reported in Chapter 9 was also a response to negative and disheartening encounters with native Swedes and majority Swedish society. The respondents interviewed by Öncel Naldemirci in Chapter 3 give vivid and often humorous accounts of such encounters, which were captured in imaginative nicknames and narratives. The humour clearly functioned as a way of making sense of the migration experience but also as a mechanism for coping with difficult or conflict laden inter-cultural encounters in a new country for these first-generation immigrants. In Chapter 4, Vera-Larrucea's 'second generation' interview subjects talk about the difficulties associated with integration and interaction with native Swedes in, for example, the Swedish military, where even mundane things like food can emphasise one's 'otherness' if, for example, you are a Muslim and the food everyone is served contains pork. It is arguably the ethnic Turkish community that has suffered the most in terms of not feeling fully accepted as a distinct group with legitimate concerns and interests, as illustrated by Altuğ Akin's case study of Radio Merhaba in Chapter 6. It is not lost on the Turkish-speaking Swedes that the only Turkish-language radio programme on Swedish public radio was shut down while Kurds have their own Kurdish-language public radio station (Radyoya Swêdê). But as many of the chapters attest, the feeling of not being fully accepted into Swedish society applies to the entire Turkey-originated diaspora in Sweden.

Hence, if one conclusion from this study is that integration is a complex phenomenon that can be measured in different ways and along different dimensions (see especially Chapters 2, 4, and 9), then a second conclusion is perhaps that integration can also be seen a two-way street that involves native Swedes as much as immigrants and their descendants. Of the several understandings of the notion 'integration' that Charles Westin discusses in Chapter 2, he prefers the one that opposes it to 'disintegration'. In this sense of the word, we can speak of an 'integrated' society as a whole that is held together. Here, it becomes less obvious that the natural focus of integration policy should be on how immigrants and their descendants should be made to integrate into an existing Swedish society that does not significantly change. Such an approach easily turns into demands for 'assimilation' and places the burden of change squarely on the immigrants. On our understanding, the achievement of a 'well-integrated society' would instead place demands on native Swedes as well as immigrants and their descendants. This hardly sounds revolutionary, but the proper acknowledgment of this would have consequences not only for integration policy but also for how both immigration and integration policies are discussed in Sweden and beyond.

In Sweden, supporters of a generous immigration policy have long sought to defend it by assuring the public that Swedish society would not change much, and claims to the contrary were not infrequently dismissed as intolerant or as little more than thinly veiled racism. But our interpretation of the research collected in this volume is that for integration – in the sense of societal cohesion – to work properly in a multicultural society, an approach of removed and benevolent tolerance towards cultural difference by majority society is insufficient. The TIES data shows not just that the Turkish (second generation) diaspora in Sweden fails to identify strongly with Sweden and is rather socially isolated from majority society, but also that native Swedes are atypical among other European nationalities included in the study in how strongly they identify with the country in which they live. Moreover, native Swedes are more socially 'isolated from Turks and other immigrant groups in terms of having friends or classmates with other ethnicities.[33] Hence, the descendants of the Turks that immigrated to Sweden are, in a sense, better trained at managing cultural interactions than most native Swedes. For integration as social cohesion, then, to be successful, the burden of adaptation and learning also falls on native Swedes.

The existence of multiple identities in Sweden (and in many similar European societies) is now a fact and certainly nothing that should necessarily be lamented. But it is easy to understand why even many people of Turkish descent who have been born and raised in Sweden can neither emotionally identify with Sweden nor describe themselves as 'Swedes' when that label in folk usage carries connotations that in many ways seem to exclude them. Like many other European societies that have seen significant immigration in the past half-century, Sweden is now a changed place, and yet we still often speak of 'Sweden' and 'Swedes' as if their denotation had not changed. And in many ways, Sweden has arguably not changed enough. Fear of losing one's traditions, whether those are 'majority' or 'heritage' traditions, has propelled many to erect barriers to the kinds of interactions and integration that would be conducive to a more fully integrated and cohesive society. So, while there is much to be happy about when it comes to the integration of the Turkey-originated diaspora in Sweden, this volume points to additional work that needs to be done when it comes to interaction, identification, and inclusion.

Notes

1. Francesco Pasetti, Corridor Report on Sweden: The Case of Iranian and Turkish Migrants, INTERACT (2015)/04.
2. Data available at the website of Statistics Sweden (accessed on 2016-07-11): http://www.scb.se/sv_/Hitta-statistik/Statistik-efter-amne/Befolkning/Befolkningens-sammansattning/Befolknings statistik/#c_li_120253.

3. Table adapted from Constanza Vera-Larrucea, *Historical and demographic considerations The Integration of Descendants of Migrants from Turkey in Stockholm,* Amsterdam University Press (Amsterdam, 2015), pp. 25–42. Sums are rounded to the nearest integer.
4. Şahin Alpay, *Turkar i Stockholm. En Studie av Invandrare, Politik och Samhälle* [Turks in Stockholm: A Study of Migrants, Politics and Society] PhD Thesis, Department of Political Science, Stockholm University (Stockholm, 1980).
5. Ingrid Lundberg and Ingvar Svanberg, *Turkish Associations in Metropolitan Stockholm,* Centre for Multiethnic Research, Uppsala University (Uppsala, 1991).
6. Ingrid Lundberg, *Kulubor i Stockholm. En Svensk Historia* [Kulu Migrants in Stockholm: A Swedish History] Sveriges invandrarinstitut och museum (Stockholm, 1991).
7. Sema Erder, *Refah Toplumunda Getto (A Ghetto in Welfare Society),* Istanbul Bilgi University Publications (Istanbul, 2006), p. 301.
8. Aylin Akpinar, 'Challenged Family and Kinship Ideals: Family Crisis and Social Networks Among Turkish Immigrants', *Swedish Institute for Social Research Working Papers,* 10, Stockholm University (Stockholm, 1988).
9. Martin Bak Jorgensen, *National and Transnational Identities: Turkish Organising Processes and Identity Construction in Denmark, Sweden and Germany,* Aalborg University: Institut for Historie, Internationale Studier og Samfundsforhold, Aalborg Universitet, Spirit PhD Series; No. 19 (2009).
10. Charles Westin, 'Young people of migrant origin in Sweden', *The International Migration Review* 37/4 (2003), pp. 987–1010.
11. Öncel Naldemirci, *Caring (in) Diaspora: Aging and Caring Experiences of Older Turkish Migrants in a Swedish Context,* Unpublished PhD Thesis, Göteborg Studies In Sociology No. 54, Department of Sociology and Work Science, University of Gothenburg (2013).
12. Altuğ Akın, *Ethnic Minority Media Production From Producers' Perspective: Case of Turkish Broadcasts in Swedish Public Service Broadcaster (SR)* (Stockholm, 2006).
13. Constanza Vera-Larrucea, *Citizenship by citizens: first generation nationals with Turkish ancestry on lived citizenship in Paris and Stockholm.* Department of Political Science, Stockholm University. Stockholm studies in politics (Stockholm, 2013), p. 150.
14. Bahar Başer, *Diasporas and Homeland Conflicts: A Comparative Perspective,* Ashgate (Farnham, 2015).
15. Paul Vedder and Erkki Virta, 'Language, ethnic identity, and the adaptation of Turkish immigrant youth in the Netherlands and Sweden', *International Journal of Intercultural Relations* 29/3 (2005), pp. 317–37.

16. Nuran Bayram, Hans Nyquist, Daniel Thorburn and Nazan Bilgel, 'Turkish Immigrants in Sweden: Are They Integrated?', *The International Migration Review*, 43/1 (2009), pp. 90–111.
17. Charles Westin (ed.), *The Integration of Descendants of Migrants from Turkey in Stockholm*. Amsterdam University Press (Amsterdam, 2015).
18. Vera-Larrucea,'*Citizenship by citizens*', pp. 35–6.
19. The other notable example of this kind of concentrated labour migration among Turks in Europe is the case of Emirdağ Turks from Afyon who migrated to Belgium in a similar manner.
20. All population figures in the remainder of this paragraph are calculated by the authors using population data from Statistics Sweden, downloaded on 24-10-16 from: http://www.scb.se/sv_/ Hitta-statistik/Statistik-efter-amne/Befolkning/Befolkningens-sammansattning/Befolkningsstatistik/
21. Karin Eriksson, "Höstens kriser fick debatten om flyktingar att tvärvända." 21 November 2015. *Dagens Nyheter*. 24 October 2016. http://www.dn.se/nyheter/sverige/hostens-kriser-fick-debatten-om-flyktingar-att-tvarvanda/ (accessed 10 July 2016).
22. "Asylsökande får inte längre hjälp att hitta bostad." 19 November 2015. *Sverigesradio*. 24 October 2016. http://sverigesradio.se/sida/ artikel.aspx?programid=83&artikel=6306364. (accessed 10 July 2016).
23. Heather Saul, "Refugee crisis: Sweden's deputy Prime Minister Asa Romson cries as she announces asylum policy U-turn." 26 November 2015. *Independent*. 24 October 2016. http://www. independent.co.uk/news/people/refugee-crisis-sweden-deputy-prime-minister-cries-as-she-announces-u-turn-on-asylum-policy-a6749531.html (accessed 10 July 2016).
24. Kerstin Holm and Anna H Svensson, "Regeringen: Ny lagstiftning för färre asylsökande." 24 November 2015. *SVT Nyheter*. 24 October 2016. https://www.svt.se/nyheter/inrikes/regeringen-utokade-id-kontroller-vid-gransen (accessed 10 July 2016).
25. Colin Freeman, "Stockholm riots leave Sweden's dreams of perfect society up in smoke." 25 May 2013. *The Telegraph*. 24 October 2016. http://www.telegraph.co.uk/news/worldnews/ europe/sweden/10080320/Stockholm-riots-leave-Swedens-dreams-of-perfect-society-up-in-smoke.html (accessed 10 July 2016).
26. External Notice of Diyanet (2007) Article 10. Downloaded from http://www2.diyanet.gov.tr/HukukMusavirligi/Mevzuat/ Foyvolant_Dis_Genelge_2007.pdf on 2016-07-25. Among the few things written on the topic of khutbas that we found useful were a Master's thesis at Bosphorus University (Saçmalı, 2013). For more information on Diyanet, see also: Ahmet Erdi Ozturk, 'Turkey's

Diyanet under the AKP Rule: From Protector to Imposer of State Ideology', *Southeast European and Blacksea Studies*, 16:4 (2016), pp. 619–35.
27. See: http://www.diyanet.gov.tr/en/category/basic-principles-and-objectives/23#.
28. "Swedish Turkish leader resigns after "death to Armenians" speech." 11 April 2016. *Sverigesradio*. 24 October 2016. http://sverigesradio.se/sida/artikel.aspx?programid=2054&artikel=6408898 (accessed 10 July 2016).
29. Staffan Axelsson, "ABF utesluter Turkiska riksförbundet." 29 June 2016. *Sverigesradio*. 24 October 2016. http://sverigesradio.se/sida/artikel.aspx?programid=83&artikel=6463741 (accessed 10 July 2016).
30. "Sweden's housing minister quits after extremism row." 18 April 2016. *The Local*. 24 October 2016. https://www.thelocal.se/20160418/swedens-housing-minister-quits-after-row (10 July 2016).
31. In a sign that the turmoil in Turkey will continue to spill over into Swedish politics, reports at the time of writing that Swedish Turks have been prompted to report suspected members of the Gülen movement living in Sweden to the Turkish authorities, has provoked outrage and comdemnation by the Swedish authorities. This could be classified as 'refugee espionage,' which is illegal according to Swedish law.
32. Andrew Brown, "This cover-up of sex assaults in Sweden is a gift for xenophobes." 13 January 2016. The *Guardian*. 24 October 2016. https://www.theguardian.com/commentisfree/2016/jan/13/sex-assaults-sweden-stockholm-music-festival (accessed 10 July 2016).
33. Alireza Behtoui, 'Educational Achievements' In Westin (ed.), *The Integration of Descendants of Migrants from Turkey in Stockholm*, Amsterdam University Press (Amsterdam, 2015).

References

Akın, A., *Ethnic Minority Media Production from Producers' Perspective: Case of Turkish Broadcasts in Swedish Public Service Broadcaster (SR)*, (Stockholm, 2006).

Akpinar, A., 'Challenged Family and Kinship Ideals: Family Crisis and Social Networks Among Turkish Immigrants', *Swedish Institute for Social Research Working Papers*, 10, Stockholm University (1998).

Alpay, S., *Turkar i Stockholm. En Studie av Invandrare, Politik och Samhälle* [Turks in Stockholm: A Study of Migrants, Politics and Society], PhD Thesis, Department of Political Science, Stockholm University (Stockholm, 1980).

Başer, B., *Diasporas and Homeland Conflicts: A Comparative Perspective*, Ashgate Publishers (Farnham: 2015).

Bayram, N., Nyquist, H., Thorburn, D., and Bilgel, N., 'Turkish Immigrants in Sweden: Are They Integrated?' *The International Migration Review*, 43/1 (2009), pp. 90–111.

Behtoui, A., 'Social capital'. In Westin, C. (ed.), *The Integration of Descendants from Turkey in Stockholm: The TIES Study in Sweden*, Amsterdam University Press (Amsterdam, 2015), pp. 57–68.

Crul, M., 'Snakes and Ladders in Educational Systems: Access to Higher Education for Second-Generation Turks in Europe', *Journal of Ethnic & Migration Studies*, 39/9 (2013), pp. 1383–1401.

Crul, M., Schneider, J., & Lelie, F., *The European Second Generation Compared: Does the Integration Context Matter?*, Amsterdam University Press (Amsterdam, 2012).

Erder, S., *Refah Toplumunda Getto (A Ghetto in Welfare Society)*, Istanbul Bilgi University Publications (Istanbul, 2006).

Jorgensen, M.B., National and Transnational Identities: Turkish Organising Processes and Identity Construction in Denmark, Sweden and Germany, Aalborg University: Institut for Historie, Internationale Studier og Samfundsforhold, Aalborg Universitet, Spirit PhD Series; No. 19 (2009).

Konyali, A., Turning disadvantage into advantage: Achievement narratives of descendants of migrants from Turkey in the corporate business sector, *New Diversities*, 16/1 (2014), pp. 107–21.

Lundberg, I., *Kulubor i Stockholm: En Svensk Historia* [Kulu Migrants in Stockholm: A Swedish History], Sveriges invandrarinstitut och museum (Stockholm, 1991).

Lundberg, I., and Svanberg, I., *Turkish Associations in Metropolitan Stockholm*, Centre for Multiethnic Research, Uppsala University (Uppsala, 1991).

Naldemirci, O., *Caring (in) Diaspora: Aging and Caring Experiences of Older Turkish Migrants in a Swedish Context*, unpublished PhD Thesis, Goteborg Studies In Sociology No. 54, Department of Sociology and Work Science, University of Gothenburg (2013).

Ozturk, A.E., 'Turkey's Diyanet under the AKP Rule: From Protector to Imposer of State Ideology', *Southeast European and Blacksea Studies*, 16/4 (2016), pp. 619–35.

Pasetti, F., Corridor Report on Sweden: The Case of Iranian and Turkish Migrants, INTERACT (2015).

Saçmalı, M.H., *Compliance and Negotiation: The Role of Turkish Diyanet in the Production of Friday Khutbas*, (Master of Arts), Boğaziçi University (2013).

Schneider, J., Fokkema, T., Matias, R., Stojcic, S., Ugrina, D., & Vera-Larrucea, C., Identities: Urban Belonging and Intercultural Relations. In M. Crul, J. Schneider, & F. Lelie (eds), *The European Second Generation Compared: Does the Integration Context Matter?* Amsterdam University Press (Amsterdam, 2012).

Vedder, P., and Virta, E., 'Language, ethnic identity, and the adaptation of Turkish immigrant youth in the Netherlands and

Sweden', *International Journal of Intercultural Relations*, 29/3 (2005), pp. 317–37.

Vera-Larrucea, C., *Citizenship by citizens: first generation nationals with Turkish ancestry on lived citizenship in Paris and Stockholm.* Stockholm: Department of Political Science, Stockholm University. Stockholm studies in politics (2013).

———, 'Historical and Demographic Considerations', in Charles Westin (ed.), *Integration of Descendants of Migrants from Turkey in Stockholm: The TIES Study in Sweden*, (Amsterdam, 2015), pp. 25–42.

Westin, C. (ed.), *The Integration of Descendants of Migrants from Turkey in Stockholm.* Amsterdam University Press (Amsterdam, 2015).

———, 'Young people of migrant origin in Sweden', *The International Migration Review* 37/4 (2003), pp. 987–1010.

Wiesbrock, A., 'The Integration of Immigrants in Sweden: a Model for the European Union?', *International Migration*, 49/4 (2011), pp. 46–66.

CHAPTER 2

REFLECTIONS ON THE ISSUE OF INTEGRATION

Charles Westin

Introduction

International policy reviews describe the Swedish state-administered welfare system as fair and square.[1] Widespread poverty has been done away with. Public housing is of a decent standard, which by European norms is quite high (apartments are equipped with running water, electricity, central heating etc.). Education at all levels is free of charge. The health care system is available to everyone. Unemployment allowances and health insurance guarantee a reasonable standard of living and the pension system is all-embracing. This welfare regime came into being through successive reforms implemented by Social Democratic governments, which were in office uninterruptedly from 1936 to 1976. Swedish industry had an advantage over many competitors during the years following World War II. Its products were in demand as the ruined cities of Europe were being rebuilt. Since Sweden had not been drawn into the war, its housing, factories, transport facilities and general infrastructure was intact.

Swedish export industry thrived, generating a surplus of taxation money for the public sector.

By the 1950s, industry's need for manpower could not be met by domestic sources alone. Labour was recruited from neighbouring Nordic countries, from Germany, Austria and Hungary, and from southern Europe (Italy, Greece, Yugoslavia and Turkey). In the early days of labour recruitment, politicians, trade unions and employers took it for granted that foreign labour recruitment was a temporary measure. It was generally assumed that foreign workers would return home when a recession set in.

However, things did not turn out that way. Foreign labourers stayed on, even when there was a downturn in the economy. And they brought their families to Sweden. By the late 1960s the Swedish authorities were aware that many foreign workers were residing in Sweden, but were not incorporated into mainstream society. This insight occasioned a tightening up of the regulations for foreign workers seeking employment in Sweden. The political objective was to reduce spontaneous immigration, but not to prevent industry from recruiting labour. Secondly, the government appointed a commission to look into conditions for migrants, to propose measures to facilitate their incorporation, and to determine what public services needed to be developed.

The commission presented its proposals in 1974. With some minor modifications the proposal was passed in parliament after having been referred to various authorities, unions and relevant organisations for consideration. The adopted policy was referred to as 'immigrant policy', but it was in fact the first comprehensive integration policy. Its aims were to bring the growing population of migrant origin into Swedish welfare society. The policy was popularised in three catchwords.[2]

- Equality: migrants who are permanent residents are to enjoy the same social, economic and educational rights as native-born Swedish citizens.
- Freedom of choice: migrants are free to identify with their native culture and they are not required to assimilate culturally into mainstream Swedish society. However, in the public sphere migrants are expected to follow Swedish rules and regulations.
- Partnership: migrants are expected to cooperate and collaborate with Swedish authorities and with Swedish civil society through their own organisations.

These fundamental principles unfolded into practical measures that were implemented in a number of policy fields. Language was one such field. Language issues included interpreter services, introductory courses in Swedish for newcomers, and home language classes in schools for children of migrant background. Another field was about organisational issues: Migrant organisations could apply for subsidised state funding if they met certain basic requirements. There were also franchise issues and naturalisation issues: Migrants with permanent residence permits were granted the right to vote in municipal and county elections. It was seen as a positive step towards incorporation to become a naturalised Swedish citizen. Sweden adopted liberal stipulations for naturalisation and there were no tests or language proficiency demands. The only requirements were five years' permanent residence and meeting a good conduct clause. For political refugees the time requirement for naturalisation was reduced to four years, and for Nordic citizens to two years. Furthermore, Swedish parliament passed an anti-discrimination law and instituted an Ombudsman to deal with ethnic and racial discrimination.

Over the 40 years that have passed the central ideas behind this integration policy have remained much the same. Later governments and commissions expanded on some practical solutions, changed the focal points of certain issues, and introduced new terminology. More teeth were put into anti-discrimination legislation at a later stage. In the 1990s the concept of multiculturalism was introduced to the discourse. Sweden was seen to be on its way to becoming a multicultural society. In recent years, however, the multicultural discourse has been downplayed, with diversity becoming the catch word succeeding multiculturalism. Diversity is about equal rights regardless of background and origin. It embraces not only cultural identities, but also identities associated with gender, sexual orientation, social class etc.

Recruitment of foreign labour was ended in 1972. This led to a temporary decrease of migrant influx to Sweden during the immediately following years. However, a gradual increase in refugee migration took place instead. Initially this was due to political unrest (authoritarian regimes, persecution of civilians and civil war) in the Middle East, the Horn of Africa and Latin America. The build-up of networks between refugee migrants who made it to Sweden and their relatives back home triggered chain migration processes through family reunification. Endangered members of the opposition in politically turbulent countries sought passage to safe countries in the West to escape persecution. In many cases this also meant escape from poverty and lack of opportunity. These movements were part and parcel of the snowballing globalisation processes. In the 1990s the Balkan wars ensuing the break-up of former Yugoslavia, triggered the largest wave of refugees in Europe since World War II. Sweden accepted some 150,000 refugees from various republics of ex-Yugoslavia over the course of a few years.

While a majority of Swedish people accepted the Balkan refugees, the influx met with opposition from right-wing extremists and nationalists. Activists associated with right wing organisations attacked refugee camps, in several instances setting barracks on fire. Other critics of Swedish migration policy organised themselves politically, eventually distancing themselves from the rowdy, neo-Nazi skinhead louts who were out in the streets to attack migrants and migrant-run businesses and to fight anti-racists. The roots of the currently third largest party in the Swedish parliament, the Sweden Democrats (SD), are to be found in the neo-Nazi, non-parliamentary groups of the 1990s that protested against all types of immigration. The present leadership of the SD took over the then small party with the objective of gaining representation in political bodies, initially at the local level but with the long-term aim of achieving representations in the national parliament. National front type parties in other European states had proved that this could be done. Election to municipal councils would mean access to public funding of party organisations which is eligible to all parties once they are elected. The SD has successfully disseminated its view of failed integration to the general public. Over the course of three national elections (eight years) the SD increased its share of votes from 2.5 per cent in 2006 to over 13 per cent in 2014. In current opinion polls close to 20 per cent say they would vote for the party today.

Migration from Turkey to Sweden started in the mid-1960s as labour migration. In later decades migrants from Turkey were granted residence permits on humanitarian grounds and even as political refugees. This chapter reports the findings from a recent study carried out on the living conditions, education and employment situation of descendants of these migrants from Turkey. We find that different ethno-cultural backgrounds and different conditions of incorporation affect integration. Against this backdrop the chapter outlines different understandings of the integration concept.

The Question

Integration is a key issue in current political debate. Two contrary views about Swedish integration policy appear in public debate. In international discussion Sweden is recognised as having developed, and implemented, a successful integration policy. This understanding is backed up by various European comparative surveys, in which Sweden comes out top-of-the-class.[3] Some reports have been commissioned by the European Union, others by the ILO. These reports may find readers among politicians and experts, possibly even researchers. However, they have not caught the attention of the general public in Sweden. Mention may be given by the media in brief paragraphs or announcements, but even then, reported findings are rarely commented on in editorials or analyses.

The other view, disseminated by the SD, and which most political analysts and molders of opinion endorse, is that Swedish integration policy has failed to incorporate migrant populations into the country.[4]

Do these divergent views about integration in Sweden really refer to the same phenomenon? This chapter seeks to problematise the concept of integration. It does so by drawing on recent research on the situation as regards education, work and living conditions of young descendants of migrants from Turkey to Sweden.

Why is this so?

When European Union analysts conclude that Sweden has a progressive and successful integration policy in place, they are alluding to the country's legislative framework. It is in this domain that the European Union can make a difference. It looks at formal and legal regulations that apply to migrants. It reviews rights and obligations that accompany the resident permit. Analysts find that in the fields of housing, health care, education, child care, labour market, social care, pensions and social benefits migrants with a residence permit enjoy equal rights with Swedish citizens. They have scrutinised anti-discrimination laws, language rights, cultural rights and the requirements for naturalisation. They have concluded that on the whole Sweden has more liberal regulations in place than other member states of the European Union.

However, these European Union reviews do not evaluate the impact on daily life of these policies as reflected in statistics regarding social indicators (unemployment rates, income distribution, social welfare dependency, educational achievement etc.).

The SD states that the integration policies have failed because most recent migrant categories have not adapted to Swedish ways. According to the SD, this applies particularly to migrants of African and Asian origin, and even to their descendants. In particular it applies to migrants who are Muslims or who have come from Muslim countries.

The SD argues that migrants of African and Asian origin do not intend to integrate in Sweden. These migrants, the party says, do not make an effort to learn the Swedish language and seek to lead their lives in cultural enclaves. Some outspoken representatives of the party even contend that migrants do not seek to earn their living through work, but are instead happy to exploit the social welfare system. The SD is especially critical of Islam. The party insists that Islam is foreign to Swedish culture. Another point that the SD is more than willing to communicate is that persons of migrant origin are overrepresented in the criminal justice statistics for offences such as armed robbery, rape, assault and murder.

One MP for the SD, Mr Kent Ekeroth, submitted a motion to parliament calling for a change in the current law so as to enable national and ethnic registration of migrants, and of descendants of migrants, who are found guilty of criminal offences. The justification for the proposed change of law is to improve statistical analysis in the name of crime prevention.[5] However, Mr Ekeroth's motion met with strong resistance in parliament and outside.[6]

While the European reports are rarely given public attention, the SD has successfully promoted its highly critical position. The good news, that Sweden at least in certain respects is doing quite well at integrating persons of migrant origin, does not make the headlines. This is because molders of opinion tend to be sceptical about European analysis. While public opinion in general seems to accept as fact that integration in Sweden is facing serious problems, not everyone is prepared to accept the solutions put forward by the SD. One proposed solution is to drastically reduce all forms of migration to Sweden. Another is to repatriate migrant categories that are seen to stand out culturally. Most recently the SD proposed a change of legislation on naturalisation with the intent of denying persons of non-European origin the right to access Swedish citizenship.

The European refugee crisis, building up during the fall of 2015 and culminating in the spring of 2016, brought about a major change in Swedish refugee policy. Along with Germany, Sweden initially chose not to close its borders to asylum seekers as virtually all European member states did. This led to a rapid increase in the number of asylum seekers, reaching tens of thousands per week at the peak in October 2015. The government found itself forced to act, as the immigration authorities could no longer handle the increasing numbers. Several parties in parliament agreed that the number of new arrivals needed to be reduced drastically. The coalition government (Social Democrats and Green Party) introduced temporary residence permits, adapted the norm for granting permits to a European minimum, and set up identity checks at border crossings. Persons seeking entry to Sweden who could not produce valid identification cards were turned back and not permitted to enter the country. These measures were criticised by the Left party and the Centre party, while other, non-socialist parties gave their tacit support. The measures proved to be effective, with the number of asylum seekers dropping significantly. An unexpected effect of this change of policy was that the SD for the first time in years saw a fall in the opinion polls, a small, but nonetheless statistically significant drop in support.

When people on the political left claim that Swedish integration policies have failed, they obviously do not endorse the SD analysis that cultural differences and unwillingness to adjust to Swedish ways is the problem. Instead they stress problems of inequality, discrimination in the labour market, segregation in the housing market, and racism in society. For the political left these are structural conditions in society that integration policy has not managed to counteract.

The Facts

What are the hard facts? What do social indicators tell us?

It is true that persons of migrant origin are over-represented in the criminal justice statistics. This has emerged repeatedly in surveys over the years.[7] It is also a fact that persons of migrant origin are overrepresented in the unemployment statistics. From this it follows that persons of migrant origin are more dependent on social welfare than native Swedes are. Another observation that should concern the authorities is that children of migrant origin show higher dropout rates from school than children of native Swedish origin.[8] An important fourth indicator is in the general health statistics. These show that people of migrant origin are harder hit by welfare diseases than others. These include cardio-vascular diseases, cancer and diabetes.[9]

These social indicators imply that problems exist in integrating persons of migrant origin and ensuring that these persons enjoy equality with the Swedish-born population. However, these indicators do not point in the direction of culture conflict as claimed by the SD.

The statistical concept of overrepresentation is often subject to misunderstanding. A majority of all criminal offences committed in Sweden are committed by native born Swedish perpetrators for the simple reason that native born Swedish people constitute the vast majority of the population. In SD propaganda, however, one is led to believe that people of migrant origin are responsible for most criminal offences. Another implicit assumption is that the victims of crimes committed by persons of migrant background are persons of native Swedish origin. However, this is not the case. The criminal justice data clearly shows that persons of migrant origin are also overrepresented among victims of crime. Criminal offences committed by persons of migrant origin are primarily directed at other persons of migrant origin.

Further analysis of the criminal justice statistics demonstrates that social class rather than ethnicity, culture or migrant origin explains the overrepresentation.[10] This means that inequality and structures that serve as obstacles to equal opportunity (discrimination, segregation etc.) are the problem, not cultural differences.

Long-term panel studies of the labour market show that unemployment rates for persons of non-Swedish origin tend to drop. Unemployment rates for descendants of migrants still tend to be higher than for young persons of native Swedish origin, but on the other hand lower than that of their migrant parents. Employment is an important indicator of integration because the labour market as a social arena brings people of non-Swedish origin into contact with an essential structure of Swedish society. From this we learn that integration is not a quick-fix. It takes time and there are many reasons why this is the case. Mastering the language, building up a network of contacts and acquiring viable qualifications are all time-consuming endeavours.

While education statistics show that children of migrant origin are overrepresented among drop-outs and among children who leave school without passing exams, statistics also show that children of migrant background are overrepresented among those doing exceptionally well at school. This applies in particular to girls of migrant origin, many of whom would not have enjoyed equal educational rights in their parents' native countries.

While migrants of non-European origin have a poorer general health status than native Swedes of the same age, this does not apply to descendants of migrants living in Sweden.[11]

One conclusion to be drawn is that integration is a time-consuming process. Many of the problems highlighted by the media as integration problems, and which the SD are quick to exploit for propaganda purposes, are not really problems of integration. They are rather difficulties associated with initial settlement and adjustment. These problems should more correctly be labelled as issues of incorporation. What we refer to as 'integration' is a complex social phenomenon, extending over several generations and with significant variations when various central variables are more closely examined.

The TIES-project

The TIES-project was an enquiry into the living conditions, educational achievements and career accomplishments of descendants of migrants from Turkey.[12] Respondents were selected from residents in the greater Stockholm metropolitan area, and the study was carried out by a research team at Stockholm University. This study was part of a comparative European project.[13] The TIES-project as a whole was endorsed by the European Science Foundation and the Swedish study was financed by the Swedish council for working life and social research. Data was collected using structured interviews with young adults aged between 18 and 35. In order to facilitate comparative analysis, most questions were the same in all participating countries. There were also some country specific questions. Additionally, the situation for the target group of descendants of migrants from Turkey was compared to corresponding data from a reference (or comparison) group consisting of native Swedish persons in the same age bracket.[14]

At first sight comparative studies between (superficially) relatively similar nations may seem a straightforward and feasible task. However, quite frequently international comparative studies come up against some hard nuts to crack, on account of deep-seated cultural, ideological and political differences between countries. Words that appear to have the same meaning in different languages may be understood in dissimilar ways depending on non-uniform socio-political contexts.

This is not to say that comparative studies should not be carried out, but it is a reminder that questions of terminology in joint comparative ventures need to be scrutinised carefully. One's choice of terminology will have a profound effect on the entire mindset. Some terminological issues within the TIES project as a whole were not in accord with Swedish understanding, two of which I shall mention.

The first one concerns the concept of generation. While it is not incorrect to speak of a first generation of migrants, with reference to persons migrating and settling in a country other than that in which they were born and raised, the concept of second generation migrants is misleading when it is used to denote descendants of migrants born in the country to which their parents migrated. Descendants of migrants are not migrants themselves. In this sense the categorisation is objectively erroneous. However, a more important consideration is that by employing generational terminology one is essentialising migrant identity, and perpetuating it. If one accepts that 'second generation migrant' is an exact categorisation there is no reason why one should not speak of a 'third generation migrant' and a 'fourth generation migrant' and so on. While there is every reason for research to assess the situation of descendants of migrants as regards health, well-being, educational achievement, labour market opportunities and so on, all this can be done without resorting to the generation metaphor.

The second issue which the TIES-project management overlooked is the fact that migrant groups originating in Turkey are of different ethnic origins and present different reasons for migrating to Europe, in our case to Sweden. The TIES-project management assumed, so it seems, that all migrants originating from Turkey are ethnic, Turkish-speaking Turks. The Swedish TIES data presents a different picture. It is true that a majority of the respondents of the Swedish sample are ethnic Turks, but a significant number of the respondents within the sample identify themselves as Kurds. This is a matter of categorisation, labelling and identity, hence a terminological issue, with empirical implications. Its importance should not be overlooked. By and large ethnic Turks came to Sweden as labour migrants, while many of the Kurds that came to Sweden from Turkey did so as refugees. These two migrant categories came at different points in time. A third ethnic category found in our sample is the Syriacs, identifying themselves as Syrianis (some refer to themselves as Assyrians). These people, speaking the language of Suryoyo, are an Eastern Orthodox Christian minority found in south-eastern Turkey and neighboring countries. They were not accepted as political refugees in Sweden, but were granted residence permits on humanitarian grounds. Subsequently, chain migration has increased the Syriac community significantly. The conditions for incorporation and integration for this community differ significantly from those applying to ethnic Turks and Kurds. Our analysis shows that these different community backgrounds, migration motives and incorporation conditions play a considerable role for the results of our study.[15] It is noteworthy that researchers participating in the TIES-project seem to have overlooked this important variable.

Findings

The Swedish study found that a majority of Muslim respondents reported personal experiences of racial discrimination and harassment.[16] We found that the schools which our interviewees had attended were

Table 2.1 Parents' ethnicity (self identification); Ethnic Turks, Kurds and Syriacs[17]

	Father	Mother
Ethnic Turks	60	59
Kurds	14	15
Syriacs	23	24
Other, don't know	3	2
	100 (n = 251)	100 (n = 251)

segregated according to national criteria, in the sense that in one category of schools pupils represented a broad range of national and cultural backgrounds whereas proportionally fewer pupils were of native Swedish background. In other schools very few pupils were of non-Swedish background. Segregation of schools and of housing tends to produce segregated social relations. This in turn affects participation in civic and political organisations. We found that the descendants of migrants from Turkey do not participate in civic organisations to the same degree as the native Swedish reference group does.[18] Partner formation and marital relations are likely to be affected. Descendants of migrants from Turkey rarely engage in social events and occasions that are typical of majority culture. Therefore identification with Sweden as a country is weak.[19]

On the other hand, identification with the suburban neighbourhood where the respondents reside is strong. We observed that educational performance was quite successful among our respondents. These descendants of migrants from Turkey are not way behind the Swedish reference group in educational achievement.[20] This means that young people with a background in Turkey have defied downward assimilation.[21] Despite successful educational achievement, young women with a background in Turkey nevertheless are in a weaker position in the labour market than male respondents. This outcome would appear to depend on an all-embracing gender discrimination within the Swedish labour market (also affecting women of the reference group), as well as on the inferior social position ascribed to women within ethnic groups emigrating from Turkey. For male respondents there are no significant differences between target group and reference group as regards labour market careers. However, respondents with a background in Turkey run a greater risk than the reference group of becoming singled out from the labour market.[22] Target group respondents tend to end up in similar un-qualified labour market positions to their parents.

In summary, the situation for descendants of migrants from Turkey is not as detrimental as critics on the extreme right-wing would have it. For several crucial indicators the target group is not behind, or at least not far behind, the Swedish reference group. The picture propagated by the SD is that migrants of non-European origin, and also their descendants, are an economic burden to society. Our data shows that this conception is incorrect as far as migrants from Turkey and their descendants are concerned. On the other hand, however, the promising image of successful Swedish integration policies presented in various European reports does not hold true for this group. They are victims of discrimination and segregation in society. Although in certain respects they are doing reasonably well, in other respects there is cause for concern about injustices affecting this group.

These findings indicate that integration is a more complex phenomenon than public debate suggests. This occasions us to reflect about what is actually meant by integration. In sociological theory we may identify three distinctly different conceptualisations: integration as identification, integration as participation and integration as cohesion. These conceptualisations emerge from different theoretical traditions in the social sciences.

Integration as Identification

The Canadian social psychologist John Berry represents the identification approach.[23] Berry's focal point is on migrants' (or minority persons') simultaneous identification (or lack of identification) with majority society/culture and minority society/culture. Berry assumes that migrants, and usually also their descendants, as well as members of an ethnic minority, need to make up their mind about how they relate to majority society/culture and to minority society/culture. *Integration* represents the option where they affirm both situations. This could mean that in the public/private divide of life one outwardly accepts, cherishes and abides by the codes and tenets of majority society (in working life, in the educational system and as regards citizenship). In the private sphere of the family on the other hand, one may honour traditions, ways of being and the language of the minority culture. This private sphere may be extended to include cultural and religious organisations associated with minority identity.

Table 2.2 Berry's Conceptualisation of Integration in Terms of Identification

Identification with		Majority Culture/Society	
		yes	no
Minority	yes	integration	separation
Culture/Society	no	assimilation	marginalisation

When a migrant, descendant of migrants or member of a minority group opts to identify with the values and mores of majority society and to disown the cultural heritage of her/his family and forebears we have assimilation. In countries of immigration such as the United States, Canada and Australia assimilation was regarded as the obvious and given solution to the incorporation of migrants. A second outcome is separation. This implies that migrants, their descendants and minority groups do not associate more than is necessary with the institutions of majority society. This option implies that they would prefer to live apart from members of mainstream society. Parents would send their children to schools run by their own community. Traditional cultural minorities present examples of this. A third outcome is termed marginalisation. In this case, both majority and minority society/culture are rejected. Berry's theoretical framework is unclear for this case. Marginalisation as Berry defines it represents failure and is an unwanted and barren solution to the issue of identification in a multicultural context. This is a consequence of Berry's operational definitions. Theoretically there need be no negative tinge to marginalisation. Rather, marginalisation may well have positive connotations in terms of cultural change, cultural development and 'hybridity'. Radical ideas put forward by the Chicago school of sociology in their groundbreaking studies of migrant communities in the American Midwest in the 1930s saw marginalisation as an opening to cultural change.

Berry's operational approach is insufficient when it comes to understanding marginalisation, but his framework has proved to be an empirically powerful tool. Numerous studies from many parts of the world have all come up with high and significant correlations with explanatory power.

Integration as Participation

The American sociologist Milton Gordon saw assimilation as a stepwise and gradually increasing participation in various domains of social life. He defined integration as active participation.[24] According to this approach integration, and ultimately assimilation, is recognised as a process over time that may extend over generations. Gordon's classic book *Assimilation in American Life* had a profound impact on the discourse of incorporation in the 1950s. It drew on surveys of European migrants' settlement in the United States.

One first sphere in which migrant participation takes place virtually right from the first day of arrival in the new country is the economy. The migrant and his/her family needs to find a dwelling, to buy food and to secure a source of income. A second domain in which migrant children will participate is the educational system. Every child, regardless of legal status, ethnic origin or cultural background, is subject to compulsory school attendance. The migrant will need to seek employment. When this is successfully achieved he or she will participate in the general workforce. In capitalist societies low-paid labour is usually in demand. When migration from Europe was at its height a century ago low-paid employment was found in branches of the manufacturing industry. Today in the USA a demand for low-paid seasonal labour dominates parts of the agricultural sector. This demand is met by undocumented Latino migrants, crossing over from Mexico. Currently in Sweden the construction industry is facing competition from low-paid labour from Poland and the Baltic states.

Language is a domain in which migrants will increase their participation as they learn to master the host country language. For adults it usually takes longer to acquire a working proficiency than for their children. Language proficiency is usually essential for educational and career achievement. It opens up opportunities to socialise across ethnic and cultural boundaries, not only between members of migrant/minority and majority communities, but also between different migrant/minority communities. Language proficiency is an essential practical condition for participation in civic organisations, social networks, unions and interest organisations, and ultimately in the political field at large. Language capability provides migrants with the tools to pursue political objectives and representation in political bodies.

By international standards, Sweden has liberal laws on naturalisation. Naturalisation is accompanied by the right to vote in national elections and also includes protection by the state in times of crisis. Acquisition of citizenship may involve compulsory national service when this is required or reintroduced. The Swedish state encourages naturalisation of those who plan to stay and who meet the requirements. Welfare statistics prove that naturalised foreign-born residents do not diverge in significant respects from comparable population segments of native born Swedish citizens.[25]

Time and again surveys bear witness to the presence of segregation in the housing market. This is not only a reality in major cities, but also in medium-sized and even small towns. Families of migrant origin tend to be referred to low-status residential areas located on the outskirts of urban areas. Housing standards are usually of an acceptable quality, but the residential areas are impoverished and often lacking in work-places. They live in rented accommodation and generally don't own their apartments. Segregation is an obstacle to socialising across social, ethnic and cultural boundaries. Migrant families who do well professionally will relocate to middle-class residential areas where people own their houses or apartments. In Sweden residential segregation is basically a social class phenomenon and has a long history going back to the times of industrialisation and rapid urbanisation. Today social-class based segregation has an added racial and ethnic element, as migrant categories are directed to housing in lower-class areas.

When persons of migrant/minority background find housing in previously native Swedish middle-class residential areas without encountering opposition, and when they are accepted as neighbours, then one may speak of residential integration.

The last stage in Gordon's model is about partner formation and marriage across earlier ethnic, cultural and religious boundaries. When this final barrier is pulled down, then we may speak of family integration. And this, Gordon says, defines assimilation.

Integration as Cohesion

In a general sense 'integration' refers to the relationship between a whole and its parts. Hence it is a systemic and relational concept. In this understanding integration represents a situation in which the parts making up the whole operate in such a way that each and every part, although performing different tasks, enables the functioning of the whole. The logical opposite of integration understood in this way is not segregation but disintegration. This approach to understanding 'integration' is holistic. We need to fathom the whole, whatever whole we have in mind and however we define it, in order to determine whether the parts are operating in concert or not. An important consideration is what whole we have in mind, what limits we set to it, and in what context it is situated.

The German philosopher and sociologist Georg Simmel posed an intriguing question: 'How is society possible?' he asked.[26] How does a society work out? Sweden is a small country in the family of nations with nearly ten million inhabitants. China at the other end of this continuum is the world's most heavily populated country with some 1.4 billion inhabitants. How is it possible that the activities of all the individual persons making up the population of a society, and all its organisations, institutions, businesses, parties and authorities at various levels somehow synchronise to make life reasonably tolerable for most people most of the time? Some societies break down under internal strains and conflicts, but these cases are exceptions rather than the rule. Problems occur, mistakes are made, sections of the population may be dissatisfied, some break the law for personal gain, conflicts occur, sometimes leading to armed struggle and war. The consequences of war may well be a breakdown of society, at least for the losing side. The war effort in itself may on the other hand serve to integrate society by spurring people to make an additional contribution to the common cause. By and large most societies are functional most of the time. The whole holds together when each and every individual member of society goes about his or her business.

Social cohesion was a central question addressed by the classic sociologists. Class division during the age of early industrialisation was seen to threaten social stability and social cohesion.

A crucial question is what we define as the social whole. Society, or to be more precise, the nation state, is an obvious candidate. Integration, defined as social cohesion, is an issue that a consolidating nation state needs to address. Social division, be it defined by class, ethnicity, religion or culture occasions unequal opportunities, unequal distribution of resources and unequal access to power. It generates strains in society.

To understand cohesion as a societal phenomenon, different levels of analysis merit consideration. A minority group may be well integrated in itself (for example the Amish community in Pennsylvania, or the Saami people of northern Scandinavia) but not in society as a whole. Should we speak of integration/social cohesion in such cases?

At the other end the European Union introduces a supranational level of analysis when it strives to achieve the goal of integration at the European level. Signal words such as 'harmonisation', 'joint solutions' and 'common interests' indicate that the European Union is aiming at cohesion between the different member states. The EU consists of 28 sovereign member states. For the European Union integration is about harmonisation of laws, in particular in fields of concern that transcend national borders. Combating organised crime is one such issue where member states need to work towards the same goals. Another common concern is environmental protection. Migration is a third concern where member states need to cooperate and pull in the same direction. In recent months we have witnessed the breakdown of solidarity between member states in sharing the burden of managing the ongoing refugee crisis, which is a serious threat to European integration.

The word for society in various European languages has different etymological roots. In English and French the word society/societé is derived from Latin socius with the meaning of friendship. In a metaphorical sense it may be read as implying good neighbourly relations. The meaning of the two German words Gemeinschaft and Gesellschaft were analysed by Ferdinand Tönnies in his classic treatise.[27] Gemeinschaft has connotations of community, while *Gesellschaft* is more about association. The Danish and also the identical Norwegian word for society is *samfund*, which translates as community. Although a Scandinvian language, the Swedish word differs from its Danish and Norwegian counterpart. The Swedish word for society is *samhälle*. This Swedish word is directly derived from the word *sammanhållning*, which literally means holding together. The Swedish word *samhälle* highlights the most crucial aspect of society – its holding together, its social cohesion, its integration.

Durkheim's analysis of social cohesion sheds light on two different approaches by means of which societies hold together – *mechanical solidarity* and *organic solidarity*.[28] Mechanical solidarity is about members of society sharing common values. Traditionally, the Church (and in a more general sense religious institutions) was the upholder of common values. Nationalism developed into a political force during the nineteenth century, and states started to define themselves as nation states. National symbols were disseminated and national sentiments were expressed in the arts, music and literature. The idea of the nation was seen as the glue that holds society together. National identity involved allegiance to the state. National movements developed complex states and institutions, but the basic principle was still about sharing common values, common language and common identity.

One could say that a social entity, be it a state, an organisation or a community, which is characterised by mechanical solidarity, sees homogenisation as the answer to how social cohesion is maintained. This is the solution advocated by the SD. The belief is that social homogenisation reduces tension and conflict. Society is organised in such a way that its members are expected to strive towards the same societal goals. It follows that a society organised in terms of mechanical solidarity will be more likely to adopt, to favour, or just slip into a political system of authoritarian rule whether this is founded on national principles, religious belief or the dictatorship of the proletariat.

Organic solidarity on the other hand is about people's interdependence upon each other. In modern society with the industrialisation of production, individual members of the workforce need to specialise. Each and every person should not have to master all necessary skills required for life in modern society. An employee sells his/her skills for wages and with the money earned s/he pays for goods and services that others provide. At an aggregated societal level the economy operates as a complex web of interdependencies. This web is what holds society together. It does so much more effectively than indoctrinated common religious or national values.

Durkheim's analysis was about the labour market, but the same principle may come into play in other societal domains. Organic solidarity points to benefits for societies that embrace diversity. People work in a wide range of trades and businesses, they pursue different objectives, they have varying interests, they have divergent priorities, and they have unique experiences. This diversity makes complementary interdependence possible. For example, diversity of ideas is thought to serve as a breeding ground for innovation, for invention, for knowledge development, and ultimately for economic development. Differences of opinion, differences of interest and differences of priority may well be at the root of social conflict, but conflict is not necessarily something inherently bad or something that must be avoided. The problem is not conflict as such but the lack of functioning mechanisms to resolve conflict.

The plea for diversity involves two basic issues. One is equality of human worth. People may differ in various respects, but they are (and should be regarded as) equal in the eyes of the law. The second issue is that conflict needs to be recognised as an adaptive social force triggering change. The presumption is that conflict needs to be handled in a 'civilised' way, that conflict resolution will usually work towards reaching settlement in terms of compromise, that the verdict of law courts carry due weight, and that the opposite party is respected. This means that agreement prevails about how to go about resolving conflict. Agreement about rules of procedure is not homogenisation by enforcing the same values.

Right before our eyes parliamentary democracy functions in accordance with principles of diversity. Decisions made by parliament are based on the will of the majority. To organise a majority may require compromise and some horse-trading. Parties in a parliamentary democracy accept and respect the verdict of the electorate. Parliamentary democracy is an example as good as any of procedural rules on how to handle differences.

Conclusion

Returning to the Swedish situation, if we look at integration as a process of identification we find strong empirical support for the integration option rather than for separation, assimilation or marginalisation.[29] In the TIES research Berry's model and methods were not used so we cannot conclusively determine that this is the case for our target group. Our TIES data suggests, however, that Kurds and Syriacs are closer to the integration option than the ethnic Turkish respondents. The latter group appears to come closer to Berry's separation option. If on the other hand we look at integration as participation we find patterns in our data that suggest that participation in the economic, social, political and residential spheres could be better than it is. We also find that in the spheres of education, language and naturalisation our target group reports a satisfactory degree of participation.

If we look at integration as a matter of social cohesion we come up with a mixed picture. Migrants from Turkey and their descendants tend to be subject to discrimination in the housing market, and to a certain extent also in the labour market. People with an origin in Turkey rank low on various measures of social (cultural) distance. The SD party has exploited undercurrents of xenophobia present in Swedish society, thus giving xenophobia a voice in parliament. This is in itself a blow to inclusion. Organic solidarity, interdependence and inclusion are compatible with a wide range of identities. Some identities, however, tend to define themselves by exclusion. This applies in particular to identities referring to ethnicity, culture, religion and nation.

The Migrant integration policy index shows that Sweden has passed a number of laws that are necessary to enable and facilitate integration both in terms of identification and participation. In this respect Sweden is on the right track. However, such legislation is in itself not a sufficient condition to secure integration in a situation where migrants of non-European origin face discrimination in the labour market and segregation in the housing sector. Greater vigilance from society is required to combat all forms of social exclusion. Most political commentators agree that unemployment needs to be reduced, and that if and when this is achieved social cohesion would improve. Reducing unemployment is not an issue of integration policy as such but rather of economic policy, both on a national level and a supranational EU-level. It is understandable that migrant groups and their descendants, having experienced many years of discrimination and social exclusion, may tend towards what Berry calls the separation option. In the public sphere, however, social cohesion is more compatible with Berry's integration option. To compete successfully in the public spheres of education and employment descendants of migrants from Turkey residing in Sweden need to attain an adequate mastery of the Swedish language. It is therefore necessary for society to counteract residential segregation. However, minority parents may also need to rethink the situation, as sending one's children to ethnically, culturally or religiously based (minority) schools does not provide the best opportunity to gain mastery of Swedish.

Notes

1. Gosta Esping-Andersen, *The Three Worlds Of Welfare Capitalism.* Polity Press (Cambridge, 1990).
2. Tomas Hammar (ed.), *European Immigration Policy: A Comparative Study,* Cambridge University Press (Cambridge, 1985). Aleksandra Ålund & Carl-Ulrik Schierup, *The Paradoxes of Multiculturalism* Avebury (Aldershot, 1991). Charles Westin, 'Equality, freedom of choice and partnership: Multicultural policy in Sweden', in Bauböck, R., Heller, A. & Zolberg, A.R. (eds), *The Challenge of Diversity. Integration and Pluralism in Societies of Immigration* Avebury (Aldershot, 1996).
3. Charles Westin, *Settlement and integration policies towards immigrants and their descendants in Sweden,* International Migration Papers ILO, 34 (Geneva, 2000).
4. SD. Bilaga A – Besparingar på invandring och integration. SD. Ur Sverigedemokraternas principprogram. *Dagens nyheter.* 'Misslyckad integration kan leda till social kris'.
5. Motion 2014/15:1106. Reformering av lag om behandling av personuppgifter. Submitted by MP Kent Ekeroth (SD) 2014-11-07.
6. *Expressen,* 'Kent Ekeroths motion möter starkt motstånd'. *Aftonbladet,* 'SD: registrera alla invandrare. Partiet lägger fram motion som kräver registrering efter nationell bakgrund'.
7. Charles Westin, 'On migration and criminal offence. Report on a study from Sweden', *IMIS-Beiträge 8/1998,* IMIS, University of Osnabrück (1998). Martin Hälllsten, Ryszard Szulkin,

Jerzy Sarnecki, 'Crime as a price of inequality? The delinquency gap between children of immigrants and children of native Swedes', *The British Journal of Criminology*, 53/3 (2013), pp. 456–81.

8. Statistics Sweden, *Integration – en beskrivning av läget i Sverige*.
9. Ibid.
10. BRÅ. *Brott bland ungdomar i årskurs nio. Resultat från Skolundersökningen om brott åren 1995–2011*.
11. Statistics Sweden, *Integration – en beskrivning av läget i Sverige*.
12. Charles Westin (ed.) *The Integration of Descendants from Turkey in Stockholm: The TIES Study in Sweden*, Amsterdam University Press (Amsterdam, 2015).
13. Maurice Crul, Jens Schneider, & Frans Leslie, *The European second generation compared: Does the integration context matter?* Amsterdam University Press (Amsterdam, 2012).
14. C. Westin (ed.), *The Integration of Descendants from Turkey in Stockholm*.
15. Costanza Vera-Larrucea, 'Historical and demographic considerations', in Charles Westin (ed.), *Integration of Descendants of Migrants from Turkey in Stockholm: The TIES Study in Sweden*, Amsterdam University Press (Amsterdam, 2015), pp. 25–42.
16. Alireza Behtoui, 'Perceptions of discrimination', in Westin, C. (ed.), *The Integration of Descendants from Turkey in Stockholm: The TIES Study in Sweden*, Amsterdam University Press (Amsterdam, 2015), pp. 69–78.
17. Ibid., p. 37.
18. Alireza Behtoui, 'Social capital', in Westin, C. (ed.), *The Integration of Descendants from Turkey in Stockholm: The TIES Study in Sweden*, Amsterdam University Press (Amsterdam, 2015), pp. 57–68.
19. Costanza Vera-Larrucea, 'Identity: Belonging, language and transnationalism', in Westin, C. (ed.), *The Integration of Descendants from Turkey in Stockholm: The TIES Study in Sweden*, Amsterdam University Press (Amsterdam, 2015), pp. 79–102.
20. Alireza Behtoui, 'Educational achievement', in Westin, C. (ed.), *The Integration of Descendants from Turkey in Stockholm: The TIES Study in Sweden*, Amsterdam University Press (Amsterdam, 2015), pp. 43–56.
21. Alireza Behtoui, 'Conclusions', in Westin, C. (ed.), *The Integration of Descendants from Turkey in Stockholm: The TIES Study in Sweden*, Amsterdam University Press (Amsterdam, 2015), pp. 125–33.
22. Lena Schröder, 'The labour market', in Westin, C. (ed.), *The Integration of Descendants from Turkey in Stockholm. The TIES Study in Sweden*, Amsterdam University Press (Amsterdam, 2015), pp. 103–24.

23. John Berry, 'Psychology of acculturation', in J. Berman (ed.), *Cross-Cultural Perspectives: Nebraska Symposium on Motivation.* University of Nebraska Press, (Lincoln, 1990), pp. 201–34.
24. Milton Gordon, *Assimilation in American life*, Oxford University Press (New York, 1964).
25. Statistics Sweden, *Integration – en beskrivning av läget i Sverige.*
26. George Simmel, *On Individuality and Social Forms*, The University of Chicago Press (Chicago, 1971), pp. 6–22.
27. Ferdinand Tönnies, *Community and Association*, Routledge and Kegan Paul (London, 1955).
28. Emile Durkheim, *The Division of Labour in Society*, Macmillan (London, 1984).
29. Erkki Virta, David L. Sam and Charles Westin, 'Adolescents with Turkish background in Norway and Sweden. A comparative study of their psychological adaptation', *Scandinavian Journal of Psychology*, 45/1 (2004), pp. 15–25.

References

Aftonbladet, 'SD: registrera alla invandrare. Partiet lägger fram motion som kräver registrering efter nationell bakgrund'. 2014. http://www.aftonbladet.se/kultur/article200/
Ålund, A., & Schierup, C.-U., *The Paradoxes of Multiculturalism*, Aldershot (Avebury, 1991).
Behrenz, L., Hammarstedt, M., & Månsson, J., 'Second generation immigrants in the Swedish labour market', *International Review of Applied Economics*, 21 (2007), pp. 151–74.
Behtoui, A., 'Perceptions of discrimination', in Westin, C. (ed.), *The Integration of Descendants from Turkey in Stockholm: The TIES Study in Sweden*, Amsterdam University Press (Amsterdam, 2015), pp. 69–78.
——, 'Social capital', in Westin, C. (ed.), *The Integration of Descendants from Turkey in Stockholm: The TIES Study in Sweden.* Amsterdam University Press, (Amsterdam, 2015), pp. 57–68.
——, 'Educational achievement', in Westin, C. (ed.), *The Integration of Descendants from Turkey in Stockholm: The TIES Study in Sweden*, Amsterdam University Press, (Amsterdam, 2015), pp. 43–56.
——, 'Conclusions', in Westin, C. (ed.), *The Integration of Descendants from Turkey in Stockholm: The TIES Study in Sweden*, Amsterdam University Press (Amsterdam, 2015), pp. 125–133.
Berry, J.W., 'Psychology of acculturation', in J. Berman (ed.), *Cross-Cultural Perspectives: Nebraska Symposium on Motivation*, Lincoln: University of Nebraska Press (Lincoln, 1990), pp. 201–34.
Berry, J.W., Phinney, J.S., Sam, D.L., & Vedder, P. (eds), *Immigrant youth in cultural transition*, Lawrence Erlbaum (London, 2006).

BRÅ, *Brott bland ungdomar i årskurs nio Resultat från Skolundersökningen om brott åren 1995–2011*, The Swedish National Council for Crime Prevention (Stockholm, 2013).

Crul, M., Schneider, J., & Leslie, F., *The European second generation compared. Does the integration context matter?* Amsterdam University Press. (Amsterdam, 2012).

Dagens nyheter, 'Misslyckad integration kan leda till social kris' (2016). http://www.dn.se/ekonomi/misslyckad-integration-kan-leda-till-social-kris/ (accessed 29 August 2017).

Durkheim, É., *The Division of Labour in Society*, Macmillan (London, 1984).

Esping-Andersen, G., *The Three Worlds of Welfare Capitalism*, Polity Press (Cambridge, 1990).

Expressen, 'Kent Ekeroths motion möter starkt motstånd' (2014). http://www.expressen.se/nyheter/politik/kent-ekeroths-motion-moter-starkt-motstand/ (accessed 29 August 2017).

Gordon, M., *Assimilation in American Life*, Oxford University Press (New York, 1964).

Hällsten, M., Szulkin, R., Sarnecki, J., 'Crime as a price of inequality? The delinquency gap between children of immigrants and children of native Swedes', *The British Journal of Criminology*, 53/3 (2013), pp. 456–81.

Hammar, T. (ed.), *European Immigration Policy: A Comparative Study*, Cambridge University Press (Cambridge, 1985).

Motion 2014/15:1106. Reformering av lag om behandling av personuppgifter. Submitted 20141107. http://www.riksdagen.se/sv/dokument-lagar/dokument/motion/reformering-av-lag-om-behandling-av_H2021106 (accessed 29 August 2017).

Sam, D.L. and Berry, J.W. (eds), *The Cambridge Handbook of Acculturation Psychology*, Cambridge University Press (Cambridge, 2006).

Schröder, L., 'From problematic objects to resourceful subjects: An overview of immigrant-native labour market gaps from a policy perspective', *Swedish Economic Policy Review*, 14/1 (2007), pp. 7–31.

——, 'The labour market', in Westin, C. (ed.), *The integration of descendants from Turkey in Stockholm: The TIES study in Sweden*, Amsterdam University Press (Amsterdam, 2015), pp. 103–24.

SD, Bilaga A – Besparingar på invandring och integration (2014), https://sd.se/wp-content/uploads/2014/11/Besparing-invandring-och-integration-141027.pdf (accessed 29 August 2017).

SD, Ur Sverigedemokraternas principprogram (2015), https://vasternorrland.sd.se/kommunpolitik/invandring/ (accessed 29 August 2017).

Simmel, G., *On Individuality and Social Forms*, The University of Chicago Press (Chicago, 1971).

Statistics Sweden, *Integration – en beskrivning av läget i Sverige*, Statistiska centralbyrån, (Örebro, 2013).

Tönnies, F., *Community and Association*, Routledge and Kegan Paul (London, 1955).

Vera-Larrucea, C., 'Historical and demographic considerations', in Westin, C. (ed.), *The Integration of Descendants from Turkey in Stockholm: The TIES Study in Sweden*, Amsterdam University Press (Amsterdam, 2015), pp. 25–42.

——, 'Identity: Belonging, language and transnationalism', in Westin, C. (ed.), *The Integration of Descendants from Turkey in Stockholm: The TIES Study in Sweden*, Amsterdam University Press (Amsterdam, 2015), pp. 79–102.

Virta, E., Sam, D.L., and Westin, C., 'Adolescents with Turkish background in Norway and Sweden. A comparative study of their psychological adaptation', *Scandinavian Journal of Psychology*, 45/1 (2004), pp. 15–25.

Westin, C., 'Equality, freedom of choice and partnership: Multicultural policy in Sweden', in Bauböck, R., Heller, A., & Zolberg, A.R. (eds), *The Challenge of Diversity: Integration and Pluralism in Societies of Immigration*, Aldershot (Avebury, 1996).

——, 'On migration and criminal offence. Report on a study from Sweden'. *IMIS-Beiträge 8/1998*, IMIS, University of Osnabrück (1998).

——, *Settlement and integration policies towards immigrants and their descendants in Sweden*. International Migration Papers 34 (Geneva: ILO. 2000).

——, (ed.), *The Integration of Descendants from Turkey in Stockholm: The TIES Study in Sweden*, Amsterdam University Press (Amsterdam, 2015).

CHAPTER 3

NICKNAMES IN DIASPORA: TRACING MIGRANT TALES OF FIRST-GENERATION TURKISH MIGRANTS IN SWEDEN

Öncel Naldemirci

Introduction

Nicknames are well-known to anthropologists who conduct research in small-scale rural communities, yet scarce attention has been paid to the roles they may play in a migration context, specifically within diasporic communities. Nicknames might offer insight into ways in which a sense of community is created and sustained, especially during dramatic changes such as migration and settlement in a new country. In this chapter, drawing upon ethnographic study with Turkish migrants who settled in Sweden in the 1960s and early 1970s and focusing on a selection and narrative analysis of nicknames, I seek to illustrate first-generation Turkish migrants' experiences and diasporic ties in Sweden. Nicknames were common among Turkish migrants, primarily among men and bear traces of their experiences as migrants in Sweden. These nicknames reflect Turkish migrants' first impressions of Swedish society, illustrate their first encounters with the local people and Swedish institutions, remind them of their pre-migratory backgrounds and highlight community-building processes in a migration context. I argue that nicknames are emblematic of the responses of migrants who sought to come to grips with the challenges of 'homing' in a new country. For older members of the Turkish community, telling the stories of these nicknames constitutes a nostalgic and humourous way of remembering their migration and settlement in Sweden. As many nicknames are rooted in stories, I will also point to the narrative environments where migrant tales and nicknames are concocted and circulated. Oral histories of individual migrants are significant to record the history of a migrant community, yet it is also of relevance to hark back to collective experiences that are shaped in diaspora space and captured in forms other than testimonies.

Notes on the Context and the Study

Turkish associations in Sweden celebrated the 50th anniversary of the beginning of Turkish immigration to Sweden in 2015. Even though it was not possible to designate an exact date, their milestone was the mid-1960s when Sweden became an immigration country receiving labour migrants from Finland and southern parts of Europe, including Turkey. Turkish migrants to Sweden were part of the exodus from Turkey to Europe in the late 1960s and early 1970s. Most Turkish migrants went to Germany where labour migration agreements had been made.[1] Some Turkish migrants chose Sweden as a destination where they would seek employment and a better life. Some travelled around the north-western

European countries, partly as adventure at the heart of Europe, and partly as a strategy to find the most receptive labour markets. Turkish migrants came to work in big industrial cities in Sweden, where they found jobs mainly in the manufacturing sector.[2] They were pioneers, launching and/or facilitating more massive immigration from Turkey in successive years, through chain migration. Sweden had signed a labour force agreement with Turkey in 1967, however its effect was slight and recruitment was mainly through unofficial networks.[3] This led to a relative homogeneity of Turkish migrants in terms of points of departure in Turkey. Kulu, a small town in Konya in Turkey, was the home town of many migrants in Sweden.[4] The chain migration organised around kinship networks undermined the relative heterogeneity of Turkish pioneers in the early 1960s. When relatively easy immigration to Sweden came to an end after 1972,[5] it became largely limited to family reunification of the former immigrants and asylum applications. In the 1980s, Kurdish and Assyrian people from Turkey came to Sweden as refugees and this further diversified the community of Turkey-born migrants. As for today, there is a highly heterogeneous community including students, highly skilled labour migrants, refugees, large families originating from the same towns in Turkey and descendants of migrants from urban families.

The arguments presented in this chapter are based on qualitative data collected as part of an ethnographic study (2011–13) with 20 Turkish migrants who settled in Sweden in the 1960s and early 1970s. The over-arching objective in the study was to investigate how cultural repertoires around ageing, caring about each other and care giving are shaped in the context of migration.[6] In order to do justice to the heterogeneity of

Turkey-born people in Sweden, their reasons and motivations of migration and the methodology of the study, I sought to contact the first-generation self-defined Turkish immigrants in a large industrial city in Sweden. I received the help of two key informants. My first informant has lived and worked as an interpreter in Sweden for more than 45 years and he initiated my first contact with a small group of first-generation Turkish migrants who emigrated from different cities in Turkey, including Istanbul, Izmir, Ankara and Eskisehir. They had come to know each other in Sweden after their immigration. My second key informant was a woman who had come to Sweden with her now ex-husband and introduced me to some other informants, who were also older members of larger families from Konya. For interviews, I identified a list of topics in advance, such as experience of age, family relations, formal care facilities and decisions in old age. I was not initially inclined to collect life stories systematically, however many embarked on telling me, a new migrant to Sweden, their life stories. Besides these formal and semi-structured interviews, I had the opportunity to participate in the everyday life of my older informants. I was invited to family gatherings, reunions and celebrations. I took notes during and after conversations, social events and meetings. My key informants helped me understand the context of the study throughout the fieldwork.

Nicknames and stories analysed in this chapter were selected from interviews and field notes taken during social gatherings, dinners and conversations. These nicknames were more widespread among the initial group of informants who presented themselves as the pioneers from urban and relatively more educated backgrounds who had achieved middle class comforts after long years in the Swedish labour market. The nicknames that I collected were in reference to a third party during interviews and informal conversations among my informants. None of my informants, except one, referred to themselves with their conferred nicknames. I met but did not interview some third parties to whom my informants referred with nicknames, some had passed away but were remembered by my informants. Rather, I concentrated on the stories about the derivation and usage of these nicknames and why they were circulating in daily conversations of my older informants. Even though most nicknames were not derogatory or insulting, for a better chance of anonymity, I decided not to give an exhaustive list of names I had collected by eavesdropping. For those related to particular plots and stories, I have avoided giving the Turkish version of nicknames and have slightly changed the story or the nickname, taking care not to lose the colourful texture of it. I decided to use a common and even trite nickname for the only interview excerpt I use.

Nicknaming in Diaspora

Nicknaming has been considered a common feature of rural communities in Europe and in the Middle East.[7] Despite the pervasive character of the phenomenon, the derivation and function of nicknames have been subject to different interpretations. David D. Gilmore suggests that nicknaming can be seen as a form of verbal aggression, 'a mechanism of community social control',[8] whilst Richard Breen considers nicknames as a type of classification and differentiation between households and families.[9] Both advance their arguments on small-scale, non-migrant and rural communities. Drawing upon the nicknaming phenomenon among Ashkenazic and Sephardi Jews in Indianapolis, Jack Glazier advances his arguments about nicknames 'in the complex, fragmented design of urban life' by taking the effects of migration and diasporisation into consideration.[10] Glazier anchors nicknaming in the representation of a mnemonic of community. According to him, by providing a window on the past and creating a sense of community beyond the domestic and religious domains, nicknames remind people of their humble beginnings, economic struggles, the sense of community and mutual support in the early years of their settlement. Nicknames among first-generation Turkish migrants I came to know resonate more with this mnemonic definition than with derogatory and classificatory explanations. However, I would also add to Glazier's understanding by highlighting the mnemonic character of nicknames being deeply rooted in their narrative nature and the circulation of stories.

Like in a boarding school

Nicknames were significant tools for my informants to make sense of and tell me about their migration, settlement and diasporic belonging. As many were retired and pondering the possibilities of mobility and return migration, referring to nicknames and their stories constituted a nostalgic and humorous way of remembering 'the old days' when they first came and settled in Sweden. Men had immigrated earlier than women and this had led to a homosocial and even fraternal space. After their immigration to Sweden, men mostly socialised at work but also in some urban localities that had never seen this type of socialisation. Some gathered in the local train station for instance, like a regular after work socialisation. As a male informant put it, they were living *like in a 'boarding school'*. This allegory translates the experience of a particular gendered bonding, nurturing some degree of reflexivity on belonging and solidarity in a new and unfamiliar place. The homeland 'roots' formed the umbrella for a diasporic attachment, yet *like in a boarding school* the very experience of finding each other facing similar regulations, jobs and challenges was more decisive than their pre-migratory origins and similarities.

Nicknames flourished in a homosocial atmosphere of creating new bonds in a migration context. Few women had nicknames and nicknaming women had not been as common as men since it was not considered appropriate for gendered subject positions and roles they were supposed to have as wives, daughters and mothers. There were some women who took nicknames, especially for their peculiar body characteristics, for example man-voiced X, but these were not mentioned or disseminated as often as male nicknames were. However, another reason could be to do with my position as a male researcher to whom it would be inappropriate to disclose stories behind these nicknames.

Unlike the general trends of nicknaming in the Mediterranean and Middle Eastern regions based on the bodily characteristics of people, I rarely heard these types of nicknames during my fieldwork. Rather, there were two main trends in nicknaming among first-generation Turkish immigrants. The first was to adjoin the titles of previous occupations in Turkey to the first names and the second was to create a nickname based on a specific event or encounter in Sweden.

Pre-Migration Occupations

This first cluster of nicknames consisted of their pre-migratory titles and marked their professional experiences in migrants' biographies. The irony in the creation and communication of these nicknames was that they had professional skills that many never used again in the host country. These titles usually turned into nicknames but they could also precede the forenames in the stream of conversation. It is worth citing some well-known nicknames like *Polis* (Police officer), *Berber* (Barber), *Terzi* (Tailor), occasionally followed by their first names. These nicknames were a reminder of professions and their social prestige in Turkey, especially after having taken standardised manufacturing jobs in Sweden. In this way, migrants could hold on to their past in an environment where they all became blue-collar workers in standard employment with migratory status within the economy of the 1960s and early 1970s.

This cluster of nicknames derived from professional titles demonstrates that Turkish migration to Sweden was much more nuanced than the mobility of unskilled labour migrants, otherwise unemployable in the labour market of Turkey at that time. Some already had some skills and jobs in Turkey and they left their jobs for a better life and an economically more favourable job market. These nicknames also support the argument that not all migrants came from rural backgrounds. The trend was initially more from rural-to-urban migration in Turkey and then from Turkey to Europe. This argument may seem controversial nowadays, especially when we recall the massive emigration from Kulu to Sweden via chain migration and the grand narrative of the Turkish exodus of unskilled labour migrants from rural backgrounds to Europe. Nevertheless, it may also be helpful for migration scholars to distinguish between different motivations behind the emigration, glossed over by these grand narratives of Turkish migration and to understand the prevalent tension within the community.

This tension unfolds mainly among Turkish migrants who are not from Kulu specifically pointing out that they are not from Kulu.

Another important note should highlight the derivation, usage and function of these nicknames in the migration context. As argued many times by my informants, people would not have used these nicknames had they stayed in Turkey where people in their social proximity were already familiar with them, their families and professions. However, when people from different socio-cultural backgrounds and geographical regions of Turkey got together in a new country, these nicknames helped to differentiate one from others. Even though one did not continue to be a police officer and became a worker like his peers in Sweden, thanks to his nickname, he could be located in the new social environment while being differentiated from others. However, these nicknames did not necessarily seek to recreate hierarchies in a new setting; everyone knew that they would have similar difficulties when it came to migration issues, work and employment. Rather, these nicknames facilitated social interaction, familiarisation and communication within the group by creating new affinities.

First Encounters with 'the Swede'

The second and more popular trend was to improvise a nickname through the stories of first encounters with the Swedish people and institutions. These nicknames were mostly linked to some transgressive events in the Swedish context. The humour underlying these nicknames was the result of estrangement, awkwardness and miscommunication when migrants faced new routines and norms in a new country. In other words, these nicknames captured migrants' initial disorientation as well as new affective attachments in a foreign land. Within the scope of this chapter, I will refer to two nicknames *Infidel Slayer* and *Ahmet the Elegant* in order to point to the first encounters of Turkish migrants with non-migrant people in Sweden.

Infidel Slayer as a nickname is deeply anchored in stories. There are two versions of the story behind this nickname. According to one, as *Infidel Slayer* was walking back from a late shift, he saw a drunken Swedish man approaching him. As he did not speak Swedish, alone in a strange place, he thought that he would be attacked or harassed by this drunken man. When the man approached him, he reacted, took his knife out of his pocket and ran after him. When he told this story to his Turkish friends, he was ridiculed by his friends who told him about the drinking habits of Swedish people. He had overreacted to a simple encounter on a Friday evening. The other story about the derivation of the nickname is less convincing. According to this second version, during the Feast of Sacrifice, *Infidel Slayer* found a butcher to kill a ram in order to fulfil his religious duties but the butcher refused to do it in the proper Islamic way. *Infidel Slayer* then wanted to do it himself but when the butcher objected he got frustrated and furious and threatened the butcher with the knife. The butcher thought he would be killed. Others thought that it was a miscommunication, and that *Infidel Slayer* was only trying to sacrifice the ram himself and that the butcher overreacted. Regardless of the veracity of these stories, my informants responded to the eccentricity and misunderstanding of their friend in a Swedish context by nicknaming him *Infidel Slayer*. This nickname highlights the fact that stories behind nicknames were responses to new rules and habits that migrants encountered in the host country. The content of the stories changed as they were narrated by different people on different occasions, but not its humourous genre. In both versions of this nickname story lie a transgression based on miscommunication with local people.

Another example is *Ahmet the Elegant*, created and ascribed by Turkish peers at work. It is known that nicknaming in male-dominated occupations ensures group cohesion and social control.[11] For many migrants, industrial work was new and the factory as a work environment was alienating. Many first-generation migrants worked to earn money not for immediate comforts and consumption in the host country but to elevate their social and financial positions in their country of origins or to prepare for marriages or emigration of their kin or spouses.[12] *Ahmet the Elegant* received his nickname because instead of saving or sending money to Turkey, he was eager to take good care of his clothes and appearance and always wanted to wear clean shirts after his shifts. This was what he also observed of his Swedish peers at the factory. Unlike migrants who spent less money on their clothes, he spent more money by buying nice shirts. While many were sending money home, as a single man at that time, *Ahmet the Elegant* had more money to spend as he wished. There was a transgression, especially to the ethos and consensus among male labour migrants at that time, in Ahmet's aspiration to conform to his Swedish peers' habits. However, it also underscored a hidden admiration by his Turkish colleagues, maybe even some kind of envy suffused with teasing.

Regardless of their origins, these nicknames contributed to a more rapid familiarisation and socialisation of first-generation Turkish immigrants. Through nicknames, the loss of previous relations and social and familial ties had been translated and transmuted into a locally produced sense of community. Avtar Brah defines homing desires as 'desires to feel at home achieved by physically or symbolically (re)constituting spaces which provide some kind of ontological security in the context of migration'[13] and conferring nicknames on some members of a potential diasporic community was one way of fulfilling these desires, by turning 'strangers' into acquaintances, if not friends.

Even today, despite the heterogeneity of Turkish community and the attenuation of the creation of new nicknames in the community, nicknames and their stories continue to circulate in social gatherings, associations and coffee houses, in order to register the early years of Turkish migration into the local history of the community. They also include some images of the native (i.e. the Swede) in diaspora space as the other (like drinkers or ignorance of Islamic rules as in the case of *Infidel Slayer* or paying special attention to their dress as in the case of *Ahmet the Elegant*) and they have become a stylised way of transmitting collective memories of migration to younger generations. Thanks to these nicknames and their amusing stories, every newcomer could be included in this local memory and storytelling. In other words, these nicknames and their stories were concocted and repeated a) vis-à-vis the host society, i.e. the real and imaginary 'Swede', b) vis-à-vis the 'community-in-making', i.e. diasporic community, c) finally, vis-à-vis newcomers and potential members.

Nicknames and Migrant Tales

This latter cluster of nicknames may also be emblematic of migrant tales. In her work with elderly Bengalis in Britain, Katy Gardner argues that 'stories – of where one has come from, and where one plans to go – seem particularly important for migrants. This is partly because they, perhaps more than others, need to give coherence and meaning to their experiences'.[14] The experience of migration can be a turning point in one's biography, it can be considered as a rupture and/or continuity in the creation of a coherent life story and subject to multiple calculations.[15] It can gain new meanings and formulations in time, in different stages of the course of life, in relation to a large array of transnational links, practices and encounters in the country of settlement. Migrant tales attempt to create a meaningful genealogy of movements and encounters. Even though each migration story is singular and personal, migrant tales are shared, activated and shaped in different settings, for different purposes. As Gubrium and Holstein argue, 'if the narratives are personal, they are worked up and conveyed with others under discernible circumstances. [...] Storytellers and listeners respond to concrete exigencies, configuring accounts in the give-and-take of the process.'[16]

A main audience for migrant tales is the real or imaginary host, 'the native' to whom stories are addressed. Not only are migrants expected to give a coherent life story during and in the eve of their settlement, but they are also reminded to repeat it in their everyday life. It is a twofold process. On the one hand, the whole range of mechanisms, practices and discourses in the regulation of migration has been to collect reasonable and intelligible migration stories, regardless of the complex motives behind the movement. Interviews with asylum seekers and refugees have become the epitome of that narrative obligation since asylum seekers have to prove officially or at least narratively their fear of persecution and need of protection. High-skilled labour migrants have to provide a

consistent career story around mobility and employment. The migration on the basis of family reunification
always goes hand-in-hand with narrative interviews by
migration officers where family members reconstruct
their family stories and prove their love and willingness
to live together. To put it simply, migrancy is something
that authorities want to hear in narrative forms. On the
other hand, migrant tales have origins in everyday life.
A particular physiognomy or a slight accent may require
a migrant to tell his or her story. It is common among
migrants to address the native people of a country of
immigration as 'significant others' in their stories. Migrant
tales are usually created vis-a-vis the real or imagined native.
Avtar Brah argues that diaspora space, 'as a conceptual
category is "inhabited" not only by those who have
migrated and their descendants but equally by those who
are constructed and represented as indigenous.'[17] Migrant
tales are repeatedly designed and narrated according to a
real or imaginary native. 'The native' is therefore a specific
construction through which a common 'we' becomes
possible to account for.

Another audience for migrant tales consists of a
common 'we' as people who share similar migration
stories, the same country of 'origin' or motivations. Not
all but many migrants tend to come together and engage
in community-building. This is organised sometimes
around a diasporic organisation based on cultural,
political and/or religious identification with others,
sometimes for practical help and sometimes as a response
to the exclusionary practices and politics in the country
of settlement. Motives and aims can differ but a common
motivation is to create a narrative environment where
people come to create a sense of identity by telling their
migrant tales. This narrative environment paves the way
for the creation of a collective identity where common

patterns and experiences are emphasised by people who participate in the interaction. For instance, Barbara Myerhoff, in her well-known ethnography with elderly Jewish people in California, highlights how narratives are actively formed and circulated to create a collective identity and a sense of community.[18]

Finally, migrant tales are solicited by people, including some researchers, who explicitly or implicitly prioritise the experience of migration, the stories of 'origins' over other possible stories. Asking for migrant tales can be seen as a simple question of curiosity but also a continuous effort to keep and reinforce the boundary between the host and the guest, the native and the non-native. Therefore, the possible narrator always evaluates and contextualises the intention of the audience and accordingly elaborates his story.

In the following section, by focusing on an informant's account about his colleague Mehmet, who never wanted to return to Turkey, unlike other labour migrants, I will show how past and present, real and imagined audiences – 'the Swede', the (diasporic) community and I as researcher and as a newly arrived immigrant – can cohabit the same narrative composition of a migrant tale, captured and embodied in a concrete nickname.

We are all Crazy: *Crazy Mehmet*

Ibrahim was one of my informants and willing to welcome me as a new potential member of the Turkish community. Ibrahim had come to Sweden in 1971 as a young man and immediately made friends with Turkish people. When we first met, before embarking on his long life story, he started by recollecting an anecdote about an older friend of his, Mehmet. I think this anecdote highlights how nicknames are created and how different audiences dwell on the same story. Here is the beginning of our first interview:

> Ask me more, whatever you want to know. Let's meet again whenever you want. I mean it, we can meet again. We can sit for a couple of hours, we can have a nice meal together. If you want to see something else, I can come with you where you want to go. Now look, my dear friend [*ciğerim*], when we came here [*short silence*] let me tell you a story: We have a brother, he is older than us and they call him *Crazy Mehmet*. His name [nickname] is *Crazy*. [*He laughs, I reciprocate in a friendly way*]. Actually, he is not crazy at all. He is a very smart guy, but his name turned out to be 'crazy'. When they [Turkish migrants] came here [Sweden], we had interpreters [he names these three interpreters]. Through them they were asked some questions: 'Where did you come from?' – Turkey, evidently. This was before the Swede employed all of them at X [a well-known factory], all got employed at X here. I also worked there. They asked him [*Crazy Mehmet*]: 'How long are you going to stay?' – 'I will stay here all my life,' he replied [*He laughs*]. All those who had said they would never ever stay here for a lifetime, those who would be back to Turkey in a couple of years passed away, most of those died here. When I say most, I mean no one is alive.

> Öncel: Maybe there are some who returned to Turkey?

> Ibrahim: There are some [returnees]. They died there [in Turkey] anyway. There are those who returned to

Turkey and live there but they are few. Many died here. All those who said they would stay two years, three years and go back, died here [in Sweden]. Their first intention was to return. They had some debts; they would work hard for two or three years and return. They did not bring their wives and children first; they [men] came alone. When *Crazy* said that he would stay for a lifetime, they asked him: [*he changes his voice in an amusing way*] 'Are you crazy? Are you a lunatic, my brother?' [*He laughs*] And they called him crazy, since then, his name has been *Crazy*. He laughs at them now, he knew in advance what would happen in the future. [*Short silence*] [*In a serious tone*] No one returned from here, my dear friend. All stayed here. People who go to Turkey are those who retired or who had retired before. They go and stay there six months and spend six months here [in Sweden]. Or they spend two or three months here. But not many people, few remained, and they are old people. Life goes on like that. One cannot return, why can one not return? Because their roots are here; their grandchildren, their children are here. It is easy, comfortable here, they get their proper (medical) treatment. I mean, they also travel for medical treatment. There was no real returnee, [*short silence*] there was a friend of ours [*he names him*] who returned definitively, he passed away recently, two years ago. I mean, the return did not happen unfortunately. They did not return, they all retired and none is a business man. They were all workers. They retired from that X factory or from some other factories. There is no one who is rich, nobody has become rich either. There is no one to provide work for other Turks. You know by now about Sweden, there are limits in Sweden, maybe there are better-off people in Stockholm, but there is no one here. No one is educated here. We all came from rural areas. Our children went to school but we, the forerunners, we are all uneducated. We have our primary school certificates or no certificate at all. People have at most a secondary school certificate, like me. That's why we did not have doctors or lawyers. Now we have some [doctors, lawyers, educated people]. At that time, no one had studied. When we brought our children, they were young, they did not study either. They prioritised pizza houses; many encouraged their children to work there. [*Short silence*] I mean, we stayed. We are all crazy, as crazy as Mehmet is.

A straightforward and naïve reading of this long account would be as follows: in the 1960s when Turkish migrants came to Sweden, there was a guy, Mehmet. He declared to the officials that he wanted to stay in Sweden for good, unlike his peers who only aspired to stay for a limited period of time. His friends thought that he was crazy and nicknamed him Crazy. In the course of time, no one returned to Turkey. Time proved Mehmet right. Not only was Mehmet crazy but all of them were crazy. Despite the overload of detail and repetition in this long account, there is a core plot and it is about temporality and the improbability of return to the homeland.

As Paul Ricoeur argues, narrative in its broadest sense is about temporality.[19] In other words, human beings make sense of time in narrative forms. Ibrahim, through this story, makes the time pass intelligibly for himself and a general audience. Moreover, this is a typical story, a regular migrant tale which is composed around the myth of return but it operates in an inverse way. The common plot is that labour migrants with strong aspirations to return to their country of departure come to understand that it is just a myth since there emerge many other reasons to continue to reside in the country of settlement as well as a wide range of forms of belonging. The story of *Crazy Mehmet* reverses this sequential order. He admitted and proclaimed, in the very beginning of his immigration, his wish to stay for good. His first unexpected attitude towards immigration retrospectively gives meaning to the improbability of return for others who had wished for it.

After this brief discussion of the plot, in the next step, I will hark back to the narrative environment and composition of Ibrahim's story and highlight the relevance of narrative embeddedness. Gubrium and Holstein argue that 'the idea of narrative embeddedness suggests that, in aiming to understand the broader meaning of accounts, it is useful to distinguish story from voice'[20]. Why and how did Ibrahim build his narrative on the story of Mehmet?

First of all, I was the main audience of this narrative performance. As it is clear in the beginning, Ibrahim embraced me as a newly arrived Turkish guy, rather than a researcher who was interested in his plans in old age. He invited me to ask him 'everything that I want to know' but he was already eager to tell me the story of *Crazy Mehmet.* This eagerness was partly because it was a humourous story and mostly because it spoke to a common experience of migration. Like my other informants who carved out a new life in Sweden for themselves and their families, Ibrahim was keen on harking back to this myth of return. The story of Mehmet turned the dramatic aspect of having once uprooted and the improbability of a definitive return into a humourous format. The eccentricity of Mehmet coloured the grey and blurred areas between belonging and not-belonging to Sweden as well as between different forms of home-making.

Another reason Ibrahim recalled this story was that he assumed that as a sociologist and a migrant, I was interested in this idea of returning to Turkey. He wanted to warn me against the easy and rosy picture of mobility. Therefore, he built a good narrative argument when he would later tell me about his wish to stay in Sweden in his old age. He also encouraged me to embrace Sweden not as a temporary sojourn but a possible and probable new home. My relative unfamiliarity with the Swedish context and the Turkish community at that time challenged the linearity of his account. Ibrahim's account therefore consisted of general information about the Turkish community, their characteristics and Sweden as he saw them. The story was interrupted by different details, sometimes very contextual, sometimes specifically addressed to me.

Another peculiarity in this account was the oscillation between pronouns 'I', 'we' and 'they'. One apparent reason was that Ibrahim came to Sweden later than the pioneers like Mehmet. 'They' as a pronoun represented mainly the forerunners while 'we' connoted the larger Turkish community. The oscillation between the pronouns 'we' and 'they' underlined how people from different migration experiences come to consider each other having similar stories in the course of time. This was the impact of merging divergent life trajectories into a sense of community. 'I', on the other hand, was interwoven in this oscillation and marked his difference from 'we' and 'they', but by underlining similar hopes and frustrations with the rest of community. What is at stake for the objective of this chapter is that Ibrahim had heard and circulated this story among his peers, older and younger Turkish people, many times. As this story generated a nickname and Mehmet was still an active member of the community, it was repeated on every occasion, especially when newcomers would join the community. Despite contextual information and repetitions, Ibrahim's narration of this nickname story was well balanced and performed with short silences, imitations and laughter. This carried the traces of previous narrations and the joy of conviviality in similar narrative environments.

A final note should be about the 'present absence' of the 'native'. The Swede appeared only once in Ibrahim's account, asking the crucial question for the moral of the story: 'How long are you going to stay?' 'The Swede' was in this narrative as the main agent to incite and activate the story. During my fieldwork, I came to realise that 'the Swede' was a specific construction through which a common 'we' came to be possible to account for. 'The Swede' was coined as the name of a typical member of a homogeneous group, mainly used in singular rather than plural form (*Isveçli*). Turkish migrants felt they were at a social distance to the native Swedish people. Even though they had had some friends and colleagues over the years, many socialised with their fellow countrymen from the very beginning of their settlement. This led to a generalisation of 'the Swedish' from the few people they came to know, and mainly from already circulating discourses about the characteristics attributed to the Swedish people. However, as was clear in this account, 'the Swede' was also the law-making host, the official at the Migration Office or some other institution, the imagined representative of how things should be done in Sweden. *Crazy Mehmet* had not only contradicted the common aspiration of his Turkish peers but also astonished 'the Swede' who was imagined by migrants to expect them to return to their home country.

Conclusion

In this chapter, by analysing some nicknames that Turkish migrants received upon their immigration to Sweden, I attempted to shed light on their experience as migrants in a new country. Some of these nicknames recall their pre-migratory backgrounds. Previous professional titles used as nicknames, for instance, highlight the different experiences of the community in a job market where they were interchangeable in terms of their skills. This also shows that not all migrants from Turkey to Sweden were unskilled labourers. It is important to seek new means to reveal the nuances of the Turkish exodus to Europe and understand the political economy of that time which turned a tailor into an unskilled worker in the textile industry. Other nicknames reflect Turkish migrants' first impressions of Swedish society, its rules, habits and institutions and record some real or imagined transgressions of the forerunners both vis-à-vis the Turkish community and the non-migrant people in Sweden, as I tried to illustrate with *Ahmet the Elegant* and *Infidel Slayer*. By turning these transgressions into humourous nicknames, many migrants tried to make sense of these intercultural encounters and their relation to and position in the host society. While creating new social bonds in a migration context, nicknames and their stories also bear traces of the experience of being in an unfamiliar context and the estrangement of the forerunners.

Finally, some nicknames emerged to capture the very experience of migration and the traces of diaspora space. *Crazy* was based on a singular story of a man, but managed to circulate among other migrants and translate their migration stories into a particular narrative. Stories of individual migrants record the history of a migrant community, yet it may be relevant to reconsider collective experiences that are shaped in diaspora space and captured in forms other than testimonies. It is no longer possible to have recourse to the testimonies of many first-generation Turkish migrants in Europe. However, tracing their migrant tales via collective and oral stories – embodied in and analysed through nicknames in this chapter – may help us to gain a better understanding of their migration, beginnings and subjective experiences.

Notes

1. Nermin Abadan-Unat, *Bitmeyen Göç: Konuk İşçilikten Ulus-Ötesi Yurttaşlığa* [Unending Migration: From Guest Workers to Post-National Citizenship], İstanbul Bilgi Üniversitesi Yayınları (Istanbul, 2002).
2. Şahin Alpay, *Turkar i Stockholm. En Studie av Invandrare, Politik och Samhälle* [Turks in Stockholm: A Study of Migrants, Politics and Society], PhD Thesis, Department of Political Science, Stockholm University (Stockholm, 1980); Ingrid Lundberg and Ingvar Svanberg, *Turkish Associations in Metropolitan Stockholm*, Centre for Multiethnic Research, Uppsala University (Uppsala, 1991).
3. Şahin Alpay and H. Sariaslan, *Effects of Emigration: The Effects on the Town of Kulu in Central Turkey of Emigration to Sweden*, (Stockholm, 1984).
4. Ingrid Lundberg, *Kulubor i Stockholm. En Svensk Historia* [Kulu Migrants in Stockholm: A Swedish History], Sveriges invandrar-institut och museum (Stockholm, 1991).
5. Charles Westin, 'Young people of migrant origin in Sweden', *The International Migration Review* 37/4 (2003), pp. 987–1010.
6. Öncel Naldemirci, *Caring (in) Diaspora: Aging and Caring Experiences of Older Turkish Migrants in a Swedish Context*, unpublished PhD Thesis, Göteborg Studies In Sociology No. 54, Department of Sociology and Work Science, University of Gothenburg (Gothenburg, 2013).
7. David D. Gilmore, 'Some notes on community in Spain', *Man (N. S.)* 17/4 (1982), pp. 686–700.
8. Ibid., p. 686.
9. Richard Green, 'Naming practices in western Ireland', *Man (N. S.)* 174 (1982), pp. 701–13.

10. Jack Glazier, 'Nicknames and the transformation of an American Jewish community: Notes on the anthropology of emotion in the urban Midwest', *Ethnology* 26/2 (1987), pp. 73–85.
11. Lucy Taksa, 'Naming bodies at work: considering the gendered and emotional dimensions of nicknaming', International Journal of Work, Organisation and Emotion 5/1 (2012), pp. 26–40.
12. Ulla-Brit Engelbrektsson, *The Force of Tradition: Turkish Migrants at Home and Abroad*, Göteborg Studies in Social Anthropology, 1, (Gothenburg, 1979).
13. Avtar Brah, *Cartographies of Diaspora: Contesting Identities*, Psychology Press (London, 1996), p. 180.
14. Katy Gardner, *Age, Narrative and Migration: The Life Course and Life Histories of Bengali Elders in London* (Oxford, New York, 2002), p. 28.
15. John Berger, *A Seventh Man: A Book of Images and Words about the Experience of Migrant Workers in Europe*, (Baltimore, 1975).
16. Jaber F. Gubrium and James A. Holstein, *Analyzing Narrative Reality* (Los Angeles, 2009), p. 42.
17. Brah, *Cartographies of Diaspora*, p. 181.
18. Barbara Myerhoff, *Number Our Days*, (New York, 1979).
19. Paul Ricoeur, 'Narrative Time', in W. J. T. Mitchell (ed.), *On Narrative*, (Chicago, 1981).
20. Jaber F. Gubrium and James A. Holstein, 'Narrative ethnography', in S. N. Hesse-Biber and P. Leavy (eds), Handbook of Emergent Methods (New York, 2008), p. 255.

References

Abadan-Unat, N., *Bitmeyen Göç: Konuk İşçilikten Ulus-Ötesi Yurttaşlığa* [Unending Migration: From Guest Workers to Post-National Citizenship], (Istanbul, 2002).

Alpay, S., *Turkar i Stockholm. En Studie av Invandrare, Politik och Samhälle* [Turks in Stockholm: A Study of Migrants, Politics and Society], PhD Thesis, Department of Political Science, Stockholm University (Stockholm, 1980).

Alpay, S., and Sariaslan, H., *Effects of Emigration. The Effects on the Town of Kulu in Central Turkey of Emigration to Sweden*, (Stockholm, 1984).

Berger, J., *A Seventh Man: A Book of Images and Words about the Experience of Migrant Workers in Europe* (Baltimore, 1975).

Brah, A. *Cartographies of Diaspora: Contesting Identities*, Psychology Press (London, 1996).

Engelbrektsson, U.B., *The Force of Tradition: Turkish Migrants at Home and Abroad*, Göteborg Studies in Social Anthropology, 1, (Gothenburg, 1979).

Gardner, K., *Age, Narrative and Migration: The Life Course and Life Histories of Bengali Elders in London* (Oxford, New York, 2002).

Gilmore, D.D., 'Some notes on community nicknaming in Spain', *Man*, New Series 17/4 (1982), pp. 686–700.

Glazier, J., 'Nicknames and the transformation of an American Jewish community: Notes on the anthropology of emotion in the urban Midwest', *Ethnology* 26/2 (1987), pp. 73–85.

Green, R., 'Naming practices in western Ireland', *Man (N. S.)* 17/4 (1982), pp. 701–13.

Gubrium, Jaber F. and Holstein, James, A. 'Narrative Ethnography', in S.N. Hesse-Biber and P. Leavy (eds), *Handbook of Emergent Methods*, Guilford Press (New York, 2008).

———, *Analyzing Narrative Reality*, Sage Publications (Los Angeles, 2009).

Lundberg, I., *Kulubor i Stockholm. En Svensk Historia* [Kulu Migrants in Stockholm: A Swedish History], Sveriges invandrarinstitut och museum (Stockholm, 1991).

Lundberg, I., and Svanberg, I., *Turkish Associations in Metropolitan Stockholm*, Centre for Multiethnic Research, Uppsala University (Uppsala, 1991).

Myerhoff, B., *Number Our Days*, Simon & Schuster (New York, 1979).

Naldemirci, Ö., *Caring (in) Diaspora: Aging and Caring Experiences of Older Turkish Migrants in a Swedish Context*, unpublished PhD Thesis, Göteborg Studies In Sociology No. 54, Department of Sociology and Work Science, University of Gothenburg (Gothenburg, 2013).

Ricoeur, P., 'Narrative Time', in W.J.T. Mitchell (ed.), *On Narrative*, University of Chicago Press (Chicago, 1981).

Taksa, L., 'Naming bodies at work: considering the gendered and emotional dimensions of nicknaming', *Int. J. Work Organisation and Emotion*, 5/1 (2012), pp. 26–40.

Westin, C., 'Young people of migrant origin in Sweden', *The International Migration Review* 37/4 (2003), pp. 987–1010.

CHAPTER 4

THE TURKISH GENERATION BORN IN SWEDEN: BRIDGE-BUILDERS OR NEW SWEDES?

Constanza Vera-Larrucea

Introduction

Today the children of the workers who arrived in Sweden 50 years ago are Swedish citizens. The story of the second generation is a story of both success and shortcomings, of integration and differentiation. Studies focused specifically on people born in Sweden with a Turkish background are rare. This is one of them, which introduces the world of the 'new Swedes' of Turkish origin. It is part of a larger study defining their position in Sweden.[1]

Researchers such as Rundblom suggest that the best ambassadors and bridge-builders between countries are not the ones who migrated but the later generations, a group of people that has already succeeded in integrating into a society that received one of their parents.[2] This could mean that immigrants' descendants have no struggles, no external pressure for assimilation or rejection to join the national community. The so- called 'second-generation' might not have inherited all the struggles of their parents but they do have to fight to find a place in their country of birth, which happens to be different to their ancestral country.

Turks' descendants born in Europe have followed different paths. In Sweden, specifically, they still have to carry the 'immigrant' baggage but they seem to have made something positive out of it. The position of 'bridge-builders' presupposes a successful integration into Swedish society and an uncomplicated relationship to Turkey. Most of the labels used to refer to this group suggest a duality constituted by the ancestral origin and the country of residence. There is an important consideration that could position them as an in-between group, i.e. dual citizenship. The many links with the 'ancestral land' are institutionalised thanks to the possibility to become dual citizens. Both Turkey and Sweden recognise second attachments among its citizens. This chapter intends to analyse whether the life of Turks who were born in Sweden is facing such duality, which might become a bridge between Turkey and Sweden, or if people adhere to a more traditional form of political participation prioritising only one of the countries of which they are nationals.

Kaya and Kentel[3] studied first and second generation Turks in France and Germany in an effort to find out whether these 'Euro-Turks' represent a driving vanguard for Turkey in the process of integration into the European Union. The authors discovered that there is no homogeneity among Turks regarding their affiliation to Turkey. There is a group that is affiliated to both the 'home-land' and the 'host-land'[4] – the 'bridging group' – another one that has a strong orientation towards the 'home-land' – the 'breaching group' – and a third one that is completely assimilated.[5] This categorisation could be used with the material at hand for this particular study in order to find out whether Swedish Turks are the bridge-builders that Rundblom predicted them to be.

This chapter uses survey data (TIES project[6]) and, more importantly, qualitative data gathered from a sub-sample of the survey respondents. Through subjective aspects associated with citizenship – identity, sense of belonging and 'home-feeling' – and objective indicators of membership – intention to naturalise, political participation and military service – dual citizenship is tested to see whether this dual status could presuppose a situation of bridge-builders. Besides, another interesting consequence of being a dual citizen – for males only – is explored here because of its strong connotations towards identity and sense of belonging, namely military service. The results show that the attachment towards Turkey does not necessarily act against people's loyalties towards Sweden.

Previous Research

The children of immigrants have been, in many cases, called 'second generation immigrants', although they have never migrated. They were born in Europe and, in this particular case, they are Swedish citizens. The study used in this paper also struggled with labels. While the TIES consortium used the term 'second generation', the Swedish TIES team used the term 'descendants of migrants from Turkey' because it is considered to be the most appropriate, correct and neutral categorisation.[7]

In Sweden, studies of the descendants of Turks have been predominantly of a qualitative nature. Early studies are focused on the struggle between traditional Turkish patterns and the new alternatives present in Swedish society. Yazgán described second generation Turkish boys[8] and girls.[9] She found that there are common aspects for young adults, such as the preservation of the culture of their parents. Studies highlight the social mobility of descendants of Turks,[10] impacts on identity[11] and language.[12] Studies indicate that when developing their identities and in their school careers, children are very much influenced by the experiences of their parents. Those parents who intended to return to Turkey did not have the incentive to encourage their children to pursue higher education, since it was considered unnecessary. Engelbrektsson[13] studied Turkish first and second generation youth in Gothenburg, finding that they are still ambivalent with regard to returning to Turkey someday or planning to spend the rest of their lives in Sweden. In spite of these confusing perspectives, most of them identified more as Swedes than Turks.[14]

According to Virta and Westin[15] descendants of Turks seem to benefit from the Swedish model of integration, especially young women. Family relations and Swedish proficiency prove to have had a great impact on the integrative attitudes assumed by young adults during their school years.

One of the latter qualitative studies is Erder's 'Ghetto and the Turks in the Welfare Society'.[16] This study was conducted in Rinkeby, a Stockholm suburb. The author analyses the discouraging role of the 'ghetto' in the integration of Turks and their descendants into Swedish society.

Although most of the previous research seems to show that descendants of Turks have difficulties in integrating into Swedish society, other studies present a different picture. Young people of Turkish ancestry are able to transgress traditional boundaries by, for example, establishing their own association – Turkish Youth Association – and by publishing a bilingual Swedish Journal – *EuroTurk* – in a way that gives expression to their transnational character.[17]

The TIES Survey shows that young people with Turkish ancestry in Sweden encounter greater difficulties in the labour market than those of native origin and their educational level is generally lower than that of their native peers.[18] However, once variables pertaining to the socioeconomic background of individuals are controlled for, the significant differences disappear, i.e. descendants of migrants have achieved the same educational goals as young people of the majority group given the same socioeconomic background.[19] Other findings of the TIES project reveal that the descendants of migrants from Turkey studied in segregated schools and neighbourhoods. But their parents' ambition, higher expectations and extra exertion have compensated for the negative effects of segregation.[20]

The existing research has centered on whether this group is integrated into Swedish society, but few studies if any investigate the relationship with Turkey and Sweden in a parallel way. This is what this study intends to do. But first, it is important to check theoretical considerations regarding dual citizenship and later the logic behind the legal arrangements that makes dual citizenship possible for the descendants of Turks.

Dual Citizenship Implications for Membership and Belonging

The generation born in Europe has been living under different conditions to the ones faced by their parents. Most European countries have relaxed their rules for naturalisation, making it much easier for the children of immigrants. Old citizenship regimes such as republican – based on territoriality – or communitarian – based on ancestry – have now blended into a mixture of the two old principles *ius soli* and *ius sanguinis* plus a new one, *ius domicili* – the right given for a long-time residency in a country. The implications of this are that children who were born in, for example, Sweden, could early in their lives be considered Swedish citizens. In most European countries, this group has the possibility to become citizens in two countries. Such dual status goes against traditional perspectives about citizenship and integration.

From a micro perspective dual citizenship means that individuals combine membership in and of several states.[21] A dual citizen might be de-coupled from the traditional exclusive national belonging but at the same time dual citizenship might contribute to the integration of immigrants by welcoming their previous national attachment and encouraging them to naturalise, become politically active and integrate further into the receiving society.

Opponents of dual citizenship denounce double membership as a threat to societal solidarity and reciprocity among citizens and within civil society, which may even threaten state security.[22] A technical concern regarding dual citizenship, which is especially interesting in the case of young people with Turkish ancestry in Sweden, is their dual military obligation. Turkey places a condition on the retention of nationality on the part of its citizens living abroad that they fulfil their military obligations. Studies and medical conditions might be grounds for exemption. Nevertheless, there is also the possibility of performing military service in the country of birth of the second generation.[23] In this case Turkish citizens who reside abroad and also possess dual citizenship may qualify for exemption from Turkish military service if they can produce written proof that they have fulfilled military obligations in their country of residence. Austria, Denmark, Finland, France, Germany, Israel, Italy, Norway, Sweden and Switzerland afford this possibility to legal residents who possess Turkish citizenship. This removes the incompatibility of duties in relation to two countries, making dual citizenship a feasible alternative for second generation Turks.

Although descendants of Turks in Sweden have the possibility to be dual citizens, this citizenship will probably not generate the same degree of active membership i.e. civic participation. It is, nevertheless, more feasible to consider that one of them acts like dormant citizenship'.[24] By 'dormant' Faist means that there is a set of rights and duties that are not used/profited/fulfilled by non-residential citizens. Dormant citizenship means that many non-residential citizens have the potential to become active members later in life, motivated by a personal, political or economic situation. Dormant citizenship acts as an alternative to Bauböck's 'external citizenship'[25] which describes the membership of those citizens who are temporarily abroad. Dormant citizenship can be applied to immigrants, emigrants' children and others who have become 'non-residential citizens'.

There is a more subjective side of citizenship which is not usually problematised. This subjective citizenship becomes relevant when analysing the everyday life of dual citizens. Belonging to two different countries runs counter to classical principles of citizenship. Is it possible to feel a sense of belonging and patriotic loyalty in relation to two countries at the same time and with the same intensity? In a diverse society, citizenship and identity are not part of an exclusive relationship. Besides, even a single citizenship does not imply a singular identity or an unbreakable loyalty.[26] Dual citizenship and the subjective dimension may be better understood by taking a view that traverses the context of the national. This plurality of belongings has been claimed to be one of the main strengths of this concept when describing new configurations of citizenship.[27] In addition, '"belonging" allows for the inclusion of sentimental, cultural, and symbolic dimensions in a discussion of what ties a collectivity together'.[28] How is belonging approached by dual citizens? The subjective side of citizenship is here operationalised through a sense of belonging, identity and the 'home-feeling'.

Method and Empirical Material

The constructivist character of the study presupposes the interpretation of these meanings in accordance with the social reality that surrounds interviewees. Such a perspective implies a definition of the problem assisted by those that are being studied. This study problematises everyday citizenship from the perspective of people born in Sweden who have Turkish parents.

As already stated in the introduction, this chapter contains both quantitative and qualitative data material, although it mostly relies on qualitative data. The idea behind giving priority to qualitative data is in line with one of the main objectives of this study, which assigns to people a fundamental function when trying to contribute to the actual debate surrounding citizenship.

The quantitative information comes from the TIES Survey, described at the introduction of this book. The survey data is only used for descriptive purposes in this chapter. The study originally compares the narratives of people with Turkish ancestry in Stockholm and Paris but for the purposes of this chapter, only the respondents in Stockholm – 18 in total – were taken into account. Personal interviews were the method chosen in this study in order to collect people's narratives. In depth interviews are appropriate sources for discovering the subjective meanings of certain phenomena.[29]

The informants were a sub-sample from the TIES survey. Some of the participants in the TIES study agreed to take part in a new interview about integration and left their contact information which was attached to the results of the survey. They were contacted for an in-depth interview and a large majority accepted. The interviews took place in different places in Stockholm (café, place of work, private housing, etc.) and had a duration of between 25 to 72 minutes. Due to several considerations regarding the complexity of topics such as sense of belonging, ethnic identity and transnational activities, only ethnic Turks were chosen for the interviews.[30] Therefore, the qualitative material is not representative of the whole Turkish community in Sweden, which is ethnically diverse.

The original questionnaire was semi-structured with topics such as self-perceived identification, other-perceived identification, relations between socio-economic status and degree of personal attachment in relation to different groups or places. This questionnaire was used as a point of reference. New questions came up when respondents formulated new insights regarding their experiences. The questionnaire was open enough to allow space for new relevant elements emanating from the interviewees that were gradually incorporated into later interviews.

The interviews were later transcribed and analysed with a software for qualitative analysis called Nvivo. The data-coding took a theme-based approach in accordance with the indicators previously chosen as relevant considering theory and previous research. Other themes were empirically informed, that is, the aspects that respondents themselves revealed to be relevant in their experiences as citizens and that had not been previously identified in the literature.

The quotations selected in this chapter were chosen because of their representativeness or uniqueness. The respondents are quoted using nicknames that they in most cases chose themselves. All interviews were undertaken with the promise of anonymity.

Citizens of Turkey and Sweden

The legal bond with Turkey

Turkey has changed naturalisation rules in order to keep the link with its emigrants and their descendants. The large Turkish diaspora represents a cultural, economic and political advantage for Turkey. Culturally, these emigrants represent a Turkish presence within European countries. They are expected to reproduce their culture by extending their practices and traditions to the new generations and promoting an encounter with Europeans. This social capital could eventually be mobilised as a bridge between Turkey and the European Union.[31]

The traditional Turkish approach to citizenship policies was civic-republican – inherited from Turkey's imperial past – but the current law is much closer to *ius sanguinis*.[32] This communitarian turn has been influenced by the large number of Turkish citizens living abroad. Since 1981, Turkey has allowed dual citizenship as long as the Turkish citizen who naturalises in a second country informs the authorities about it.[33] Turkish citizenship can be lost not only through a formal renouncement. Lack of contact with Turkey and its diplomatic representation offices can also lead to the loss of nationality, as well as unjustified absence from military service.

While Turkey has accepted dual citizenship, the ban on this double status in some European countries – most notably Germany and Austria – created problems for Turkish citizens that wanted to naturalise or to pass Turkish citizenship on to their children. Thus, Turkey amended its citizenship law in 1995 so as to institute a privileged non-citizen status for former citizens.

Holders of the 'pink card' acquired the right to reside, to acquire property, to be eligible for inheritance, to operate businesses and to work in Turkey on the same basis as any other citizen. 'Pink card' holders are only denied the right to vote in Turkey. Ten years later, in 2004, the 'pink card' was renamed the 'blue card', and it was stipulated that privileged non-citizens were not only deprived of their right to vote but also of their right to work in the Turkish public sector and to be elected to office.[34] This status given to Turks who are not citizens shows that Turkey embraces a transnational model of citizenship motivated by the desire of the Turkish state to maintain contact with citizens living abroad. In this sense, the attitude towards dual citizenship is instrumental. Other allegiances are less important than retaining the bond with citizens living abroad.

Swedish citizenship rules and integration policies

Sweden has tried to make naturalisation rules easier for immigrants. Although citizenship acquisition is, in principle, linked to ancestry, naturalisation is relatively easy for migrants who have lived in the country for at least five years, which constitutes an approach closer to *ius soli*. The requirements for acquiring citizenship are today also based on domicile, on grounds of residence. Those who acquire citizenship by birth must have Swedish citizens as parents. Since 1979, a child automatically acquires citizenship if the mother is a Swedish citizen. A child might also acquire Swedish citizenship during its first years if the father is a national. Descendants of immigrants without naturalised parents become Swedish nationals by notification – a simplified naturalisation – after corroboration that they have been living in the country for more than five years. In general, people who have permanently lived in the country for at least five years may apply for citizenship.

Sweden developed a de facto toleration of dual nationality through relaxed naturalisation requirements and exemption from renouncing one's original citizenship[35] and now legally accepts dual nationality.[36] This reflects the reduced significance of national citizenship for residents in Sweden, a country that seeks to equalise the rights of citizens and long-term residents from abroad.[37]

Integration policies and citizenship paradigms make it possible to classify Sweden as a multicultural state. In 2010 Sweden appeared at the top among European countries in the Multiculturalism Policy Index. The historically strong Swedish state has played an active role in trying to 'help' migrants 'maintain their culture'.[38] In this sense, traditional cultures are enabled by the state to survive. Nevertheless, some researchers believe that multicultural policy, with an emphasis on the right of immigrants and minorities to retain their cultural inheritance, seems to be behind social and economic marginalisation and that these problems tend to be reproduced in the second generation.[39]

Citizenship status of people with Turkish ancestry in Europe

According to the TIES Survey, descendants of Turks[40] are not only nationals in Sweden, but even in Germany they have become citizens.

A large majority of second generation Turks stated that they were naturalised in the country of birth. Germany has the lowest percentage of individuals with Turkish ancestry who are naturalised. In Sweden, 56.8 per cent of the people who participated in the survey declared they had acquired Swedish citizenship by birth.

Dual citizenship appears to be characteristic of second generation Turks whenever this is possible. A majority of

Table 4.1   National citizens in survey country (country of birth), second generation Turks in Europe

Austria	Switzerland	Germany	Belgium	Netherlands	Sweden	France
87.6	73.1	53.0	96.5	94.4	98.8	98.0

Source: TIES Survey

descendants of Turks who participated in the TIES survey are dual citizens, with the exception of those in Germany and Austria. In Sweden 57 per cent of individuals with Turkish parents possess citizenship in both their country of birth and the country of their parents.

In the qualitative part of this study, all the respondents who participated in the interviews except for one were dual nationals. Is this dual status an engine to become 'bridge-builders' between Sweden and Turkey? To some extent yes, because these are citizens that might well reside in the two countries and have social, economic and political interests in both countries. Nevertheless, as in this case they are all residents in Sweden, Turkish citizenship might be better characterised as the 'dormant' citizenship. The qualitative data will shed more light on the role that both legal statuses play in people's lives.

Being a Dual Citizen

Identification, sense of belonging and the 'home' feeling
During the in-depth interviews, people were asked about their personal feelings behind their dual citizenship and, moreover, of their everyday lives in Sweden with a non-Swedish origin. The large majority of the interviewees emphasised their Turkish origin as a plus that makes them more complete citizens, persons that have 'more in their baggage'.

The respondents presented a positive mixture formed by different elements that are difficult to separate and that have permeable boundaries. The fact that they could not speak of one source without referring to the other shows how mutually embedded they are.

How does it feel to be a Swedish citizen with Turkish background?
It is that pride of having another origin. But at the same time, I feel Swedish as well. Considering that I have grown up here ... I don't know. It feels like 50–50.
Eddie (24)

I know much more I believe. I have track of two cultures at the same time. Not everybody has that chance. Because I am familiarised with the Swedish society but I still have my culture and traditions.
Pia (20)

Despite the discouraging situation described by previous research all the respondents emphasised the positive side of having a Turkish origin. There were very few negative

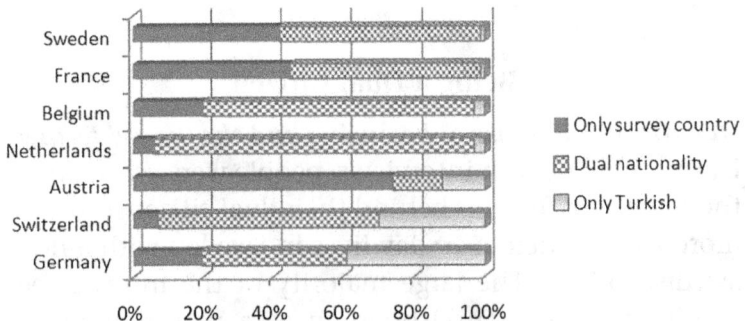

Graph 4.1 Citizenship Position of Second Generation Turks in Europe. Source: TIES Survey.

connotations related to the Turkish origin among the interviewees. People experience and regard their origin as something positive for the society in which they live. This is an important characteristic of their integration experience. At the same time it becomes relevant for the focus of studies regarding the integration of migrants and their descendants. Firstly, it shows that they are able to surpass the difficulties that a migrant origin could carry when trying to integrate into Swedish society. Secondly, they disregard the issue of segregation and discrimination as coupled to their origin. Having a Turkish background does not mean that one is less of a citizen, quite the opposite. But there were also dissonant voices which could not describe themselves as Swedes at all. However, this minority still believes that their home is in Sweden.

> I was born in Sweden but I still say that we are from Turkey. Although I was born in Sweden I learned Swedish when I was six years old because my mother was at home so she did not take us to a daycare or preschool. But I do not know. I do not feel Swedish. I always say that I come from Turkey ... Ok I am used to being here, my life is here too. When I go to Turkey I long for Sweden.
> *Do you feel at home here in Sweden?*
> Yes, oh yes.
> *But you do not feel Swedish.*
> No, I don't.
> Sehra (27)

All the respondents declared that their home was in Sweden, in Stockholm. Although their personal identities seem complex and far from homogeneous within the group, all the respondents answered that they belong in

Stockholm, not Turkey. The fact that they are not recognised as Turks when in Turkey leads to a feeling of permanent foreignness. Still, home is Stockholm, which might be a reason to prefer their membership of Sweden.

> I am happy to be a Turk. I feel myself strongly Turkish. But when I am on vacations in Turkey then I feel much more Swedish.
> Gulseli (23)

> I feel myself Turkish anyways ... That is how it is and I always say that I come from Turkey. But I belong in Stockholm.
> *Do you feel that you belong in Turkey?*
> Hmmm, no. That was a difficult question. Well no, I feel that I belong there only when I am on vacations. But [even then] people there make me feel different. He is from Europe, they say. I do not feel in-between here in Sweden, I feel Turk in here ... Somehow I am from Turkey, but I was born in Sweden and I grew up in Spånga.
> Eddie (24)

The term *EuroTurk* that has previously been used by Kaya and Kentel[41] to characterise descendants of Turks in other parts of Europe seems to work well in this case. Many respondents declared that they feel Turkish in Sweden, but not 'Turks from Turkey'. Although they are considered foreigners in both cases, they are more comfortable and feel more accepted as Turks in Sweden, where they belong. They decouple their Turkish identity from a sense of belonging and, especially, the home-feeling. The experiences of young Turks in Stockholm let us know that it is somehow allowed to be a Turk in

Sweden and still be a good Swedish citizen. Is this an imprint of the multicultural policy which celebrates diversity but emphasises difference? A deeper analysis would be needed to draw a causal relation between multiculturalism and identification.

The results of this section suggest that the Turkish side is not regarded as something that weakens their local belonging in Sweden. Turkish identity is not equated with a feeling of belonging in Turkey or feeling at home in Turkey. All interviewees felt at home in Stockholm, independently of their identity. In this sense, the residential citizenship is stronger for the home feeling. The main message seems to be that one does not need to feel at home in a country in order to identify with that category.

Being a dual citizen: practical concerns

The previous section disentangled the complex subjective aspects towards identification and belonging. What are the consequences of this for membership? Is the preference for Sweden translated into a more active membership in Sweden? The question we need to start an analysis of membership is why people decide to become a dual citizen if their lives seem to be predominantly in Sweden.

Becoming a dual citizen has been most of the time a family decision. Respondents said that the whole family naturalised as Swedes together, or the parents prepared the paperwork so their children could become Turkish citizens. Although their Turkish side was initially presented as full of symbolic meaning, Turkish citizenship is more of a practical matter.

I have always been a Swedish citizen. But I got Turkish citizenship five years ago. It was only

because we drove to Turkey both ways. And in the Balkans countries it is very, well, if they see that we have a European passport and driving licence then [they] haggle ... That is why we applied for Turkish citizenship. It is much easier in those circumstances.
Pia (20)

Like Pia, most of the respondents said they had acquired Turkish citizenship later in life for practical reasons. Besides this sense of practicality there were also reflections about the knowledge and sense of familiarity behind the two citizenships.

The rights are similar ... But it only counts if you know what your rights are. In that case I am Swedish, but on the other hand [In Turkey] I do not know how it is actually. Then I feel that I am Swedish, that I have a Swedish passport and I belong to the Swedish state in that sense.
Merkan (28)

Turkish citizenship seems more like a 'plus' in people's lives than a status that they embrace. A better way to test whether Turkish citizenship is an active or dormant status is to investigate whether some of the rights and duties attributed to it are exercised by Turkish citizens born in Sweden.

Electoral participation

Among the many objections to being a dual citizen, the breaking of the rule 'one citizen, one vote' seems one of the strongest arguments to discourage such dual status. Hence, it is important to know what happens in the case of Swedish citizens who are also Turkish citizens. Moreover, if they are really bridge-builders then they should be politically integrated at both sides of the bridge. Is that the case?

Given that the great majority of the people participating in the TIES survey were Swedish citizens, they are able to participate in all forms of elections. When asked whether they have voted in past elections, 72.5 per cent of the respondents who were able to do so, considering their age, declared that they had voted. This is lower than the turnout of respondents with a Swedish background (84.2 per cent). Still, it is not low enough to support the old theory of political quiescence of migrants and their descendants.[42]

Turkish Law has made electoral participation for registered citizens living abroad possible since 1987 but it was originally only possible to vote in polling stations set up at the border. Today the conditions have changed and after a couple of amendments to the 1987 Law[43] Turkish citizens living in different countries have been able to vote twice.[44] The first time was for the presidential elections in August 2014 and the second was the General Elections in June 2015.[45]

The interviews were conducted before it was possible to vote from Sweden in Turkish elections. Therefore, the interviewees were asked for a potential vote intention from Sweden or whether they have travelled to Turkey to participate in elections. When confronted with these questions the interviewees showed an inclination to participate in Swedish elections but not Turkish ones. Residence in Sweden seems to be more relevant for their political participation. This seems to show that young people with Turkish ancestry are well integrated into Swedish society from a sociopolitical perspective.

It is really important for me to vote. To be active in the political arena. One must also take note of what

is happening ... If I vote but another person doesn't, others might become the majority and choose someone who is not good for me. So everybody must vote. Otherwise, it does not work.
Do you vote in Turkey?
No ... There are several processes one must go through in order to [do it]. It is a complicated process ... I think it's unimportant to me.
Smek (20)

The fact that people's narratives put Sweden first when it comes to political participation is very revealing in terms of loyalties. Although Smek believes that voting is very important and that everybody should participate in the process, he does not vote in Turkey. Like Smek, many other respondents considered it unnecessary for them to participate in an electoral process in Turkey. There was a small group who did show interest in the electoral processes in their ancestral land but it was a matter of being there at the right time and with the right documentation. In general, people were not so familiar with political processes in Turkey. Participation in the Turkish elections was portrayed as complicated for those living abroad. Only two respondents – both living in Stockholm – claimed to have voted in Turkey. However, it was neither something that they would regularly do nor an informed action.

I did it once when I found out that I had the right to vote in Turkey ... But when I voted I realised almost immediately that it was not the right thing. The error is that I vote here in Sweden because I live here and I am here! And back then I was on a holiday. Even if it was Turkey I was on holiday. And perhaps I do have these other feelings and the closeness and

other important sentimental issues. But it is a whole different matter and it is based on my background and nationality. But I have no right to vote ... [in Turkey]. It is those who live there who should determine and decide and it is their voice which is important not mine ... Their votes are the ones that are important ... I am an active citizen here in Sweden and a passive one in Turkey.
Ali (29)

Ali participated in Turkish elections because he happened to be in Turkey at the right time but, in general, the participants in this study do not show much interest in electoral participation there. The relative ignorance regarding electoral participation was also mentioned when talking about other forms of participation in Turkey. This is a sign of the different kinds of affiliation that people express towards the countries in which they are citizens.

A double duty: Military service
A new element that appeared among the narratives as a relevant experience linked to being a dual citizen is military service. Failure to perform military service in Turkey may lead to problems with the authorities. Some informants even mentioned the possibility of losing their Turkish citizenship if they failed to enlist for military service or if they did not pay the amount required to be exempted from it. Although this is not the case, it does make life complicated for male Turkish citizens who want to visit Turkey. However, the Turkish government established the 'Exemption for those with Dual Nationality'.[46] This exemption is applicable to those that are residents abroad and in addition to Turkish nationality also have citizenship in their country of residence, if they

can produce written proof of having already completed military service in that country corresponding more or less to a similar period of time as in Turkey. Therefore, second generation Turks can be exempted from military service in Turkey and avoid problems with the Turkish authorities that could cause the loss of citizenship. Although most young men said they had done military service in Sweden because it would allow them to avoid it in Turkey, the experience brought something more than what they expected.

> It was the coolest thing I have ever done in my life. Eleven months in Luleå. I did not feel like a proper soldier, because there is not such a thing as war in Sweden. So that was a huge advantage. I must say that there were quite a lot of Swedes there and only I and somebody else with a foreign background ... They took care of us so well and we formed a good fellowship. I have met them [fellows at the military service] often after that.
> Smek (20)

Smek illustrates how this experience became a positive way of interacting with Swedes. This outcome could lead to the conclusion that military service could represent a means of integration. Such an assumption, nevertheless, can only be investigated through more detailed work with regard to the outcomes of those months spent doing military service. It is indeed a fact that they share their daily lives with more people with Swedish ancestry than they usually do, since most second generation Turks in Stockholm live in the outskirts of the city among other young people of an immigrant background. Young men stated that during this period they needed to speak more Swedish than usual and discuss daily issues with young adults of Swedish background, which was both interesting and fun.

> I feel that I am 'försvenskad' [too Swedish] given that I was born here in Sweden and adjusted my life and living conditions in Sweden. But somewhere I feel that I do not embrace a Swedish nationality because I have a foreign background. You are not disappointed because you have not done military service in your homeland, but conscription service abroad in other countries is significantly harder and longer. Therefore, I chose to do it here in Sweden.
> Koray (22)

Interestingly Koray refers to his lack of attachment to the Swedish nationality at the same time that he describes his foreign background. He calls Turkey his homeland but still Sweden seems to be prioritised. Although in many other interviews Turkey was described as 'homeland' it is in Sweden where young people study, work, pay taxes, vote and even do military service. Turkey seems to have a more symbolic role in their lives. Such a role does not compete with allegiances towards Sweden.

Not all the respondents are aware of the possibility of avoiding their military service in Turkey if this is fulfilled in Sweden. The characteristics of the military service in Turkey seem to be unclear. The duration and compensation that a person needs to pay in case of exemption from it is not known by all the interviewees. Some of them were even unaware of the Turkish 'Exemption for Dual Citizens'.

The perception of military service in Sweden as a positive experience found among the participants of the study is not shared by other voices within the community. The magazine *EuroTurk*, produced by the Turkish Youth Association in Sweden, compiled the experiences of young men who performed military service and had negative experiences with regard to the food.[47] Young Turks avoid pork for religious, and even cultural and health reasons. Despite the fact that they informed the people in charge of their dietary preferences before the *Värnplikt* started, the constant presence of pork in the meals led many of them to avoid eating, to feel undernourished, and most of all different. *Euroturk* questions the capacity of the Armed Forces in Sweden to be responsive to the various requirements of different people. Military service meant, in the cases described by the article in *Euroturk*, a sign of their difference in relation to Swedish society. *Försvarsmakten*, the military Forces in Sweden, responded to this[48] by referring to a specific equality policy with regard to dietary preferences and religious affiliation that has been in place since 2009. However, in some cases this is not implemented due to a lack of knowledge of the policy, the non-traditional character of special dietary requirements or simply because the number of young people with another diet preference that are enrolled at a given time is low.

Military service in this specific case is a direct consequence of being a dual citizen. Boys with Turkish background wish to avoid having trouble with the Turkish authorities when travelling to Turkey. Due to special agreements they can perform this service in Sweden. This leads to unexpected experiences in terms of belonging, difference and identity. In this sense, military service illustrates the consequences of being a dual citizen which might be experienced differently by individuals.

This empirical section showed that from a perspective of subjective aspects – identity, feeling of belonging and 'home feeling' – and objective aspects – practical concerns, voting from abroad and military service – people transform a duality that could be problematic into a situation that they can handle and profit from in their everyday lives. Besides, the subjective aspects showed that by emphasising the qualities that they gain from their origin when being Swedish citizens people show that they can actually become a bridge. However, they are not a bridge between two countries, but between the migrant generation and the Swedish population without immigrant ancestry.

Conclusion

From the data presented in this chapter – a shorter version of a much broader study – it is possible to observe that young people of Turkish background are predominantly active as Swedish citizens. Although that status makes them legally entangled with the country, as regards their interest in Turkey in terms of sense of belonging and political participation their 'residential citizenship' i.e. Sweden is stronger than the blood ties towards Turkey. Therefore, there is no perfect division or duality between Sweden and Turkey but a Swedish citizenship with a plus.

This chapter aimed to answer whether descendants of Turks in Sweden can be considered as bridge-builders between the two countries. Although the qualitative character of the study does not allow for generalisation, it is possible to conclude that the participants of the study are not bridge-builders in a transnational sense, understood as trans-state bridge-builders. They are not active members in Turkey in a way that allows them to be informal ambassadors of the country in front of Swedish society. However, the fact that so many respondents of the study regard their Turkish origin as something positive shows that they can be bridge-builders, but between cultures within the country. They are bridge-builders between their ethnic ancestry and their 'everyday' belonging. At the same time, they are a bridge between their parents – the migrant generation – and the national society – where they grew up. The Turkish and Swedish sides are not parallel tracks as in a hybrid perspective. Instead these are integrated into everyday life. The empowerment that people see in their cross-cultural experiences shows that they are good ambassadors of the Turkish community in Sweden. In this sense, they are closer to the 'breaching group' that Kaya and Kentel[49] explored in other European countries. But a breaching group that is proud of being a Turk. They refer to themselves as another kind of Turks and they have been regarded as 'European Turks' when being in Turkey. Therefore, they are a new generation of Turks, the 'Euro Turks', first generation of nationals in their parents' receiving country. Interestingly, the identification that a person might feel does not influence membership. Even people who declared they did not identify as Swedes at all feel at home in Stockholm. This shows the importance of the concept of belonging and 'home feeling' which shows a degree of integration that is not possible to understand if one only looks at identity.

The results show that the attachment towards Turkey does not compete with the allegiance towards Sweden. Is this a matter of age or generation? Most interviewees had only recently started their work careers and family life. There are many factors in their lives that could change, making them look at Turkey with different eyes.

There is, nevertheless, no fixed pattern for being a Swedish citizen with Turkish ancestry. People organise their feelings of belonging differently in order to construct an identity that allows them to feel comfortable with their origins, their citizenship and their loyalties. Having a non-Swedish ethnic background might be regarded as a negative thing when facing discrimination or become an excuse for avoiding integration into national society. However, descendants of Turks in Stockholm show that having another origin can also be a source of empowerment from a citizenship perspective.

The case of young men with Turkish background is particularly interesting for the debates around dual citizenship. An ironic consequence of the wish to maintain Turkish citizenship is the fact that many young Turks do their military service in Europe. The respondents of this study manifested this experience as a very positive one which even contributed to their integration into Swedish society.

Finally, it is important to take into account that the interviews were carried out in 2009. Nowadays, it would be interesting to gauge interest in the latest political developments in the country. It is highly possible that their dormant Turkish citizenship awoke with incidents such as the Gezi Park protests in May 2013.

Notes

1. Costanza Vera-Larrucea, *Citizenship by citizens: first generation nationals with Turkish ancestry on lived citizenship in Paris and Stockholm*. Department of Political Science, Stockholm University. Stockholm studies in politics; p. 150 (Stockholm, 2013).
2. Harald Runblom, *Migrants and the homeland: Images, symbols and realities*, Uppsala: Centre for Multiethnic Research [Centrum förmultietniskforskning] (Uppsala, 2000), p. 14.
3. Ayhan Kaya & Ferhat Kentel, *Euro-Turks: A Bridge, or a Breach, between Turkey and the European Union?* Bilgi University (Istanbul, 2005).
4. The terms host-land and home-land are presented here within quotation marks because these are not appropriate terms for the second generation. They were born in their parents' host-land, and there is no evidence that they consider Turkey to be their homeland.
5. Kaya & Kentel, *Euro-Turks*, p. 69.

6. TIES is the acronym of 'The Integration of the European Second Generation'. The aim of this Survey is to describe immigrants' descendants' living conditions in 17 European cities. For more info see www.tiesproject.org.
7. Charles Westin et al., 'Introduction'. In Westin (ed.), *The Integration of Descendants of Migrants from Turkey in Stockholm*, Amsterdam University Press (Amsterdam, 2015), p. 13.
8. Ayla Yazgan, *Turkiska flickor: andra generationen invandrare*, Statens Invandrarverk [National Immigration Board] (Norrköping, 1983).
9. Ayla Yazgán, *Turkiska pojkar: andra generationens invandrare*, CEIFO Publications (Stockholm, 1993).
10. Reza Eyrumulu, *Turkar Möter Sverige. En studie om turkisktalande elevers skolgång i Göteborg*, Carlssons (Stockholm, 1992).
11. Magnus Berg, *Seldas andra bröllop. berättelser om hur det är: turkiska andragenerationsinvandrare, identitet, etnicitet, modernitet, etnologi.* Göteborg: Etnologiska Institutionen (Göteborg, 1994).
12. Judith Narrowe, *Under one roof: on becoming a Turk in Sweden*, AlmqvistWiksell International (Stockholm, 1998).
13. Ulla Engelbrektsson, *Tales of Identity: Turkish Youth in Gothenburg*, CEIFO Publications (Stockholm, 1992).
14. Ibid., p. 356.
15. Erkki Virta and Charles Westin, *Psychosocial adjustment of adolescents with immigrant background in Sweden.* CEIFO Publications (Stockholm, 1999).
16. Sema Erder, *Refah Toplumunda 'Getto' ve Turkler* (Ghetto and Turks in the Welfare Society), İstanbul Bilgi University Press (Istanbul, 2006).
17. Sven E O. Hort, 'The Growing Strength of the Euroturk in Pro-Turkish and Euro-Sceptical Sweden', in Kucukcan, T. & Gungor, V. *Turks in Europe: Culture, Identity and Integration*, The Netherlands Turkevi Research Centre (Amsterdam, 2009) p. 432.
18. Westin (ed.) *The Integration of Descendants of Migrants from Turkey in Stockholm*, Amsterdam University Press (Amsterdam, 2015).
19. Alireza Behtoui, 'Educational Achievements', in Westin (ed.), *The Integration of Descendants of Migrants from Turkey in Stockholm*, Amsterdam University Press (Amsterdam, 2015).
20. Ibid., p. 55.
21. Thomas Faist, 'The Fixed and Porous Boundaries of Dual Citizenship', in Th. Faist (ed.), *The Politics of Dual Citizenship in Europe: From Nationhood to Societal Integration*, Aldershot, Avebury (London, 2007), p. 3.
22. Ibid.
23. UNHCR, Directorate for Movement of Persons, Migration and Consular Affairs. Asylum and Migration Divisions.

24. Thomas Faist, *Dual citizenship as overlapping membership*, Malmö Högskola (Malmö, 2001).
25. Rainer Bauböck, 'The rights and duties of external citizenship' *Citizenship Studies*. 13/5 (2009), pp. 475–99.
26. Miriam Feldblum, 'Citizenship matters: Contemporary Trends in Europe and the United States,' *Stanford Electronic Humanities Review*, 5/2 (1997).
27. Hakan Sicakkan and Y. Lithman, 'Politics of identity, modes of belonging and citizenship: An overview of conceptual and theoretical challenges', in Sicakkan, H. and Lithman, Y. (eds) *Changing the Basis of Citizenship in the Modern State*, The Edwin Mellen Press (USA, 2005).
28. Ibid., p. 27.
29. Norman Denzin, *Interpretive Biography*, Sage Publications (California, 1989).
30. People with Kurdish or Syriani origins also participated in the TIES questionnaire. However, their ethnic belonging is more complex – though no less interesting – to analyse. Due to time constraints they were not included in the study.
31. Talip Kucukcan, 'Bridging the European Union and Turkey: The Turkish Diaspora in Europe,' *Insight Turkey*, 9/4 (2007), pp. 85–99.
32. Zeynep Kadirbeyoglu, 'National Transnationalism: *Dual Citizenship* in Turkey', in Faist (ed.) Dual Citizenship in Europe. Aldershot (Ashgate, 2007), pp 128–32.
33. Fuat Keyman and Ahmet İçduygu 'Globalization, Civil Society and Citizenship in Turkey: Actors, Boundaries and Discourses'. *Citizenship Studies*, 7/2 (2003), pp. 219–34.
34. Zeynep Kadirbeyoglu, Report on Turkey. EUDO, Robert Schuman Centre for Advanced Studies. European University Institute (2009), pp. 4–8.
35. Faist 'The Fixed and Porous Boundaries of Dual Citizenship', p. 103.
36. SFS 2001Svensk författningssamling 2001:82 Law about Swedish citizenship p. 82.
37. H. Lokrantz Bernitz, 'Country Profile: Sweden', in European Union Democracy Observatory. http://eudo-citizenship.eu/docs/CountryReports/Sweden.pdf (2012).
38. Lisa Åkesson, 'Multicultural Ideology and Transnational Family Ties among Descendants of Cape Verdeans in Sweden'. *Journal of Ethnic and Migration Studies*. 37/2 (2010), pp. 217–35.
39. Grete Brochman & Idun Seland, 'Citizenship Policies and Ideas of Nationhood in Scandinavia,' *Citizenship Studies*. 14/4 (2010), pp. 429–43.

40. In this case the statistics show those whose parents were Turkish citizens at the time of their arrival in Sweden. However, they belong to different ethnic groups, though predominantly ethnic Turks.
41. Kaya and Kentel, *Euro-Turks*.
42. The thesis of the political quiescence of immigrants emerged to explain migrants' apathy and lack of civic commitment. However, migrants proved to be involved in politics in the receiving country although their involvement in politics was not considered to be strong enough to classify them as a political force (See Mark Miller, 'The political impact of foreign labor: A Re-evaluation of the Western European Experience'. *The International Migration Review*, 16/1, Spring, 1982). Today, non-traditional forms of political participation among immigrants have demonstrated that the thesis of migrant political quiescence was far from accurate (See Marco Martiniello, 'Political Participation, Mobilisation and Representation of Immigrants and Their Offspring in Europe'. *Willy Brandt Series of Working Papers in International Migration and Ethnic Relations*, School of International Migration and Ethnic Relations, Malmö University (Malmö, 2005)).
43. The first Amendment (no. 4121) to Article 67 of the Constitution in 1995 aimed at promoting new legislation enabling citizens residing abroad to vote from their country of residence. Still, due to technical and legal obstacles, in the four general elections between 1995 and 2007, voting at the border remained the only method. The Law was amended again in 2008 to enable citizens living abroad to vote in general elections through different methods of voting. But it was not until 2012 when a final amendment (no. 6304) to the electoral law created an overseas voters' registry. After this last amendment it was possible to organise an electoral process from abroad with the help of the Turkish diplomatic representations.
44. Zeynep Kadirbeyoglu & Asli Okyay, 'Turkey: Voting from abroad in 2015 general elections'. EUDO Citizenship (European University Institute, Florence). Published on Thursday, 6 August (2015).
45. In the 2015 elections 12,588 votes were cast in Sweden. Source: http://secim.aa.com.tr/YurtDisiENG.html (accessed 11 January 2016).
46. Website of the Directorate for the Admission of Conscripts (Askeri Alma Daire Başkanlığı) of the Ministry of Defence (www.asal.msb.gov.tr/webersikcasorulan.htm).
47. *EuroTurk* No. 2 (2010).

48. *Euroturk*, No. 3 (2010), p. 17.
49. Kaya and Kentel, *Euro-Turks*.

References

Åkesson, L., 'Multicultural Ideology and Transnational Family Ties among Descendants of Cape Verdeans in Sweden,' *Journal of Ethnic and Migration Studies*, 37/2 (2003), pp. 217–35.

Bauböck, R., 'Stakeholder citizenship and transnational political participation: A normative evaluation of external voting,' *Fordham law review*, 75/5 (2007), pp. 2393–447.

——, 'The rights and duties of external citizenship' *Citizenship Studies*, 13/5 (2009), pp. 475–99.

Behtoui, A., 'Educational Achievements' in Westin (ed.), *The Integration of Descendants of Migrants from Turkey in Stockholm*, Amsterdam University Press (Amsterdam, 2015).

Berg, M., *Seldas andra bröllop. berättelser om hur det är: turkiska andragenerationsinvandrare, identitet, etnicitet, modernitet, etnologi*, Etnologiska Institutionen (Göteborg, 1994).

Bloemraad, I., 'Who Claims Dual Citizenship? The Limits of Postnationalism, the Possibilities of Transnationalism, and the Persistence of Traditional Citizenship,' *The International Migration Review*, 38/2 (2004), pp. 389–426.

Denzin, N., *Interpretive Biography*, Sage Publications (Newbury Park, CA., 1989).

Engelbrektsson, U., *Tales of Identity: Turkish Youth in Gothenburg*, CEIFO Publications (Stockholm, 1992).

Erder, S., *Refah Toplumunda 'Getto' ve Turkler* [Ghetto and Turks in the Welfare Society], İstanbul Bilgi University Press Series on Sociology (Istanbul, 1992).

Eyrumulu, R., *Turkar Möter Sverige. En studie om turkisktalande elevers skolgång i Göteborg*, Carlssons (Stockholm, 1992).

Faist, T., *Dual citizenship as overlapping membership*, Malmö Högskola (Malmo, 2001).

——, 'The Fixed and Porous Boundaries of Dual Citizenship, in Th. Faist (ed.), *The Politics of Dual Citizenship in Europe: From Nationhood to Societal Integration*, Aldershot (UK: Avebury, 2007).

Feldblum, M., 'Citizenship matters: Contemporary Trends in Europe and the United States,' *Stanford Electronic Humanities Review*, 5/2 (1997).

Hort, Sven E. O., 'The Growing Strength of the Euroturk in Pro-Turkish and Euro-Sceptical Sweden,' in Kucukcan, T., & Gungor, V. *Turks in Europe: Culture, Identity and Integration*, The Netherlands Turkevi Research Centre (Amsterdam, 2009).

Kadirbeyoglu, Z., 'National Transnationalism: Dual Citizenship in Turkey', in Faist (ed.), *Dual Citizenship in Europe*, Aldershot: Ashgate (Farhnam, 2007), pp. 128–32.

————, Report on Turkey. EUDO, Robert Schuman Centre for Advanced Studies, European University Institute (Florence, 2009). http://eudo-citizenship.eu/docs/CountryReports/Turkey.pdf.

Kadirbeyoglu, Z., and Okyay A., 'Turkey: Voting from abroad in 2015 general elections,' EUDO Citizenship, European University Institute (Florence, 2015).

Kaya, A., and Kentel, F., *Euro-Turks: A Bridge, or a Breach, between Turkey and the European Union?* Bilgi University (Istanbul, 2005).

Keyman, E.F., and Içduygu, A., 'Globalization, Civil Society and Citizenship in Turkey: Actors, Boundaries and Discourses,' *Citizenship Studies*, 7/2 (2005), pp. 219–34.

Kücukcan, T., 'Bridging the European Union and Turkey: The Turkish Diaspora in Europe,' *Insight Turkey*, 9/4 (2007), pp. 85–99.

Martiniello, M., 'Political Participation, Mobilisation and Representation of Immigrants and Their Offspring in Europe,' *Willy Brandt Series of Working Papers in International Migration and Ethnic Relations*, School of International Migration and Ethnic Relations, Malmö University (Malmo, 2005).

Miller, M., 'The political impact of foreign labor: A Re-evaluation of the Western European Experience,' *The International Migration Review*, Vol. 16, No. 1 (1982).

Narrowe, J., *Under one roof: on becoming a Turk in Sweden*, Almqvist & Wiksell International (Stockholm, 1998).

Runblom, H. (ed.), *Migrants and the homeland: Images, symbols and realities*, Centre for Multiethnic Research [Centrum förmultiet-niskforskning] (Uppsala, 2000).

Sicakkan H., and Lithman Y., 'Politics of identity, modes of belonging and citizenship: An overview of conceptual and theoretical challenges' in Sicakkan H., and Lithman Y. (eds), *Changing the Basis of Citizenship in the modern State*, The Edwin Mellen Press (USA, 2005).

Vera-Larrucea, C., *Citizenship by citizens: first generation nationals with Turkish ancestry on lived citizenship in Paris and Stockholm*, PhD Thesis at the Department of Political Science, Stockholm University. Stockholm studies in politics (Stockholm, 2013).

Virta, E., and Westin Ch., *Psychosocial adjustment of adolescents with immigrant background in Sweden*, CEIFO Publications (Stockholm, 1999).

Westin, Ch., 'Young people of migrant origin in Sweden,' in E. Zeybekoglu, & J. Johanson (eds), *Migration and labour in Europe: Views from Turkey and Sweden*, (Istanbul, 2003), pp. 173–5.

Westin Ch. and Behtoui; Vera-Larrucea, 'Introduction,' in Westin (ed.), *The Integration of Descendants of Migrants from Turkey in Stockholm*, Amsterdam University Press (Amsterdam, 2015).

Yazgan, A., *Turkiska flickor: andra generationen invandrare*, (Norrköping, Statens invandrarverk [National Immigration Board] 1983).

————, *Turkiska pojkar: andragenerationensinvandrare*, CEIFO Publications (Stockholm, 1993).

Other Sources

Svensk författningssamling (SFS), Law (2001:82) about Swedish
    citizenship
Euroturk, No. 3, 2010
Anadolu Ajansi, http://secim.aa.com.tr
TIES Project, www.tiesproject.org

CHAPTER 5

TURKISH MAINTENANCE AND BILINGUALISM AMONG SECOND-GENERATION TURKS IN MULTICULTURAL STOCKHOLM

Memet Aktürk-Drake

Introduction

In the last three decades, the interest in the role of language in the acculturation and integration of immigrants and their descendants has been on the rise, not only among researchers but also among journalists and policy makers. Coupled with the ubiquity of Turkish speakers in Western Europe, this interest has generated considerable research on Turkish-speaking communities' proficiency and use regarding both Turkish and the majority language in their countries of residence. Turkish children and adolescents in Swedish cities had previously been included in large-scale international comparative studies on the second generation.[1] However, similar studies on young adults were missing in Sweden until the recent publication of the results of the project *The Integration of the*

European Second Generation.[2] Relying on data from this project (henceforth TIES), this chapter aims to investigate how the maintenance of Turkish and the bilingual profiles of adult ethnic Turks in Stockholm can be accounted for by Sweden's multicultural policies and by several different background factors.

Language Development and Bilingualism

Heritage-language maintenance refers to the transgenerational maintenance of languages that are part of the ancestral heritage in a context where they are only shared by a minority. The engine of heritage-language maintenance is the interplay between language use and language proficiency. The foundation of proficiency in the heritage language is laid prior to school age mainly by parents who help the young generation in acquiring the main skills involved in spoken communication by using their heritage language with their children. Through continued and diversified use of the heritage language from school age (ages six–seven) until the end of their adolescence, the young generation can increase their proficiency by extending their vocabulary and by increasing their grammatical mastery, as well as by developing literacy skills, which are typically linked to formal education.[3] Depending on the linguistic composition of their family, kindergarten and neighbourhood, children may already get exposure to the majority language and start acquiring it before school age.

Most heritage-language speakers will become bilingual by also acquiring proficiency in the majority language. Depending on the structures and discourses in the larger society and on the local conditions in their neighbourhood and school, the introduction of the majority language as a second language can potentially have negative effects on the children's development in their heritage language. If the macro- and micro-conditions encourage or compel children and adolescents to stop using their heritage language once they have acquired proficiency in the majority language, we speak of *subtractive bilingualism.*[4] However, in many diasporic contexts and language communities, heritage languages maintain their vitality over several generations.[5] In such cases, where the majority language does not undermine the heritage language but constitutes an addition to the speaker's language repertoire, we speak of *additive bilingualism.*[6]

Multicultural Sweden as a Special Context for Bilingual Development

Today, multiculturalist integration policies towards immigrants and a pluralistic ideology supporting the maintenance of heritage cultures and languages are most strongly associated with *settler nations* such as Canada and Australia. Nonetheless, since the 1970s Sweden has made the most serious attempt in Europe at establishing multiculturalist policies towards immigrants and their descendants. According to the *Multiculturalism Policy Index*[7], since 1980 Sweden has been following a gradual path of multicultural policies towards the highest scores, which were attested in Canada and Australia. Moreover, Sweden has the highest score in the *Migrant Integration Policy Index* (MIPEX) today.[8] These facts make Sweden a unique historical case because it is the only historically ethnicity-based nation (without a colonial past) that has combined a decidedly multiculturalist outlook with a well-developed social welfare state.

In terms of the education and language development of immigrants and their descendants, currently Sweden has the highest MIPEX score for education policy and has had the highest Multiculturalism Policy Index (MPI) score regarding funding for ethnic organisations, bilingual education and mother-tongue instruction since 1980. This leading position has also been confirmed by the results of the TIES project where one of the most promising educational results among the second generation with background from Turkey was found in Sweden.[9] Several factors have contributed to this outcome and set Sweden apart from the rest of Western Europe in terms of the language development of immigrants and their descendants, a fact that is often overlooked in studies on Turks and Turkish in Europe.

Firstly, the Swedish educational system set additive bilingualism as one of its goals very early on. This gave rise to the parallel development of the school subject Swedish as a second language and mother tongue instruction (MTI), which started in the mid-1960s and were cemented through gradual legal reforms in 1975, 1977, 1982 and 1995.[10] Secondly, the first generation of Turkish immigrants were not treated as guest workers but as new members of Swedish society. Therefore, the acquisition of Swedish by adult immigrants started to receive public funding as early as the mid-1960s, labour-force immigrants obtained the right to receive a minimum of 200 hours of Swedish courses in 1968 and the hours were gradually raised to 700 in the reform of 1986.[11] Hence, the multiculturalist integration infrastructure that makes Sweden the leading country in recent international comparisons was principally in place by the mid-1970s.

Although Sweden's 'welfare multiculturalism' has ensured that immigrants and their descendants are better off in many respects compared to other Western European countries, they are still not viewed and treated as equal members of Swedish society.[12] This is partly due to the slower transition from assimilationist to pluralistic ideology in key institutions and among the general public compared to official policies. This gives rise to ideological tensions or covert conflicts and to implementation problems in practice.[13] Behtoui describes the resulting situation today as one of *subordinate inclusion*, which means that 'stigmatised migrant groups are included in the institutional system in general, but placed in subordinate positions in all spheres of life'.[14]

Previous Findings on Turkish Maintenance Among Second-Generation Turks

Several studies have investigated language issues among second-generation Turkish speakers with a comparative approach by using the same methodology in countries such as Germany, France, the Netherlands, Belgium and Sweden as well as in Australia and the USA. These comparative studies have provided two important general findings concerning the maintenance of Turkish. Firstly, the Turkish diaspora communities' attitudes towards the Turkish language have consistently been found to be very positive as an important marker of Turkish identity in all countries that were studied.[15] Secondly, the results point to a big divide between settler nations and other nations where migration is a more recent and less pervasive phenomenon. In Western Europe, Turkish is one of the immigrant languages with the highest degree of maintenance across all countries examined.[16] In this context, where national identities tend to be narrowly defined due to historical roots in common ethnicity and religion, second-generation Turks' feelings of belonging to the country of residence turned out to be rather weak while their Turkish sense of belonging was usually quite strong. In contrast, a much stronger sense of belonging to the country of residence and rather low degrees of Turkish maintenance were observed in the settler nations Australia and the USA.[17]

Although Sweden is a historically ethnicity-based Western European nation, it has a pluralist ideology similar to some settler nations and it would be interesting to know if Turkish maintenance patterns and bilingual profiles in Sweden are more similar to those found in Western European nations or in settler nations. Previous international comparative studies of second-generation Turkish speakers, which also included Swedish cities, have shown that the community in Sweden is quite similar to other communities in Western Europe, at least in their childhood and adolescence. The *Multilingual Cities Project* on children with Turkish background between ages six and 12 in five Western European cities, including Gothenburg in Sweden, revealed similarly high degrees of Turkish maintenance across all cities. Among the 20 languages covered in Gothenburg, Turkish had the fifth highest degree of maintenance.[18] A further finding of the project in Gothenburg was that 'there [was] a significant relationship between reported literacy (reading and writing skills) and [mother tongue] instruction for all of the 20 most frequently reported home languages'.[19] This latter finding was recently confirmed in a study which found that Somali reading and vocabulary knowledge among children of Somali background in Sweden benefitted significantly from participating in weekly MTI.[20]

The *International Comparative Study of Ethnocultural Youth* (ICSEY) included ethnic Turkish adolescents between ages 15 and 18.[21] They largely belonged to the second generation and resided in five Western European countries with comparable Turkish communities, including Sweden (Stockholm). Based on ICSEY data, Vedder and Virta found that Turkish proficiency was an important part of Turkish identity in Sweden and contributed positively to the adolescents' psychological and sociocultural adaptation.[22] Further ICSEY results showed that more than half of all adolescent Turks in each of the five countries displayed acculturation profiles where the maintenance of Turkish heritage played a central role.[23]

Methodology

The present data comes from a large Western European survey conducted as part of *The Integration of the European Second Generation* (TIES) project.[24] The survey covered *inter alia* the second generation with origins in Turkey in 13 cities in seven European countries. Two cities per country were included in France, Germany, Austria, Switzerland, the Netherlands and Belgium but only Stockholm in Sweden. Through random sampling from the Swedish Population Register, Statistics Sweden identified 2,250 persons between the ages of 18 and 35, who were born in Sweden, resided in Stockholm County and whose parents were born in Turkey. Questionnaire-based interviews were subsequently conducted with this group in 2007 and 2008 until the number of 250 participants was reached.[25] Of these, 145 (58 per cent) reported that both their parents were ethnic Turks and will henceforth be referred to as second-generation Turks. The interviews included detailed questions on a number of different subjects such as occupation, education, socialisation and identity.[26] Here, the focus will be on the few questions concerning language skills and use as well as on a wide range of background variables.[27] The raw TIES data was reorganised and analysed statistically by the author with mainly non-parametric tests.

Following the general theoretical approach of the TIES project,[28] in this chapter being employed (or in education), having higher levels of education and majority-language proficiency as well as greater degrees of socialisation with members of the majority society (in the neighbourhood and in school as well as in friendships and partnerships) are assumed to facilitate integration into the country of residence. For the parents, it is furthermore assumed that higher degrees of urbanisation in their home areas in Turkey facilitate integration due to the greater occurrence of cultural Westernisation and social structures pertaining to industrialised societies in such areas.

Results and Discussion

Background variables

Half of the 145 participants had finished or were still enrolled in upper secondary education, while 30 per cent had received university education. Most of their parents were born between 1950 and 1970. The median age of immigration was 19 for the fathers and 18 for the mothers. The parents were raised in home areas in Turkey with varying degrees of urbanisation. Thirty-eight per cent were raised in a village, 30 per cent in a small town and 32 per cent in a city. For 24 per cent of the parents, the home area corresponded to the Western Turkish metropolitan cities of Istanbul, Ankara and Izmir (and for a few the Swedish capital Stockholm). Among the parents, the highest level of education was primary school for 29 per cent, lower secondary school for 29 per cent, upper secondary school for 22 per cent and university for 19 per cent. Ninety per cent of the parents could read and write in Swedish while 67 per cent of the mothers and 75 per cent of the fathers spoke Swedish well or very well. Seventy per cent of the mothers had had some type of employment when the participants were 15 years old.

According to Schneider et al., in eight TIES cities (Amsterdam, Rotterdam, Vienna, Frankfurt, Paris, Strasbourg, Brussels and Antwerp) the communities with a background from Turkey consisted predominantly of ethnic Turks (i.e. included few members of ethnic minorities from Turkey).[29] This makes these cities comparable with the present data on ethnic Turks in Stockholm and they will henceforth be referred to as TIES8. Comparisons with TIES8 revealed that second-generation Turks in Stockholm had some of the least Turkish and most multi-ethnic socialisation networks.[30] However, their social networks tended to become more Turkish in adulthood. They also had one of the lowest levels of contact with Turkey, although the level was absolutely speaking not very low.[31] The Stockholm Turks' highly multi-ethnic socialisation patterns are likely to be due to Stockholm being Sweden's most multi-ethnic county, the small size of the Turkish community there (ca. one per cent) and its neighbourhood patterns with a relatively low density of fellow Turks. The relatively low levels of contact with Turkey can be explained by two factors. Firstly, Sweden's welfare multiculturalism is likely to have enabled Turks to feel more at home, which made them less oriented towards Turkey compared to other Western European cities. Secondly, despite the increased accessibility of airline travel in Europe in the last two decades, in earlier periods Turkey was less easily accessible from Stockholm than from many continental European cities, when travelling by car, bus or train was the norm.

Belonging

Graph 5.1 presents an overview of four types of belonging investigated among second-generation ethnic Turks in Stockholm. The feeling of belonging to the minority categories Turk and Muslim were rather strong, closely followed by city belonging, while national belonging was rather weak. This pattern mimics the general results in the TIES project, but there were some subtle differences too. Compared to TIES8, Turkish belonging was the lowest and Muslim belonging the second lowest in Stockholm.[32] This means that while minority identities were absolutely speaking strong in Stockholm, they were somewhat weaker relative to comparable TIES cities. This is probably due to the multi-ethnic atmosphere of Stockholm, especially in the Turks' neighbourhoods, which together with the pluralistic public discourse in Sweden made heritage identities relatively less important as they were not openly challenged. The lack of a significant correlation between Swedish and Turkish belonging in Table 5.1 confirms that multiple belongings were facilitated in multicultural Stockholm. Moreover,

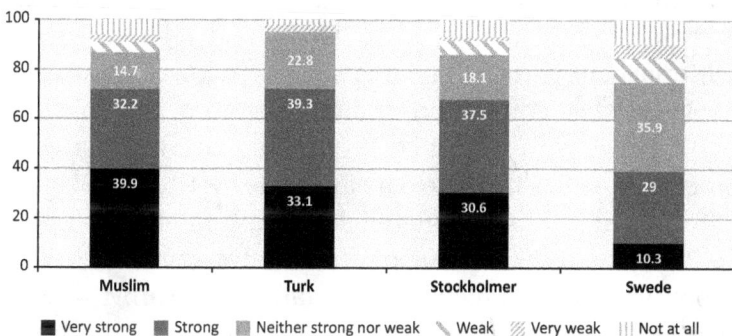

Graph 5.1 Strength of belonging to different groups among second-generation Turks in Stockholm in response to the question 'How strongly do you feel that you belong to these groups?' (in per cent).

Table 5.1 Correlations between variables concerning belonging and language proficiency (two-tailed Spearman)

	Turkish belonging	Muslim belonging	Mean Swedish proficiency	Mean Turkish proficiency
Swedish belonging	r = −.057 p = .497	r = −.160 p = .057	**r = .227** **p = .006**	r = .002 p = .978
Turkish belonging		**r = .468** **p = .000**	r = .010 p = .908	**r = .192** **p = .021**
Mean Swedish proficiency				**r = .246** **p = .003**

Bold style = Correlation is significant at the 0.05 level.
Following established statistical conventions, the r value indicates the strength and direction of the correlation while the p value indicates the significance of the correlation.

the moderate positive correlation between the language proficiencies in Table 5.1 suggests that we have a case of additive bilingualism in Stockholm.

Furthermore, there was an interesting contrast in Stockholm between very strong city belonging, which was the highest compared to TIES8, and relatively weak national belonging, which was the fourth lowest compared to TIES8.[33] A correlation analysis between the share of participants with strong or very strong city belonging in Stockholm and TIES6 (no data available for the two Belgian cities), and the accumulated Multicultural Policy Index (MPI) score (1980–2010) of their states revealed a very robust positive correlation (two-tailed Pearson: $r = .927$, $p = .003$). Thus, the stronger multicultural national policies were, the stronger the second generation's city belonging was. In contrast, no significant correlation was found between strong or very strong national belonging and MPI scores ($r = .057$, $p = .884$).

A plausible interpretation of the contrast between national and city belonging is that national identities are much more rigid and closed in Western Europe (in contrast to settler nations) and therefore much less affected by multicultural policies compared to the more open and inclusive city identities, which have not been the subject of intensive propaganda and therefore reflect the positive effects of multiculturalism much better.

Proficiency in Turkish and bilingual profiles

Graph 5.2 summarises the percentage of participants who reported different levels of Swedish and Turkish proficiency in three language skills.

In the diasporic context, it is not surprising to find higher reported proficiency in the majority language (Swedish) than in the heritage language (Turkish). However, the proficiency differences are quite marked in the Swedish context when we compare the share of participants who reported excellent or very good skills across the two languages (as indicated by the dashed lines in Graph 5.2). The reported proficiency difference was smaller in speaking skills with 31.8 percentage points and

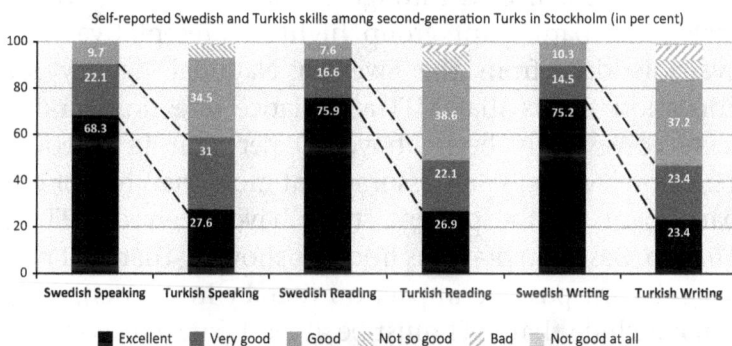

Self-reported Swedish and Turkish skills among second-generation Turks in Stockholm (in per cent)

Legend: Excellent | Very good | Good | Not so good | Bad | Not good at all

Graph 5.2 Self-reported Swedish and Turkish skills among second-generation Turks in Stockholm (in per cent).

greater in literacy skills with 43.5 and 42.9 percentage points in reading and writing respectively. Such bilingual profiles with a very clear dominance in the majority language are rather unusual among Turks in the Western European context. Coupled with the relatively high levels reported for the majority language, the bilingual profiles are more reminiscent of settler societies such as Australia.

Overall, approximately half of the participants in Graph 5.2 reported having excellent or very good skills in Turkish. A Friedman Test was conducted in order to compare the different skills of the same speaker. The results indicated that there was a significant difference between the participants' three skills ($\chi^2 = 33.39$, p = .000) with the level 'very good' being the median for speaking and 'good' for reading and writing. The subsequent Wilcoxon Signed Rank test showed that each of the three skills were significantly different from the others but that the effect sizes were rather small (Speaking-Reading: p = .001, r = .19; Speaking-Writing: p = .000, r = .28; Reading-Writing: p = .004, r = .17). The TIES project did not record the participants' attendance of mother-tongue instruction (MTI). However, the data in Sweden was collected through random sampling, which makes the participant group highly representative. The available data from the Swedish National Agency for Education shows that MTI attendance rates for Turkish have consistently been above 50 per cent in Sweden. Therefore, we can safely assume that more than half of the participants of the present study have received MTI in Turkish. Based on previous findings showing that MTI had a significant positive impact on literacy in Sweden,[34] we can conclude that MTI must be at least partly responsible for the small size of the difference between Turkish speaking and the two literacy skills in Graph 5.2.

A mean Turkish proficiency score was calculated based on speaking skills and the mean of reading and writing skills in order to give the oral and written modalities equal weight. The correlations between mean Turkish proficiency and different types of background factors are presented in Table 5.2.

Variables related to the participants' general integration and socialisation with other Turks in Sweden from upper secondary school until today had no significant impact on Turkish proficiency. In contrast, variables concerning relation to heritage, early socialisation and parental background as well as contact with Turkey displayed moderate positive correlations with mean Turkish proficiency. These findings reveal that a positive stance towards the heritage and interactive communication with Turkish speakers who were raised in Turkey play the most important roles for Turkish proficiency. The later the participants had joined Swedish public education and consequently the more time they had spent at home with their mothers (and siblings) in early childhood, the higher they reported their Turkish proficiency to be. All the same, age of onset had no significant correlation with their mean Swedish proficiency (one-tailed Spearman: $r = -.134$, $p = .072$). This pattern can be explained by the fact that the foundation of heritage language proficiency is laid in this period. The fact that participants with parents from more urbanised areas and with university education reported higher proficiency is likely to be due to the fact that these parents were able to provide better support for the extension of their children's vocabulary as well as for their formal and academic registers. Based on these results, the fact that the mean levels of contact with Turkey and Turkish belonging were relatively weaker and the age of onset for public education was relatively earlier

Table 5.2 Correlations between mean Turkish proficiency and background factors (one-tailed Spearman)

	General integration		Relation to Turkish and Muslim heritage			Early socialisation and parents' background		
	Occupation (Working/studying versus neither)	Highest level of education	Turkish belonging	Preference for heritage preservation	Intensity of religious practice	Highest degree of urbanisation among parents' home areas	University education among parents	Age of onset for public education
	r = .071 p = .199	r = .113 p = .087	r = .208 p = .006	r = .142 p = .045	r = .209 p = .016	r = .210 p = .006	r = .163 p = .025	r = .199 p = .015

Table 5.2 *Continued*

| | Socialisation with other Turks in Sweden from upper secondary school until today | | | Contact with Turkey | | |
	Share of Turks among 3 best friends now	Share of Turks in current neighbourhood	Frequency of contact with relatives in Sweden (excl. parents & household)	Frequency of visits to Turkey in the last five years	Partner raised in Turkey	Share of Turkish channels in TV watching
Share of Turks among 3 best friends in upper secondary school	r = .071	r = .066	r = −.108	**r = .259**	**r = .213**	r = −.077
r = −.016	p = .209	p = .218	p = .098	**p = .001**	**p = .027**	p = .182
p = .432						

Bold style = Correlation is significant at the 0.05 level.

in Stockholm compared to TIES8, offers some explanation for the fact that we did not find higher levels of Turkish skills in Graph 5.2.

Language use

Graph 5.3 summarises the second generation's language use with different interlocutors in the private sphere. As can be seen at the bottom of Graph 5.3, the answer scale was designed to include both Swedish and Turkish use in an inverse relationship.

As in previous studies on second-generation Turks, the highest degree of Turkish use was found with the parents and the lowest with friends. The degree of Turkish use with the partner was closer to the degree with the parents, while language use with siblings was more similar to that with friends.

For statistical analyses, mean Turkish use was calculated based on Turkish use with parents (mean of mother and father due to their high correlation), partner, siblings and friends. An ascending scale for mean Turkish use was constructed based on the answer alternatives in Graph 5.3, where 'mostly Swedish' was given the value one and 'mostly Turkish' the value four. The resulting

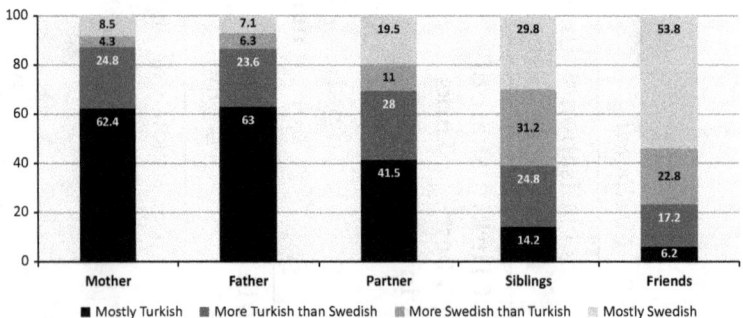

Graph 5.3 shows a stacked bar chart with values:

	Mother	Father	Partner	Siblings	Friends
Mostly Swedish (top)	8.5	7.1	19.5	29.8	53.8
More Swedish than Turkish	4.3	6.3	11	24.8	22.8
More Turkish than Swedish	24.8	23.6	28	31.2	17.2
Mostly Turkish (bottom)	62.4	63	41.5	14.2 / 24.8	6.2

■ Mostly Turkish ■ More Turkish than Swedish ■ More Swedish than Turkish ▨ Mostly Swedish

Graph 5.3 Language use with different interlocutors among second-generation Turks in Stockholm (in per cent).

mean Turkish use was normally distributed (Kolmogorov-Smirnov test of normality: Significance = .200; Skewness = .034; Kurtosis = −.833). Table 5.3 presents a straight-forward linear regression model with mean Turkish use as the dependent variable and mean proficiency in both languages as well as national and heritage belonging as independent variables.

As the last column of Table 5.3 shows, all four types of independent variables made significant contributions to the regression model. The beta values in the penultimate column demonstrate that the greatest unique contribution was made the variable mean Turkish proficiency, followed by mean Swedish proficiency. Due to the inverse relationship between Turkish and Swedish use, the Swedish variables had negative values. As the R Square value in the middle column illustrates, this model could account for 28.1 per cent of the variance in language use.

Although the model is reasonably successful in explaining the observed language use patterns, it misses one crucial type of variable: the specific interlocutor's background. After all, both the interlocutors' proficiency in the two languages and their identity and language attitudes based on several background factors influence the participant's language choice with them. In order to complement the results of the general regression model, Table 5.4 presents the correlations between Turkish use and a selection of background factors for different types of interlocutors.

The left-hand side of Table 5.4 includes the participants' relation to their heritage as expressed by their preference for preserving their heritage and the intensity of their religious practice. Those participants who had higher preference for heritage preservation displayed higher Turkish use with all interlocutors. The correlation was strongest for partners and friends. Similarly, the

Table 5.3 A linear regression model with mean Turkish use (reverse of mean Swedish use) as the dependent variable and different language proficiencies and types of belonging as independent variables

Independent variables	F	Sig. F	R Square	B	SE B	β	Sig. B
	$F(4,140) = 13.703$	.000	.281				
1) Mean Turkish proficiency				.255	.059	.335	.000
2) Turkish belonging				.119	.057	.156	.039
3) Mean Swedish proficiency				−.332	.097	−.262	.001
4) Swedish belonging				−.135	.041	−.243	.001

Table 5.4 Correlations between Turkish use (reverse of Swedish use) with different interlocutors and background factors (one-tailed Spearman)

	Relation to Turkish heritage and Muslim heritage		Socialisation with Turks in adulthood		Variables that facilitate integration in Sweden				
Interlocutor	Preference for heritage preservation	Intensity of religious practice	Partner's degree of connection to Turkey	Share of Turks among 3 best friends now	Highest level of own education	Age of onset for public education	Urbanisation degree of parents' home area	Parents' Swedish proficiency	Interlocutor's highest level of education
Mother	**r = .181** **p = .016**	r = .051 p = .305			r = .054 p = .261	**r = .238** **p = .005**	r = −.098 p = .124	**r = −.321** **p = .000**	**r = −.240** **p = .003**
Father	**r = .229** **p = .005**	r = .160 p = .068			r = −.059 p = .254	**r = .217** **p = .012**	r = −.021 p = .409	**r = −.221** **p = .006**	**r = −.298** **p = .000**
Sibling	**r = .232** **p = .003**	**r = .191** **p = .028**			r = −.086 p = .156	**r = .202** **p = .014**			*older siblings* **r = −.385** **p = .001**
Partner	**r = .288** **p = .005**	**r = .412** **p = .000**	**r = .688** **p = .000**		**r = −.228** **p = .020**	r = .179 p = .078			
Friends	**r = .338** **p = .000**	**r = .236** **p = .008**		**r = .568** **p = .000**	r = −.134 p = .054	**r = .195** **p = .016**			

Bold style = Correlation is significant at the 0.05 level.

participants whose religious practice was more intense also used most Turkish with their partners and friends. When we take into consideration the next two columns in Table 5.4 concerning socialisation with Turks in adulthood, which show participants with partners raised in Turkey and more close Turkish friends who also use more Turkish with them, a pattern emerges. Those participants who have close ties with their heritage choose similarly inclined partners and friends, with whom they also tend to speak more Turkish.

Let us now turn to variables that facilitate integration on the right-hand side of Table 5.4. We can see that the participants' own level of education played a significant role for Turkish use with the partner. Further analysis with Mann-Whitney U Tests revealed that this was due to the fact that participants with a non-Turkish partner had a significantly higher level of education compared to those with Turkish partners raised in Turkey and the effect size was medium ($p = .012$; $r = .33$). Since education is generally viewed as a good predictor of integration, it could be argued that the more integrated members of the second generation showed a higher tendency to choose non-Turkish partners (of Swedish or non-Swedish heritage), with whom they used mostly Swedish.

As previously mentioned in the introduction, the parental first generation has quite high proficiency in Swedish due to the fact that their Swedish acquisition was facilitated by public policies. As the results in Table 5.4 show, the parents' Swedish proficiency had a moderately negative effect on Turkish use with parents. Moreover, the higher the parents' level of education was, the more their children tended to use Swedish with them. A similar pattern was observed with older siblings, too. Furthermore, entering public Swedish education later, and thus having early socialisation in the Turkish-intensive environment of the home, seems to promote a significantly stronger preference for using Turkish with all interlocutors except for with the partner. Overall, those factors that facilitated integration in Sweden also tended to have an indirect, positive effect on Swedish use and, simultaneously, a negative effect on Turkish use.

In addition to MTI in primary and secondary schools, mother-tongue support (MTS) can be offered in Swedish kindergartens (ages one to six). Firstly, it should be noted that the fact that MTS is offered does not make a kindergarten bilingual, as Swedish typically constitutes the dominant language of communication. Secondly, after a peak with more than 60 per cent of eligible children receiving MTS in Swedish kindergartens in the late 1970s, this proportion had gradually dropped to 13 per cent in 2001.[35] Between 1990 and 2001, the proportion in Stockholm decreased from 45 to 13 per cent.[36] Thirdly, the share of MTS receivers was typically lower for the age group one to four.[37] Against this background of gradual decline, one of the goals of the new Swedish school law of 2010 is to provide better support for the children's mother tongue in kindergartens.

In the ethnic Turkish group in Stockholm, 80 per cent had attended kindergarten for more than a year and another 12 per cent for less than a year while 8 per cent had not attended kindergarten at all. Mann-Whitney U tests showed that there were no significant differences between attenders and non-attenders in mean Swedish proficiency ($p = .905$) or in mean Turkish proficiency ($p = .158$). However, those who had attended kindergarten for more than a year reported significantly lower Turkish use with their mothers with a small effect size ($p = .028$, $r = .19$). No significant differences were observed in Turkish use with other interlocutors. Taken together with the effect of age of onset for public education in Tables 5.2 and 5.4, these findings clearly show that the environment of early language development has a crucial long-term impact on heritage-language proficiency and use, as also concluded by previous research on heritage-language speakers.[38] Given that only 20 per cent of the second-generation Turks in Stockholm had spent their early childhood in a Turkish-intensive home environment, it is not surprising that only slightly more than half of them reported excellent or very good skills in Turkish.

Fifty-one per cent of the participants were between ages 18 and 26 while 49 per cent were between ages 27 and 35. Mann-Whitney U tests showed that there were significant differences between these two age groups regarding mean Turkish use ($p = .002$), parents' year of immigration ($p = .000$ for both), highest level of education among mothers ($p = .015$) and fathers ($p = .000$), as well as the level of Swedish proficiency among mothers ($p = .006$) and fathers ($p = .012$). The older group's parents simply belonged to an older cohort of Turkish immigrants, most of whom had arrived between the late 1960s and the mid-1970s, while the younger group's parents belonged to a later cohort, most of whom had arrived between the 1970s and the early 1980s. Thus, the older group's parents had immigrated early on when most multiculturalist integration policies were still being developed, while the younger group's parents had arrived when both the integration infrastructure and the Turkish community were principally established. The younger group's parents were better educated due to a combination of greater diversity among later cohorts of immigrants from Turkey (especially among mothers) and better opportunities for complementing their education in Sweden (especially among fathers). They also attained higher Swedish proficiency, which must be mostly due to the qualitative and quantitative improvements in Swedish courses for immigrants after 1973.[39]

The older group, which started preschool 1975–1983 and finished compulsory education 1987–1995, is also very likely to have had Turkish as a medium of instruction to a greater extent than the younger group. This is partly due to the aforementioned decline in the extent of mother-tongue support in preschools, which would have affected the older group less. Moreover, the older group is more likely to have been placed in so-called 'mother-tongue classes' or 'bilingual classes' to a larger extent. These involved large cohorts with the same mother tongue being placed in the same class where the mother tongue was used in the teaching of different subjects. Such classes were relatively common in compulsory education for large immigrant languages like Turkish in the 1970s and 1980s,[40] a period that largely overlaps with the older group's period in compulsory education. Mann-Whitney U tests showed no significant differences in proficiency in either language between these age groups but revealed significant differences with small effect sizes concerning language use with several interlocutors. The older group used more Turkish with their fathers ($p = .020$, $r = .21$), siblings ($p = .007$, $r = .13$) and friends ($p = .028$, $r = .18$). Together, these findings demonstrate the impact of the recipient society's integration infrastructure on language use patterns in the private sphere.

Although the participants' parents were all born in Turkey, only 54 per cent of the participants reported that both their parents were only raised in Turkey (G2) while 8 per cent reported that both their parents were partly raised in Sweden (G3). A comparison between G2 and G3 could provide us with important clues regarding the maintenance of Turkish beyond the second generation. Mann-Whitney U tests showed that there were no significant differences at the 5 per cent level between G2 and G3 in terms of proficiency in both languages, the four belonging variables, parents' home areas and highest level of education as well as Turkish use with siblings, friends and partners. However, there were significant differences concerning the fathers' level of Swedish (p = .003) and the mothers' level of Swedish (p = .024). The Swedish level of G3's parents was on average 15 percentage points higher than that of G2's parents. Consequently, G3 used significantly less Turkish than G2 with their mothers (p = .007) and fathers (p = .008), and the effect sizes were medium (r = .31 and r = .32 respectively). G2's Turkish use level with parents was closest to 'mostly Turkish', whereas G3's level was closest to 'more Turkish than Swedish'. On average, G3 used 21 percentage points less Turkish with parents compared to G2, but crucially Turkish was still the dominant language at home.

A further Mann-Whitney U test concerning Turkish use with partners revealed a significant difference with a large effect size (p = .000, r = .51) between participants with partners raised in Turkey and those with Turkish partners raised in Sweden. The medians indicated that the former group tended to use 'mostly Turkish' with their partners while the latter group used 'more Turkish than Swedish'. These findings suggest that the children of the second generation are most likely to be raised in predominantly Turkish-speaking homes since 78 per cent of the second-generation had Turkish partners. Based on these facts, we can draw the conclusion that Turkish will most likely be successfully transmitted to the third generation in Stockholm. This is in line with previous findings on the first cohort of the third generation in Gothenburg[41] and in several other Western European cities.[42]

Conclusion

The results of this study have illustrated that second-generation Turks in Stockholm occupied an intermediate position between similar communities in settler nations and in Western Europeans nations. Their bilingual proficiency profiles with clear majority-language dominance at a high proficiency level were reminiscent of settler nations while their belonging profiles and heritage-language maintenance patterns were generally more similar to other communities in Western Europe. However, a comparison with eight cities within the TIES project revealed that Sweden's multicultural policies were partly responsible for the Stockholm community's relatively stronger city belonging as well as for its weaker minority belonging and weaker contacts with Turkey. Hence, while clearly following the Western European type concerning belonging and maintenance, second-generation Turks in Stockholm were nevertheless situated at the least heritage-oriented margin within this type.

Similar to other pluralistic societies, the use of Turkish among second-generation Turks in Sweden can be said to suffer from the 'paradox of linguistic pluralism', that is the phenomenon that less heritage-language use is found in societies that explicitly support heritage maintenance. Lower degrees of Turkish use with parents as well as with older siblings and partners were observed due to the successful integration of the first generation in the former case and of the second generation in the latter. If these patterns persist, we might observe lower degrees of Turkish maintenance in Sweden in future generations compared to other Western European countries.

All in all, language policies and practices in Sweden had a tangible effect on Turkish proficiency and use, albeit not a uniformly positive one. The official goal of additive bilingualism and positive public attitudes towards heritage languages contributed to substantial levels of Turkish use with siblings, friends and partners in adulthood. Furthermore, it was argued that mother-tongue instruction in Swedish schools had a positive impact on keeping Turkish literacy skills on a comparable level to speaking skills. However, generally low ages of onset for public education in Swedish-dominant kindergartens had long-lasting negative consequences not only for Turkish use with most interlocutors but also for Turkish proficiency in adulthood. Considering that kindergarten attendance did not have a significant effect on Swedish proficiency in adulthood, bilingual kindergartens could probably mitigate such negative effects on the heritage language without jeopardising the children's development in Swedish. It remains to be seen if the new school law can accomplish this.

Notes

1. Guus Extra and Kutlay Yağmur (eds), *Urban Multilingualism in Europe: Immigrant Minority Languages at Home and School*, Frankfurt Lodge (Clevedon, 2004); Berry, John W., Phinney, Jean S., Sam, David L. and Vedder, Paul (eds), *Immigrant Youth in Cultural Transition: Acculturation, Identity, and Adaptation across National Contexts*, Taylor & Francis (London, 2006).
2. Charles Westin (ed.), *Integration of Descendants of Migrants from Turkey in Stockholm: The TIES Study in Sweden*, Amsterdam University Press, (Amsterdam, 2015).
3. Silvina Montrul, *The Acquisition of Heritage Languages*, Cambridge University Press, (Cambridge, 2016), pp. 99–109.
4. Wallace E. Lambert, 'Culture and language as factors in learning and education', in Frances Aboud and Robert D. Meade (eds), *Cultural Factors in Learning and Education*, Western Washington University (Bellingham, 1974), pp. 91–122.
5. Memet Aktürk-Drake, 'Det flerspråkiga Konstantinopel' [Multilingual Constantinople], *Dragomanen* 13 (2011), pp. 28–35; Kutlay Yağmur & Fons J. R. van de Vijver, 'Acculturation and Language Orientations of Turkish Immigrants in Australia,

France, Germany, and the Netherlands', *Journal of Cross-Cultural Psychology* 43/7 (2012), p. 1113.

6. Lambert, 'Culture and language', pp. 91–122.
7. MPI (Multiculturalism Policy Index), http://www.queensu.ca/mcp/ (accessed 30 April 2016).
8. Thomas Huddleston, Özge Bilgili, Anne-Linde Joki and Zvezda Vankova, *Migrant Integration Policy Index* (2015), http://www.mipex.eu/key-findings (accessed 9 December 2015).
9. Maurice Crul and Jens Schneider, 'Conclusions and implications: The integration context matters', in Maurice Crul, Jens Schneider and Frans Lelie (eds), *The European Second Generation Compared: Does the Integration Context Matter?* Amsterdam University Press, (Amsterdam, 2012), p. 378.
10. Kenneth Hyltenstam and Tommaso Milani, 'Flerspråkighetens sociopolitiska och sociokulturella ramar [The sociopolitical and sociocultural frame of multilingualism]', in Kenneth Hyltenstam, Monica Axelsson and Inger Lindberg (eds), *Flerspråkighet: en forskningsöversikt* [Multilingualism: a research overview], Vetenskåpsrådet (Stockholm, 2012), pp. 57, 61, 77.
11. Ibid., pp. 83–4.
12. Alireza Behtoui, 'Conclusions', in Charles Westin (ed.), *Integration of Descendants of Migrants from Turkey in Stockholm: The TIES Study in Sweden*, Amsterdam University Press (Amsterdam, 2015), pp. 125–33.
13. Hyltenstam and Milani, 'Flerspråkighetens sociopolitiska och sociokulturella ramar', pp. 17–152.
14. Alireza Behtoui, 'Conclusions', p. 132.
15. Yağmur and van de Vijver, 'Acculturation and Language Orientations of Turkish Immigrants', pp. 1110–30.
16. Extra and Yağmur (eds), *Urban Multilingualism in Europe* (Clevedon, 2004); Yağmur and van de Vijver, 'Acculturation and Language Orientations of Turkish Immigrants, pp. 1110–30.
17. Yağmur and van de Vijver, 'Acculturation and Language Orientations of Turkish Immigrants', pp. 1110–30; Kutlay Yağmur and Gülcan Çolak-Bostancı, 'Intergenerational acculturation orientations of Turkish speakers in the USA', in Deniz Zeyrek, Çiğdem Sağın Şimşek, Ufuk Ataş and Jochen Rehbein, (eds), *Ankara Papers in Turkish and Turkic Linguistics*, Harrassowitz Verlag (Wiesbaden, 2015), pp. 514–29.
18. Lilian Nygren-Junkin, 'Multilingualism in Göteborg', in Guus Extra and Kutlay Yağmur (eds), *Urban multilingualism in Europe: Immigrant Minority Languages at Home and School*, Frankfurt Lodge (Clevedon, 2004), p. 148.
19. Ibid., p. 160.

20. Natalia Ganuza and Christina Hedman, 'The impact of weekly mother tongue instruction for the development of biliteracy – evidence from Somali-Swedish bilinguals in the early school years' (under review).
21. Berry et. al., *Immigrant Youth in Cultural Transition*.
22. Paul Vedder and Erkki Virta, 'Language, ethnic identity, and the adaptation of Turkish immigrant youth in the Netherlands and Sweden', *International Journal of Intercultural Relations* 29 (2005), pp. 328, 330.
23. Jean S. Phinney, John W. Berry, Paul Vedder and Karmela Liebkind, 'The Acculturation Experience: Attitudes, Identities and Behaviors of Immigrant Youth', in Berry et al. (eds), *Immigrant Youth in Cultural Transition* (London, 2006), pp. 91–2.
24. For an overview, see Maurice Crul, Jens Schneider and Frans Lelie (eds), *The European Second Generation Compared: Does the Integration Context Matter?* Amsterdam University Press, (Amsterdam, 2012).
25. Charles Westin, Alireza Behtoui, Constanza Vera-Larrucea, Ali Osman, 'Introduction', in Charles Westin (ed.), *Integration of Descendants of Migrants from Turkey in Stockholm: The TIES Study in Sweden*, Amsterdam University Press, (Amsterdam, 2015), p. 19.
26. For an overview, see Charles Westin, (ed.), *Integration of Descendants of Migrants from Turkey in Stockholm: The TIES Study in Sweden*, Amsterdam University Press, (Amsterdam, 2015).
27. For a similar discussion, see Constanza Vera-Larrucea, 'Historical and Demographic Considerations', in Charles Westin (ed.), *Integration of Descendants of Migrants from Turkey in Stockholm: The TIES Study in Sweden*, Amsterdam University Press, (Amsterdam, 2015), pp. 25–42.
28. Crul, Schneider and Lelie (eds), *The European Second Generation Compared*, Amsterdam University Press, (Amsterdam, 2012).
29. Ibid., pp. 298, 306.
30. Ibid., pp. 263–4, 318–19, 326–30, 389.
31. Ibid., pp. 326–30.
32. Ibid., pp. 298, 339.
33. Ibid., pp. 292–3, 392.
34. Nygren-Junkin, 'Multilingualism in Göteborg', p. 160; Ganuza and Hedman, 'The impact of weekly mother tongue instruction'.
35. Ulla Nordenstam, 'Tre decenniers modersmålsstöd – om modersmålet i förskolan 1970–2000. Bilaga 5. [Three decades of mother-tongue support – on the mother tongue in preschool. Appendix 5.]' in Skolverket, *Flera språk – fler möjligheter – utveckling av modersmålsstödet och modersmålsundervisningen 2002*, Statens skolverk (Stockholm, 2003), p. 39.
36. Ibid., p. 29.

37. Ibid., p. 39.
38. Silvina Montrul, *The Acquisition of Heritage Languages*, Cambridge University Press (Cambridge, 2016), pp. 98–9, 113, 121.
39. Hyltenstam and Milani, 'Flerspråkighetens sociopolitiska och sociokulturella ramar', p. 85.
40. Ibid., p. 59.
41. Nygren-Junkin, 'Multilingualism in Göteborg', pp. 133–62.
42. Extra and Yağmur (eds), *Urban Multilingualism in Europe*.

References

Aktürk-Drake, M., 'Det flerspråkiga Konstantinopel' [Multilingual Constantinople], *Dragomanen* 13 (2011), pp. 28–35.
Behtoui, A., 'Conclusions', in Charles Westin (ed.), *Integration of Descendants of Migrants from Turkey in Stockholm: The TIES Study in Sweden*, Amsterdam University Press (Amsterdam, 2015), pp. 125–33.
Berry, J.W., Phinney, J.S., Sam, D.L., and Vedder, P. (eds), *Immigrant Youth in Cultural Transition. Acculturation, Identity, and Adaptation across National Contexts*, Taylor & Francis (London, 2006).
Crul, M., and Schneider, J., 'Conclusions and implications: The integration context matters', in Maurice Crul, Jens Schneider and Frans Lelie (eds), *The European Second Generation Compared. Does the Integration Context Matter?*, Amsterdam University Press (Amsterdam, 2012), pp. 375–404.
Crul, M., Schneider, J., and Lelie, F. (eds), *The European Second Generation Compared: Does the Integration Context Matter?* Amsterdam University Press, Amsterdam University Press (Amsterdam, 2012).
Extra, G. and Yağmur, K. (eds), *Urban Multilingualism in Europe: Immigrant Minority Languages at Home and School*, Frankfurt Lodge (Clevedon, 2004).
Ganuza, N. and Hedman, C. 'The impact of weekly mother tongue instruction for the development of biliteracy – evidence from Somali-Swedish bilinguals in the early school years' (under review).
Huddleston, T., Bilgili, Ö., Joki, A.L. and Vankova, Z. *Migrant Integration Policy Index* (2015), http://www.mipex.eu/key-findings (accessed 9 December 2015).
Hyltenstam, K. and Milani, T., 'Flerspråkighetens sociopolitiska och sociokulturella ramar [The sociopolitical and sociocultural frame of multilingualism]', in Kenneth Hyltenstam, Monica Axelsson and Inger Lindberg (eds), *Flerspråkighet: en forskningsöversikt [Multilingualism: a research overview]*, Vetenskåpsrådet (Stockholm, 2012), pp. 17–152.

Lambert, W.E., 'Culture and language as factors in learning and education', in Frances Aboud and Robert D. Meade (eds), *Cultural Factors in Learning and Education*, Western Washington University (Bellingham, 1974), pp. 91–122.

Montrul, S., *The Acquisition of Heritage Languages*, Cambridge University Press (Cambridge, 2016).

MPI (Multiculturalism Policy Index), http://www.queensu.ca/mcp/ (accessed 30 April 2016).

Nordenstam, U., 'Tre decenniers modersmålsstöd – om modersmålet i förskolan 1970–2000. Bilaga 5. [Three decades of mother-tongue support – on the mother tongue in preschool. Appendix 5.]' in Skolverket, *Flera språk – fler möjligheter – utveckling av modersmåls-stödet och modersmålsundervisningen 2002*, Statens skolverk (Stockholm, 2003).

Nygren-Junkin, L., 'Multilingualism in Göteborg', in Guus Extra and Kutlay Yağmur (eds), *Urban multilingualism in Europe: Immigrant Minority Languages at Home and School*, Frankfurt Lodge (Clevedon, 2004), pp. 133–62.

Phinney, J.S., Berry, J.W., Vedder, P. and Liebkind, K., 'The Acculturation Experience: Attitudes, Identities and Behaviors of Immigrant Youth', in John W. Berry, Jean S. Phinney, David L. Sam and Paul Vedder (eds), *Immigrant Youth in Cultural Transition: Acculturation, Identity, and Adaptation across National Contexts*, Taylor & Francis (London, 2006), pp. 71–116.

Vedder, P. and Virta, E., 'Language, ethnic identity, and the adaptation of Turkish immigrant youth in the Netherlands and Sweden', *International Journal of Intercultural Relations* 29 (2005), pp. 317–37.

Vera-Larrucea, C., 'Historical and Demographic Considerations', in Charles Westin (ed.), *Integration of Descendants of Migrants from Turkey in Stockholm: The TIES Study in Sweden*, Amsterdam University Press (Amsterdam, 2015), pp. 25–42.

Westin, C. (ed.), *Integration of Descendants of Migrants from Turkey in Stockholm: The TIES Study in Sweden*, Amsterdam University Press (Amsterdam, 2015).

Westin, C., Behtoui, A., Vera-Larrucea, C., Osman, A. 'Introduction', in Charles Westin (ed.), *Integration of Descendants of Migrants from Turkey in Stockholm: The TIES Study in Sweden*, Amsterdam University Press, (Amsterdam, 2015), pp. 11–23.

Yağmur, K., and Çolak-Bostancı, G. 'Intergenerational acculturation orientations of Turkish speakers in the USA', in Zeyrek, D., Sağın Şimşek, C., Ataş, U. and Rehbein, J., (eds), *Ankara Papers in Turkish and Turkic Linguistics*, Harrassowitz Verlag (Wiesbaden, 2015), pp. 514–29.

Yağmur, K. and van de Vijver, F.J.R., 'Acculturation and Language Orientations of Turkish Immigrants in Australia, France, Germany, and the Netherlands', *Journal of Cross-Cultural Psychology* 43/7 (2012), pp. 1110–30.

CHAPTER 6

TURKISH MEDIA SPACE IN SWEDEN: THE CASE OF TURKISH BROADCASTS IN SWEDISH PUBLIC SERVICE RADIO

Altuğ Akın

In 1976, when Turkish broadcasts began in Swedish public service radio, we tried to find a balance between the expectations of the Swedish authorities and the Turkish community. On the one hand, we made programmes about, for instance, how to celebrate Christmas or *Midsommar* day. On the other hand, we made debate programmes in order to provide crucial information to our community to ease their difficulties in everyday lives in their new land, Sweden. (*Merhaba* producer 1)

After 50 years of being in Sweden, sufficient experience of the Turkish community has accumulated through which some conclusions can be drawn. In this paper experiences from the media field will be discussed, focusing on a particular case – Turkish broadcasts in *Sveriges Radio* (SR), namely *Merhaba*, meaning 'Hello' in

Turkish. With a lengthy historic span between 1976 and 2006, the case of Merhaba provides valuable insights especially thanks to its crucial position between the needs of the Turkish community and the expectations of the Swedish authorities, clearly reflected in the above quotation from a former Merhaba staff member.

Accordingly, in this paper, the media space for the Turkish community in Sweden in general and the case of Merhaba in particular are presented, highlighting the roles such media organs have played and the dynamics underpinning them. Then the suspension process of Merhaba in 2006 is discussed, as it reveals the intricate relationship and conflict between the needs of the Turkish community in Sweden and changing understandings of handling diversity in Sweden. Finally, some conclusions regarding the success of relevant institutional actors in this particular media field are discussed.

Detailed study was conducted in SR, mainly in the Immigrant Languages Unit (which Turkish broadcasts were a part of), as well as other Turkish media initiatives and Turkish community associations in Sweden, employing qualitative methods, namely in depth interviews, participatory observations and document reviews. In total, 14 formal in depth interviews were conducted, in addition to four complementary informal interviews, all of which were conducted between 2005 and 2006, the period when the Turkish service in SR was suspended after almost 30 years. Theoretically, the diaspora notion, based on transnational theory, is utilised as the lens to define/ describe the research object and discuss the findings.[1]

Media Spaces, Diaspora, Diasporic Media

Media and communications have become spaces in which both political and cultural identities are mobilised, but also spaces where the continuities between identity and citizenship are regularly reproduced and used as tactics to navigate the complex world these participants occupy.[2] Such an understanding of media and communication as tactical or strategic spaces of political and cultural mobilisation as well as identity/citizenship reproduction applies even more to diasporas.

The majority of studies in the last two decades regarding immigrant/migrant/ethnic minority groups and their media, centre their theoretical basis on the notion of diaspora. Contemporary utilisation of the diaspora concept, on the one hand relates to 'realisation of the concept to serve as a theoretical tool for the advancement of qualitatively different perspectives and outlooks in the study of human migration',[3] while on the other hand reflects an analytical rebuttal of problematical expressions, such as migrant or ethnic minority.[4] In response to the ethnicisation of societies around concepts like immigrant, migrant or ethnic minority, contemporary theorisations of diaspora are grounded on ideas of transnationalism and aim to challenge exclusion grounded on cultural differences. Referring to the development of dense networks across borders,[5] transnationalism implies processes by which migrant and diasporic communities forge and sustain multi-stranded social relations across geographical, cultural and political borders.[6] Based on this under-standing, diaspora as a concept aims to deconstruct the reifications of race, ethnicity and nationhood as signifying categories of mobile populations.[7]

Diasporas are located in the midst of, or include, diverse circulations. Borrowing Appadurai's notions, it can be argued that diaspora is the intersection point of ethnoscapes, financescapes, ideoscapes, technoscapes and mediascapes.[8] For the particular purpose of this research the mediascape of diaspora is of immense importance: The role of the media and communication, either as a bridge to the homeland or as a link between the diaspora communities at local, national and transnational levels, has been increasingly vital in the diaspora experiences. 'No diaspora without media' argues Murphet, as the concept of diaspora can be applied 'to a minority collective, only with the existence of media to make that affirmation tangible. Otherwise, a displaced collective is simply absorbed into the host culture, or eradicated altogether.'[9] Indeed, from the earliest diasporic experiences, such as scattered Jewish communities' recuperation of their national identity and ethno-religious continuity via the Torah, medium of a book,[10] to the recent possibilities opened up by internet-based social networking, different forms of media technologies have helped the imagination of forms of community across borders and the consolidation of diasporic identities connected to different spaces.

Diasporic media cultures emerge in the juncture of local, national and transnational spaces; diasporic media are of various sizes, levels of professionalism, success and lifespan; they use different technologies and have different entrepreneurial, cultural and political objectives. Yet as Georgiu argues, 'what they all have in common is that they address particular ethnic, linguistic and/or religious groups that live within broader and diverse multicultural societies'.[11] They all have some connection (imagined or real) and share a sense of belonging within a larger community spreading beyond national boundaries. However, their audiences are based within localities and nation states. They are citizens and minorities of these nation states,[12] the Turkish community in Sweden being one example, discussed in this paper.

Media Spaces of the Turkish Community in Sweden

Five major types of diasporic media cultures have developed among the Turkish community in Sweden through the following media, presented in chronological order:

Sweden originated print media

Mostly functioning as the publications of the Turkish community associations in Sweden, this form of media has a long historical tradition. For instance, *Yeni Birlik* (New Union), the journal of the Federation of Turkish Workers' Associations in Sweden, has been published since 1977, which qualifies it as the longest-running print media of Turkish communities in any European country. Some titles, such as *Belleten* (Reminder), are the pioneering media of the Turkish community in Sweden, initiated long before the introduction of broadcasting and web-based media,[13] while others, such as *Euro Turk*, launched in 1999 by the Turkish Youth Federation in Sweden in a bilingual style – Swedish and Turkish, reflect the concerns and demands of second- generation members of the community.

Turkish broadcasts in Sveriges Radio: Merhaba

Within the Swedish Public Service Radio, programmes in Turkish were broadcast from 1976 until 2006. In January 2006, Turkish broadcasts on Swedish Radio were suspended by a managerial decision. The case of *Merhaba* is discussed in detail in the rest of this chapter.

Turkey originated print media

Except for a few titles, such as *Hürriyet* (Liberty), that have been sold in Sweden on a daily basis since the late 1990s, Turkey originated newspapers and magazines could be obtained on subscription. In parallel to the establishment of Turkish communities in diverse European countries, almost all such newspapers have begun devoting special pages to European coverage. Soon European versions of these papers emerged with a particular focus on European countries with Turkish populations. Varying in degree, the content is a combination of news from Turkey and news about Turkish communities in various European countries, including Sweden.

Turkey originated TV channels

From the mid-1990s on, thanks to the spread of satellite technology and the end of the state monopoly of broadcasting in Turkey, Turkish populations living abroad gained increasing access to Turkey's TV channels. In this period, first commercial TV channels in Turkey and then the Turkish public service broadcaster TRT launched their specific channels targeting Turks abroad. Similar to the Turkey originated print media, these channels have employed correspondents in various countries and they have reserved a quite limited segment of their broadcasts to certain countries where the correspondents are located. In addition to these special TV channels – so called 'European versions', Turkish populations abroad began enjoying daily Turkish television – the 'Turkey version', which have had significant implications on how migrants experience their lives, how they think and feel about their experiences, and not least, how they imagine the homeland, Turkey.[14]

Web-based digital media

Especially popular amongst second- and third-generation members of the Turkish community, web-based media is relatively new and played a transformative role in the diasporic media space since the early 2000s. Similar to Turkey originated TV channels, web-based media have

provided the unique opportunity of having an immediate synchronisation with Turkey and among members
of the Turkish diaspora all over the globe. Besides, the
convergent media environment, where all earlier forms
converge on web-based platforms, furthers mobility
between media, as well as between ideological and
linguistic environments, in a way defined as 'media
nomadism' by Georgiou.[15]

Turkish Broadcasts in Sveriges Radio

Out of these five main media spaces of the Turkish
community in Sweden, the focus of this chapter is on
Turkish broadcasts on *Sveriges Radio*, as it enables the
problematising of the roles of a Turkish community
institution and the dynamics that impacted on it, for a
longer time period.

Until 2006, when it was suspended, Turkish broadcasts
were a part of the P6 channel of SR, namely 'Radio Sweden
International', presented on the radio's website as the
'international and multicultural channel of SR'. Under
Radio Sweden International, the Immigrant Languages
Unit (*Minoritetspråksredaktionen*) produced programming
in Albanian, Arabic, Aramaic, Farsi, Kurdish, Polish,
Serbian/Croatian/Bosnian, Somali, Spanish, Swedish and
Turkish, languages of immigrant groups in Sweden.
Merhaba was the Turkish section of Immigrant Languages,
one of the oldest sections, beginning its operations in
1976, roughly a decade after the arrival of Turkish migrants
in Sweden.

The table below (Table 6.1) provides a digest of the
period between 1976 and 2006, presenting *Merhaba*'s
production and operation environment, followed by a
discussion of the roles *Merhaba* played throughout its
existence.

Table 6.1 Outline of production environment of Turkish Broadcasts in *Sveriges Radio* from 1976 until 2006

	Introduction (1976–80)	Military regime in Turkey (1980–mid 80s)	Post-military regime (Mid 80s–early 90s)	Kurdish issue (Early 90s–mid 90s)	Winds of change (Mid 90s–2000)	Decline (2001–6)
Number of staff (permanent)	2 4	4	4–5	4–5	4	3 1
Format of programmes	5 to 25 min/day, news	15 min/day, news & children and music shows	15 min/day, news & children and music shows & magazine programmes	15 min/day news & magazine programmes	15 min/day news & magazine programmes	120–70 min/week, 3-2 magazine programmes/week
Programmes focus (geographic)	Turkey (TR), Sweden (SWE), World (W)	Mainly TR, SWE, W	Mainly SWE (a particular focus on the Turkish community in Sweden), TR, W	More focus on TR, SWE, W	More focus on SWE, TR, W	Only SWE
Newsroom atmosphere	Harmony	Pro vs. Anti military regime tension	Conflicts of various reasons	Conflicts of various reasons	Conflicts of various reasons	Harmony

Relations between staff and management	Alternative diasporic media
Editorial independence, managerial support	Publications of Turkish community associations in SWE (New Union, Forward, Homeland); Public Service local radio (Radio Stockholm); partially Voice of Turkey, BBC Turkish Service
Managerial support, suggestions from management to follow transformation process to democracy in TR	New Union, Radio Stockholm, Voice of Turkey
Introduction of editorial assistant and relevant problems	New Union, Radio Stockholm, videotapes from TR
Problems with editorial assistant, suggestions from management to report more about Kurdish issue in TR	New Union, Radio Stockholm, videotapes from TR, community radio stations in SWE (Radio Rainbow)
Introduction of Swedish perspective[16] and relevant conflicts	Satellite channels from TR, web based media, daily arriving TR originated newspapers, Euro-Turk, New Union, Radio Rainbow
Swedish perspective	Satellite channels from TR, European version of these channels, web based media, European versions of daily TR newspapers, Euro-Turk, New Union, Radio Rainbow

Turkish Broadcasts on Sveriges Radio:
Roles and Dynamics

In this section, the roles fulfilled by *Merhaba* are classified under four main categories related to information, connection, identity and integration.

Information-related roles

As the Turkish service in the Immigrant Languages Unit (ILU) in SR, *Merhaba* was a newsroom where journalistic practice, according to its most general definition, was conducted. Despite its definition as 'ethnic minority' or 'immigrant' media in the Swedish media landscape, for a considerable time *Merhaba* functioned as the media for the Turkish community in Sweden as an everyday news resource:

> When *Merhaba* was started, the Swedish authorities perceived it as an information channel to act accurately, impartially, and to answer the needs of the audience. So they expected exactly the same service they expect from other journalists, say the Swedes. Nothing different was expected due to our 'immigrantness'. How the Swedish authorities thought about *Merhaba* was: Turkish immigrants don't know Swedish, they don't have access to Swedish media. So it was *Merhaba*'s duty to provide the news, that's it. (*Merhaba* producer 3)

The content and form of the information-related service of *Merhaba* were primarily determined by the needs of the Turkish community in Sweden. For instance, although *Merhaba* began primarily as a channel to inform its audiences about developments in Turkey, the urgency of news from Turkey decreased by the mid-1980s, in parallel to the relative normalisation of life in

Turkey with the transformation to a parliamentary regime from a military regime. Hence, *Merhaba* began to devote more coverage to Sweden rather than Turkey, a change also related to changing group dynamics of the community in Sweden:

> After 1980, the organisation process of the Turkish community was completed, as associations and federations were established and advanced. So other social questions like identity, native language or unemployment were being covered more frequently in our programmes. (*Merhaba* producer 2)

Not only the focus of content switched from information-providing to discussing social questions, but also programme formats were revised, in accordance with the transformation of the Turkish community and its needs. For instance, weekend programmes were introduced in addition to daily news programmes:

> After 1983, we believed that 1970s programme formats with short sound bites about a lot of different topics mostly with informative concerns should be replaced with longer, more analytical programmes which could cover fewer topics, but in a more detailed way. What the audience needed was not how to get social help from a health authority anymore. Priority was given to programmes that could satisfy people instead of only inform them. Therefore 'magazine' programmes were introduced in addition to existing news programmes. (*Merhaba* producer 1)

Issues covered in magazine programmes were as diverse as experiences of the Turkish community in Sweden.

Marriages and divorces, problems about military service, Turkish football clubs and their problems, Turkish prisoners in Swedish prisons, psychological problems of immigrants, particular difficulties experienced by political refugees, Turkish artists living in Sweden and cultural activities organised by community associations were among the social topics covered in these magazine programmes of *Merhaba*.[17]

In a nutshell, *Merhaba*'s information-related role facilitated a flow not only between Turkey and Turks in Sweden, but also within the geographically and socio-economically dispersed Turkish community in Sweden. The original function, referred to as a 'bridge between Turkey and Sweden',[18] was crucial as the only news source about Turkey until the nineties when alternative access channels to Turkey appeared. This development, enabling information flow between members of the Turkish community in Sweden, gradually gained more dominance, as the Turkish community became established and its internal fragmentation and geographical diversity increased. This latter function is closely related with the following group of roles, that is the connectivity-related roles.

Connectivity-related roles
Another function of *Merhaba* was about providing a connection platform for the Turkish community in Sweden and beyond, in different forms. Primarily, merely listening to *Merhaba* programmes was a way of connecting with other members of the Turkish community, as a radio-phonic imagined community. Audience numbers from a 1986 survey attest that such a function was pretty much fulfilled: In 1986, 74 per cent of the Turkish audience followed *Merhaba*'s daily news programme (17.00–17.45), while 26 per cent listened to weekly magazine programmes.[19]

However, the loyalty of the audience did not mean they were uncritical towards *Merhaba* programmes. For instance, although a majority of the audience was satisfied with the content, many listeners complained about broadcasting hours, while some found the programmes insufficient, politically biased or focused only on adults, rather than kids. In short, *Merhaba* enabled an imagined community to be connected via its programming, but this connectivity was never a straightforward and uncontested one. As stated by a *Merhaba* producer '*Merhaba* functioned as a bridge between the dynamic sections of Kulu people and relatively integrated Turkish immigrants, and enabled a considerable communication amongst them.' (*Merhaba* producer 2) Although the dichotomy of 'Kulu people and integrated Turks' is highly problematical, noting the fragmentation of the Turkish community in Sweden, what can be interpreted from the above quotation is that *Merhaba* staff were aware of the social heterogeneity of the Turkish community and tried to form a common platform on which different sections of the community could connect to one another.

Secondly, *Merhaba* initiated physical connection, platforms for meetings. Although Turkish community associations and federations were responsible for this function, *Merhaba* contributed to these attempts, especially on the occasions where existing community organisations were insufficient. Most of the cultural activities for Turkish groups in Sweden in the 1970s and 1980s, especially music concerts, were arranged with the active involvement of *Merhaba*. Sporting events, in which Turkish sports clubs in Sweden competed, were given high priority in *Merhaba* programmes with the same rationale. Such activities were seen as meeting points for single individuals where they could break their isolation, first by socialising with other Turkish people, and then creating meaningful social bonds with them and the rest of Swedish society. Regular audience meetings, where *Merhaba* staff and listeners got together, had a similar aim. Turkish community members living around the locations where the audience meetings were held used to gather for meeting with *Merhaba* staff either to celebrate or criticise them. These physical meeting points were to assist the commencement of further social relations.

Furthermore, *Merhaba* functioned as a public discussion forum for the Turkish community, especially when they did not have a chance to participate in the Swedish majority public sphere. By giving them a voice in the programmes or in events such as public meetings, *Merhaba* provided the Turkish community with a platform to participate. Before general or local elections, for instance, *Merhaba* organised meetings in different regions of Sweden where there were Turkish populations, at which candidates with a Turkish background met the public to discuss their needs and proposed solutions.

Finally, *Merhaba* programmes in the Turkish language functioned as an information channel for many ethnic groups other than Turks, which could understand Turkish either as a cross over language or native language. Iranian Azeris, Kurds, Bulgarian Turks, Macedonians, Syrians, Iraqi Turkmens, among others, enjoyed *Merhaba* as their only information source for a considerable time period.

Identity-related roles

As a defining characteristic of diasporic cultures, 'images and imagination have been central in sustaining a sense of belonging in a diaspora and in shaping shared diasporic cultures. In this sense, the role of the media and communication has become increasingly important.'[20] When the Turkish group in Sweden is understood within the framework of diaspora, the significance of the identity-related role played by *Merhaba* becomes more obvious. Especially around the mid-1980s, in response to the difficulties experienced by the Turkish community regarding ethnic cohesion and cultural maintenance, *Merhaba* focused more on identity related issues. Maintenance of the Turkish language, as a means of communication as well as an expression of cultural identity and heritage, was one of the main functions of *Merhaba*. In particular for second-generation Turks, born and raised in Sweden, *Merhaba* played a significant role, with regard to their familiarity with Turkish. Weekend programmes for children functioned as complementary language courses, in addition to a few hours of optional native language classes they attended in schools:

> Once at a meeting in Gothenburg, a member of our audience said 'my son listens to your voice three times a day at least.' I was surprised, because we had one programme in the morning and a repeat programme in the afternoon, so 'How come you can listen to *Merhaba*, three times a day?' I asked. 'We tape your programmes everyday and play them again and again during the day so that my son can hear Turkish and doesn't lose his identity' he answered. (*Merhaba* producer 1)

Culture, as another significant layer of identity, also had a high priority on *Merhaba*'s agenda. Contemporary or traditional music, literature, cinema and drama produced by Turkish artists were deployed in *Merhaba* programmes not only as cultural events or products, but also as a means of sustaining the Turkish component of a new, hybrid diasporic identity.

Furthermore, realising the significance of the feeling of solidarity generated by involvement in a group, *Merhaba* mirrored diverse examples of Turkish immigrants in different countries, in order to encourage such a feeling of group belonging:

> The stories of Turkish immigrants were noteworthy. If you consider our audiences' very complex immigrant sentiments, programmes had a psychologically supportive function by making them aware of the fact that there were many others just like themselves, from the north of Sweden to the south. Secondly, as immigrants, most of our audiences had a feeling of outcasts, who were segregated, disadvantaged, disrespected and forgotten by Swedish society. We tried to show that there was still hope, or some paths they could follow, a chance that they could break this isolation. You can do this by telling success stories from the Turkish community in Sweden and in other European countries (*Merhaba* producer 4)

Integration-related roles

Beside these three roles, there was another crucial function of *Merhaba*, which was about integration. Especially until the mid-1990s, as a media channel that could reach Turkish immigrants more than any other channel, *Merhaba* took on the mission of familiarising the Turkish community with Sweden, from different perspectives.

Providing details of regulations and bureaucratic procedures, crucial for the daily lives of Turkish immigrants in Sweden, *Merhaba* functioned as a 'social information desk'. Details about the status of Turkish citizens in the Swedish social security system, rights and obligations of dual citizenship holders, military service duty of Turkish citizens, retirement in Sweden, juridical processes and even regulations about circumcision were some of the issues extensively covered by *Merhaba*:

> Most of the Turkish immigrants who originated from rural areas had enormous difficulties in adapting to Swedish society. They needed to learn Swedish, but prior to this, if they could have strong ties with Turkey they would be able to learn about the urban life in Turkey, which would speed up their integration into the Swedish way of life, which is basically an urban way of living [...] So these people faced the European urban culture before they had experienced the necessary transformation from rural life to urban life in Turkey. Therefore they kept a distance from it. The immigration board or Swedish authorities saw the opportunity to close this gap via public service broadcasts in Turkish. (*Merhaba* producer 1)

In a different, but relevant way, 'magazine' programmes about Swedish culture, traditions, values and ways of living aimed to generate an understanding of 'Swedish-ness' among Turks, in order to make their lives easier. According to producers who worked during the early years, the initial role of *Merhaba* was determined by a combination of the crucial needs of Turkish immigrants with the expectations of the Swedish immigration policies/authorities dealing with the integration of immigrants into Swedish society:

> Integration was the main role. A radio programme aiming at immigrants must serve the integration of these immigrants into society. With the style, content and message you aim for this. It is wrong if you make them hate Sweden and dream nostalgically about the good old homeland. Also, if you start with the

journalistic ethic, it doesn't matter if it is public service or commercial, you realise that in order to make your audience happier and more successful, you have to make them feel as part of the community, not an outcast. They don't have to be Swedish, don't have to speak Swedish, emotionally don't have to love Sweden, but they have to walk with the rest of society. And as a journalist I would like to help this. If you are a patriot you do it the other way round. But I can say honestly that *Merhaba* has helped this mission to a great degree, of course not by hiding the truth. If Sweden had a xenophobic immigrant policy for instance, we criticised it severely. (*Merhaba* producer 4)

The above statements from the producers broaden and at the same time challenge Riggins' claim that 'ethnic minority media may unintentionally encourage the assimilation of their audiences to mainstream values.'[21] *Merhaba*, operating within the frame of a Swedish public service institution and inevitably aiming to support audiences' integration into Swedish society, was intentional about this function from the beginning. According to accounts of *Merhaba* staff regarding its introduction period, such a 'supportive role for speeding up integration' was crucial for the Swedish authorities dealing with immigrants, therefore it can be argued that since the beginning integration was on the agenda of *Merhaba* as well as other immigrant language services within SR.

Suspension of *Merhaba*

On 14 January 2006, almost 30 years of continuous Turkish broadcasting on SR ended, with the airing of the last *Merhaba* programme. The decision to suspend *Merhaba*, poorly prepared reports on which the decision was based, and some declarations by the SR Management during the suspension process were criticised in both the Swedish and Turkish media;[22] protest letters and e-mails were received by *Merhaba* staff and SR management, mostly from Turkish people, both from Sweden and Turkey. However, the decision was not revoked. A former programme director at the Immigrant Languages Unit sums up the suspension decision as follows:

> From my perspective, if you have a certain amount of money and if you want to do good broadcasting in immigrants' languages, you have to use these resources for fewer languages rather than more languages with less money. Of course it's always a question of if we treat people fairly by dropping *Merhaba* after so many years. But now we have new people from different origins, so we have to do this. (Former programme director)

Then manager of SR International explained the decision in a nutshell: 'We just needed to make a decision between languages. And Turks were not the ones who were in the most need.'

Although Turkish broadcasts on SR ended in 2006 with these justifications, the critical break point for *Merhaba* as well as the other migrant or diasporic media in Sweden seems to be the integration policy announced in 1996. The new policy set the direction of integration as an individual project for immigrants, mostly relying on economic and social sufficiency of the individuals themselves.[23] Accordingly the measures directed at immigrants as a group were to be confined to provisions solely concerning the immigrants' first years in the country, and their aim should be their integration. Consequently, immigrant groups that are assumed to be integrated or 'established', faced negative consequences. For instance, the grant system that was initiated in 2001 resulted in reduced funding for media production by such established groups' organisations. *Merhaba's* case that resulted in its suspension as well as earlier suspended languages in SR, such as Greek, Portuguese and Polish, are victims of this redundant dichotomy: newly arriving immigrant groups vs. 'established' ones.

Around the same time, in 2001, Christensen argued that minority and multicultural divisions and programmes, both in the radio and television (SVT) branches of Swedish public service broadcasting existed because they had to, not necessarily because they should.[24] Camauër attributes this period's cutbacks in the Finnish Unit of SVT and the closing of the *Mosaik* Unit, a multicultural programme aiming to reflect on and examine multicultural and multilingual Sweden, to what Christensen calls the schizophrenia of public service: minority and multicultural units and their programmes are hailed as part and parcel of the very meaning of public service, but were the most likely to suffer cutbacks were it not for regulations and quotas.[25]

As Horsti and Hultén demonstrate, the early 2000s was also a period when discourses and accordingly the policies regarding how to handle the question of ethnic minorities was shifting. Multicultural policies aimed at providing specific services for minority groups were replaced with 'mainstreaming cultural diversity', by most of the Nordic public service broadcasters.[26] And authors argue that the shift from multicultural to a vague diversity policy, beginning in Sweden in 2004 – the same year *Merhaba* was suspended, has resulted in a collapse of the opposition between 'public' and 'market' values. For instance, a key word in the diversity discourse was 'mainstreaming', signifying that ethnic and cultural diversity should be taken into account in SVT's programmes, and that they should target a broader audience. And 'of course', as stated by the then head of SVT's division of culture 'there is a business value to diversity. The more people whose backgrounds are included in our programmes the more they are likely to watch them.'[27]

In short, Turkish broadcasts on SR ended in the context of a change in the integration policy of the Swedish state on the one hand, and its implications on Swedish public broadcasting on the other. The 1996 integration policy contradicted largely with the dominant policy towards immigrants in Sweden in the 1970s – the introduction period of broadcasts in immigrant languages on SR, which perceived the broadcasts in immigrant groups' native languages as their right, although integration to Swedish society was an equally important intention. Changing discourses about integration was coupled with growing pressure on public service broadcasters from commercial media outlets, relatively new players in the Swedish media environment. With a shrinking budget for immigrant languages, SR made the decision to suspend its Turkish section, which they deemed in less need of support in comparison with broadcasts in languages of immigrant groups who had recently arrived. With this decision, SR not only lost its agency in Turkish media space in Sweden, but also left the destiny of this space to market dynamics. However, research proves that business-driven media policies do not necessarily respond to the democratic needs of a multicultural society.[28] Instead, Isabel Awad Cherit argues, a laissez-faire approach to cultural diversity in the media, relying on commercial instead of normative justifications, reduces diversity to a business asset but does not secure a wider diversity of voices and social perspectives in the media.[29] Throughout the decade after the suspension of *Merhaba*, the Turkish community's usage of web-based diasporic media has mushroomed in

Sweden, mostly via social media platforms, as well as the influence of Turkish television channels. Although it has not been studied systematically, it can confidently be argued that the Swedish public service institution is not considered as a diasporic media space by the Turkish community in Sweden anymore, a characteristic it possessed between 1976 and 2006.[30]

Conclusion

The quotation at the beginning of this paper from a *Merhaba* producer was about the balance they tried to find between the needs of the Turkish community in Sweden and the demands of the Swedish authorities. In other words, Turkish broadcasts on SR existed as a diaspora media space shaped by specific community and institutional dynamics. Therefore, its success and failure must be evaluated in relation to these two axes. As the above presented roles fulfilled by *Merhaba* imply, in the operational zone provided by SR, it contributed, in varying degrees, to the Turkish community's access to information both from Turkey and from Sweden. It thus enhanced connectivity among its members and sustained, discussed and reformed the multiple identities of the Turkish community in Sweden (Turkish, Swedish-Turkish, Turkish-Swedish and others). Moreover, it served to further the Turkish community's integration into Swedish society in line with the demands of SR. On the latter issue, however, the evaluation of success/failure becomes more complicated as the question relates to the broader institutional context of *Merhaba*, that is, the integration policy of the Swedish state and transformations in such policy. The fact that *Merhaba* was suspended due to such a transformation in Sweden's integration policy renders such an assessment awkward, if not futile.

Still, an attempt may be made by concluding this chapter with a quotation from SR's culture programme, *Kulturnytt*, devoted to the end of *Merhaba's* journey. A producer, a second-generation member of the Turkish community in Sweden, shared her personal views about *Merhaba*, as follows:

> *Merhaba's* penultimate broadcast on Tuesday was a retrospective of its history. It also provided insight into the Swedish-Turks' history and affairs in Sweden. *Merhaba* outlined, with an inside perspective, stories of people establishing themselves in a new country. Stories of the hands that helped build the Swedish welfare system, of those who were forced to flee to Sweden and those who came for the sake of love. There was also the story of myself, their children, and thousands of others who have grown up with feet in the two countries. Some of Sweden's history and its present. For 28 years, the programmes for many have been a gateway to Sweden in Turkish, while at the same time a Swedish link back to Turkey. On Saturday, the gate was closed. Hoşçakal, *Merhaba* [Farewell to *Merhaba*].[31]

Notes

1. Studies about media cultures of Turkish-speaking populations in Europe and elsewhere have been conducted in various countries ranging from Germany (See Ayse Caglar, Encountering the state in migration-driven transnational social fields: Turkish immigrants in Europe (Berlin, 2003) and Kira Kosnick, *Migrant Media: Turkish Broadcasting and Multicultural Politics in Berlin*. Indiana University Press, (Bloomington, 2007)), to Britain Asu Aksoy and Kevin Robins, 'Banal transnationalism: The difference that television makes', in: K.H. Karim (eds) *The Media of Diaspora*, (London, 2003), to France (See Isabelle Rigoni, 'Turkish and Kurdish Media Production in Europe: An Overview' (2002)), and to Australia (See Gokcen Karanfil, 'Pseudo-exiles and reluctant

transnationals: disrupted nostalgia on Turkish satellite broadcasts' *Media Culture Society*, Vol.31, No.6, (2009)). The research on
which this chapter is based is the first one studying Turkish media
culture Sweden (See Altuğ Akın, *Ethnic Minority Media Production
From Producers' Perspective: Case of Turkish Broadcasts in Swedish
Public Service Broadcaster (SR)* (Stockholm, 2006)).

2. Myria Georgiou, *Media and the City: Cosmopolitanism and
    Difference*, Polity Press, (Cambridge, 2013), p. 88.

3. Roza Tsagarousianou, 'Rethinking the Concept of Diaspora:
    Mobility, Connectivity and Communication in a Globalised
    World', *Westminister Papers in Communication and Culture* 1/1
    (2004), p. 53.

4. Ato Quayson and Girish Daswani, *A Companion to Diaspora and
    Transnationalism*, Wiley-Blackwell, (West Sussex, UK, 2013), pp. 4–5.

5. Alejandro Portes, 'Immigration theory in the new century: Some
    problems and opportunities', *The International Migration Review*,
    31/4 (1997), pp. 799–825.

6. Nina G. Schiller, Linda Basch and Christina S. Blanc, 'From
    immigrant to transimmigrant: Theorizing transnational migration',
    Anthropological Quarterly, 68/1 (1995) pp. 48–63.

7. Myria Georgiou, 'Diasporic media across Europe: Multicultural
    societies and the universalism-particularism continuum', *Journal
    of Ethnic and Migration Studies* 31/3 (2005), p. 489.

8. Arjun Appadurai, *Modernity at Large: Cultural Dimensions of
    Globalization*, University of Minnesota Press, (Minneapolis and
    London, 1996).

9. Julian Murphet, 'The media of diaspora' in Ato Quayson and
    Girish Daswani (eds), *The Blackwell Companion to Diaspora and
    Transnational Studies*, Wiley-Blackwell, (Oxford, 2013), p. 55.

10. Ibid., p. 55.

11. Georgiou, *'Diasporic media across Europe'*, p. 490.

12. Ibid., p. 490.

13. Debuting in autumn 1967, 13 issues of *Belleten* were published by
    a group of volunteers recently arrived from Turkey. The magazine
    borrowed its name and ideological position from an earlier
    publication of the Turkish Communist Party (TKP) in Turkey. It
    was a monthly, tabloid-sized, 24-page publication in Turkish with
    a socialist perspective based on class struggle, almost without any
    emphasis on migrant questions or subjectivity.

14. With the introduction of live access to TV channels in Turkey,
    two major transformations were observed in Turkish commu-
    nities living abroad. Firstly, increasing synchronisation with the
    daily actuality of Turkey had a negative effect on the diasporic
    populations' nostalgic feelings for the homeland they left

behind. Real time access to the banality of 'there' worked against the idealisation of homeland and nostalgic feelings for Turkey. Secondly, this conventional spatial nostalgia transformed into a contemporary temporal one, the nostalgia for the early days of arrival in Sweden. Elsewhere (See Altuğ Akın, 'Revisiting diasporic condition: New patterns of nostalgia among Turks in Sweden', in J. Fornäs, Johan and M. Fredriksson (eds), *Electronic Proceedings of the Inter: A European Cultural Studies: Conference in Sweden 11–13 June 2007* (Sweden, 2007)), I argued that the sum of these two transformations signalled normalisation of a 'transnational way of being'.

15. Georgiou argues that the medium of the internet itself, perhaps more than any other, makes media nomadism possible: 'Always available and enhancing individuals' sense of power to control the flow of information and the sources of information they turn to, it provides a common framework for identities that are not fully dependent on Cartesian geography and the boundedness of the nation-state' (Myria Georgiou, 'Diaspora in the digital era: Minorities and media representation', *Journal on Ethnopolitics and Minority Issues in Europe* 12/4 (2013), pp. 91–2). For diasporic subjects, internet also brings along, what Castells (See Manuel Castells, *Communication Power* (Oxford, 2009)) defines as 'networked communalism', an attempt to find community at a distance rather than in proximity as a response to the marginalisation that many migrants and diasporic people feel (Georgiou, 'Diaspora in the digital era', 2013, p. 93). For studies on diasporas and internet see Dana Diminescu, 'The Connected Migrant: an Epistemological Manifesto', *Social Sciences Information*, Vol.47, No.4, (2008), Jennifer M.Brinkerhoff, *Digital Diasporas: Identity and Transnational Engagement* (Cambridge, 2009) and, Anna Everett, *Digital Diaspora: A Race for Cyberspace*, SUNY Press (Albany, 2009).

16. Swedish perspective principle is defined by the manager of the Immigrant Languages Unit as 'reporting about the home country in a way that is very relevant to the person living in Sweden, so there will be a Swedish link, a Swedish perspective.' This principle is perceived critically by ILU staff, for minimising contact of the community with the homeland.

17. *Merhaba* programme broadcast on 1 January 1987. Archival number 2353-86/5101.

18. Experienced especially during the 1980s, another pattern of information dissemination in which *Merhaba* was actively involved can be conceptualised as 'circular information flow'. During the military regime in Turkey, *Merhaba* was reaching expelled political actors in Turkey via telephone and then

broadcasting these interviews in Sweden. Subsequently, these programmes were being sent to Turkish broadcasts on German Public Service Radio and from Germany back to Turkey. Eventually declarations of banned politicians were being published on the front pages of national daily newspapers and reaching the Turkish public, while *Merhaba* was cited as the source (Akın, *Ethnic Minority Media Production*, 2006).

19. SR Report *Turkiska Hushåll om Radio och Teve* (Turkish households about Radio and TV) by Aulis Gröndhal (1986) was the first and the last detailed audience survey conducted on the audiences of *Merhaba* by SR. Surprisingly, until its suspension in 2006, no other formal surveys were carried out by the institution.

20. Myria Georgiou, *Mapping minorities and their media: Studying The Media. Investigating Inclusion And Participation In European Societies, European And Transnational Communities*, Working Paper, (London, 2001), p. 16.

21. Stephen Harold Riggins, *Ethnic Minority Media: An International Perspective*, Sage Publications, (California, 1992).

22. For instance, in the prestigious Swedish daily paper *Dagens Nyheter*, three articles were devoted to the decision during the week after its announcement. Articles drafted by Dan Jönsson were entitled 'Bad Timing: Radio marginalises Turkish language' and 'Political grounds may not even be suspected'.

23. Christer Lundh and Rolf Ohlsson, *Från arbetskraftsimport till flyktinginvandring* (Stockholm, 1999). Leonor Camauër, 'Ethnic Minorities and their Media in Sweden. An Overview of the Media Landscape and State Minority Media Policy'. *Nordicom Review* 2003/2 (2003).

24. Christensen, Christian 'Minorities, Multiculturalism and Theories of Public Service', in Ullamaija Kivikuru (ed.), *Contesting the Frontiers: Media and Dimensions of Identity* (Göteborg, 2001), p. 97.

25. Leonor Camauër, 'Ethnic Minorities and their Media in Sweden. An Overview of the Media Landscape and State Minority Media Policy', *Nordicom Review* 2003/2 (2003), pp. 84–5.

26. Karina Horsti and Gunilla Hultén, 'Directing diversity: Managing cultural diversity media policies in Finnish and Swedish public service broadcasting' *International Journal of Cultural Studies* 14/2 (2011), pp. 209–27.

27. Ibid, p. 220.

28. Isabel Awad Cherit, 'Cultural Diversity in the News Media: A Democratic or a Commercial Need?' *Javnost – the Public* 15/4 (2008) pp. 55–72.

29. Gunilla Hultén, 'Diversity disorders: Ethnicity and newsroom cultures' *Conflict & Communication online* 8/2 (2009), pp. 1–14.

30. Such a strong dependency of a diasporic media space to receiving a nation's policy context presents the limitations of not only the transnational characteristic of such spaces, but also diasporic media conceptualisation. See Arif Dirlik, 'Intimate others: [private] nations and diasporas in an age of globalization,' *Inter-Asia Cultural Studies*, 5/3 (2004) and John Budarick, 'Media and the limits of transnational solidarity: Unanswered questions in the relationship between diaspora, communication and community', *Global Media and Communication*, 10/2, (2014).

31. Ülkü Holago, *Hoşçakal, Merhaba!* (Stockholm, 2006). http://sveriges radio.se/sida/artikel.aspx?programid=478&artikel=772613 (accessed 16 January 2016).

References

Akın, A., *Ethnic Minority Media Production From Producers' Perspective: Case of Turkish Broadcasts in Swedish Public Service Broadcaster (SR)* (Stockholm, 2006).

———, 'Revisiting diasporic condition: New patterns of nostalgia among Turks in Sweden', in J. Fornäs, Johan and M. Fredriksson (eds), *Electronic Proceedings of the Inter: A European Cultural Studies, Conference in Sweden 11–13 June 2007* (Sweden, 2007). http://www. ep.liu.se/ecp/025/ (accessed 12 January 2016).

Aksoy, A. and Robins, K., 'Banal transnationalism: The difference that television makes', in K.H. Karim (ed.), *The Media of Diaspora*, (London, 2003).

Appadurai, A., *Modernity at Large: Cultural Dimensions of Globalization* (Minneapolis and London, 1996).

Brinkerhoff, J.M., *Digital Diasporas: Identity and Transnational Engagement* (Cambridge, 2009).

Budarick, J., 'Media and the limits of transnational solidarity: Unanswered questions in the relationship between diaspora, communication and community', *Global Media and Communication* 10/2 (2014), pp. 139–53.

Çağlar, A., *Encountering the state in migration-driven transnational social fields: Turkish immigrants in Europe* (Berlin, 2003).

Camauër, L., 'Ethnic Minorities and their Media in Sweden. An Overview of the Media Landscape and State Minority Media Policy', *Nordicom Review* 2003/2 (2003), pp. 69–88.

Castells, M., *Communication Power* (Oxford, 2009).

Christensen, C., 'Minorities, Multiculturalism and Theories of Public Service', in Ullamaija Kivikuru (ed.), *Contesting the Frontiers: Media and Dimensions of Identity* (Göteborg, 2001), pp. 81–102.

Diminescu, D., 'The Connected Migrant: an Epistemological Manifesto', *Social Sciences Information*, 47/4 (2008) pp. 565–79.

Dirlik, A., 'Intimate others: [private] nations and diasporas in an age of globalization' *Inter-Asia Cultural Studies*, 5/3 (2004) pp. 491–502.

Everett, A., *Digital Diaspora: A Race for Cyberspace*, SUNY Press (Albany, 2009).

Georgiou, M., *Mapping minorities and their media: Studying The Media. Investigating Inclusion And Participation In European Societies, European And Transnational Communities* (London, 2001).

———, 'Diasporic media across Europe: Multicultural societies and the universalism-particularism continuum', *Journal of Ethnic and Migration Studies* 31/3 (2005), pp. 481–499.

———, 'Diaspora in the digital era: Minorities and media representation', *Journal on Ethnopolitics and Minority Issues in Europe* 12/4 (2013), pp. 80–99.

Holago, Ülkü, *Hoşçakal, Merhaba!* (Stockholm, 2006). See http://sverigesradio.se/sida/artikel.aspx?programid=478&artikel=772613 (accessed 16 January 2016).

Horsti, K. and Hultén, G., 'Directing diversity: Managing cultural diversity media policies in Finnish and Swedish public service broadcasting', *International Journal of Cultural Studies* 14/2 (2011), pp. 209–27.

Hultén, G., 'Diversity disorders: Ethnicity and newsroom cultures' *Conflict & Communication online* 8/2 (2009), pp. 1–14.

Karanfil, G., 'Pseudo-exiles and reluctant transnationals: disrupted nostalgia on Turkish satellite broadcasts' *Media Culture Society* 31/6 (2009), pp. 887–99.

Kosnick, K., *Migrant Media: Turkish Broadcasting and Multicultural Politics in Berlin*, Indiana University Press, (Bloomington, 2007).

Lundh, C. and Ohlsson, R., *Från arbetskraftsimport till flyktinginvandring* (Stockholm, 1999).

Murphet, J., 'The Media of Diaspora' in Ato Quayson and Girish Daswani (eds), *The Blackwell Companion to Diaspora and Transnational Studies*, (Oxford, 2013), pp. 54–67.

Portes, A., 'Immigration theory in the new century: Some problems and opportunities', *The International Migration Review*, 31/4 (1997), pp. 799–825.

Quayson, A. and Daswani, G., *A Companion to Diaspora and Transnationalism*, Wiley-Blackwell (West Sussex, UK, 2013).

Riggins, S.H., *Ethnic Minority Media: An International Perspective*, SAGE Publications (United States, 1992).

Rigoni, I., 'Turkish and Kurdish Media Production in Europe: An Overview' (2002). http://www.lse.ac.uk/collections/EMTEL/Minorities/case_studies.html (accessed 13 January 2016).

Schiller, N.G., Basch, L. and Blanc, C.S., 'From immigrant to transimmigrant: Theorizing transnational migration', *Anthropological Quarterly* 68/1 (1995), pp. 48–63.

Tsagarousianou, R., 'Rethinking the Concept of Diaspora: Mobility, Connectivity and Communication in a Globalised World', *Westminster Papers in Communication and Culture* i/1(2004) pp. 52–66.

CHAPTER 7

ORGANISING OF TURKISH MIGRANTS IN METROPOLITAN STOCKHOLM: FROM NATIONAL FEDERATION TO WOMEN, YOUTH AND OTHER ASSOCIATIONS[1]

Yasemin Akiş Kalaylıoğlu and
Mahir Kalaylıoğlu

Introduction

Since the 1970s when multiculturalism was accepted as the official integration policy, Sweden has encouraged immigrants to organise themselves along with their ethnic identities. Turks are among the immigrant communities with the widest network of migrant associations in Sweden, with respect to quantitative indicators such as the number of associations and members. In this study, general characteristics of the Turkish migrant associations in Stockholm and the issue of organisational differentiation since the beginning of the 1990s (as illustrated by the emergence of women's and youth associations, religious foundations and Alevi associations, etc.) are investigated. We focus on three types of association: sociocultural associations (or Turkish cultural associations), women's and youth associations. Turkish cultural associations, which started to appear in the 1970s, are defined by their being the most predominant type of Turkish association in Sweden. The development of women's associations represents women's attempt to make their own voices heard within the network of Turkish associations, which are patriarchal in structure. Youth associations, on the other hand, are important with regard to understanding fundamental issues and the organising of the second generation. Furthermore, the National Federation formed by the local Turkish cultural associations continues to maintain its claim of representing both women and youth and this means the organising of women and youth is not free from conflict and tensions. In this sense, we suppose that focusing on these three types of associations enables us to address the organising of the Turkish migrants in terms of gender relations, generational differences, organisational representation as well as the conflicts brought about by them.

Methodologically, the study is a quantitative analysis based on in-depth interviews. We conducted forty semi-structured in-depth interviews with the representatives of Turkish associations (chairmen and/or executive board members) in Stockholm between March and June 2008. Additionally, using participant observation technique, we joined several official meetings, holiday celebrations and dinner parties, which were organised by the Turkish associations during the period of our field research. Through these activities, we gained more extensive knowledge of the activities of the associations. Another method we applied for the same purpose was to scan periodicals, handouts and introductory or informational booklets, which were published by national federations or local associations. In in-depth interviews, with regard to issues of organisational differentiation and main charac-teristics, we prioritised the following questions: What kinds of activities are organised by Turkish associations? What is their profile with respect to such indicators as leadership, financial support and membership? What is the rate of participation of the members in the activities organised by their local associations and is it possible to speak of differentiation depending on the age groups or gender? What can be said concerning the issue of participation in women's and youth associations and the role of state subsidy in selection of the activities and organisational differentiation of the associations? Finally, what is the future prospect of Turkish immigrants' organising? Although the data of this research dates back to 2008, most of the associations under question in this study are still active and the study has been updated from recent secondary sources to maintain the validity of the findings.

People from Kulu and Others

As also mentioned in other chapters of this book, people from Kulu (a district of Konya in Turkey), are one of the first and most well-known immigrant communities in Sweden. Although the beginning of labour migration from Turkey to Sweden coincided with the period when Sweden actively pursued a foreign labour recruitment policy, most of the Turkish workers made their way to Sweden through *spontaneous chain immigration* rather than official channels. The first group of workers was composed of young men from Kulu who received work and residence permits in 1966. The key characteristics of these pioneering groups were rural background and a low level of education. Due to the restrictions brought to non-Nordic labour immigration, labour immigration from Turkey was formally ended in the early 1970s and replaced by family reunification which continued to a lesser extent in the following periods.

Despite the numerical majority of the people from Kulu, it would be mistaken to suppose that the Turkey-origin population in Sweden is a homogeneous group. On the contrary, they constitute a complex population composition with different ethnic, religious and political identities. This composition is usually simplified as Turks and Kurds in ethnic terms, Muslims (Sunni and Alevi) and Christians (Assyrian Orthodox) in religious terms. However, in reality the picture is more complicated. In addition to Turks, other major groups are Kurds and Assyrians. Assyrians, who migrated to Sweden from the south-eastern part of Turkey in the second half of the 1970s, sought asylum on the grounds of religious persecution and were accepted by Sweden on humanitarian grounds. Kurdish refugees, on the other hand, started to immigrate to Sweden at the beginning of the 1970s and their migration together with their family members has been the main population movement from Turkey to Sweden in the post-1980 period.[2] In addition, Sweden has also become a destination for a large number of political refugees from Turkey, who fled the country following the military coups of 12 March 1971 and 12 September 1980.

This overall migration pattern makes Turkey-born immigrants one of the largest foreign-born groups in Sweden. According to 2007 figures, the number of the Turkey-born people in Sweden is 38,158 (20,422 men, 17,736 women) (vide supra, Table 7.1) and it is slightly over 60,000 when the second generation is included (54 per cent first and 46 per cent second generation). More than half of this population (35,000) lives in the Greater

Table 7.1   Turkey-born population in Sweden, from 1960 to 2016

1960	1970	1980	1990	2000	2007	2015
202	3,768	14,357	25,528	31,894	38,158	46,373

Source: Westin, 2006; 2007 and 2015 figures from Statistics Sweden, Population statistics.

Stockholm metropolitan area. The number of Turkey-born immigrants who became Swedish citizens increased after Sweden accepted dual citizenship in 2001. It is estimated that the Turkey-born population is equally distributed among ethnic Turks, Kurds and Assyrians.[3] By 2015, while the number of the Turkey-born population increased to 46,373 (25,520 men, 20,853 women), the percentage of those among them who have become Swedish citizens is almost the same as in 2007, 75 per cent (34,710). Due to their rural background and low education level, the areas of employment of Turkish migrants, to a major extent, have been limited to cleaning and industrial work. Although Turks in Sweden are largely satisfied in terms of living conditions and material wealth, they have been regarded by native Swedes as ethnically distant and foreign.[4]

Swedish Multiculturalism and Migrant Associations

As Freeman indicated, multiculturalism is 'less a choice than an unintended and often most unwelcome outcome' in the West.[5] Choosing multiculturalism as an official integration policy, Sweden became one of the few countries that are an exception to this general tendency, along with Australia, the Netherlands and Canada. With the regulations of the 1970s, the traditional assimilationist attitude towards foreigners was abandoned and

Sweden began to be viewed as an ethnically pluralist society. Most important of all, the 1974 constitution recognises the right of religious and ethnic minorities to preserve their culture and promises to provide a remarkable amount of financial support for this purpose. As a further step, the 'Immigrant and Minority Policy', adopted in 1975 and resting upon three aims formulated as, with reference to the ideals of the French Revolution, equality, freedom of choice, and cooperation, officially declared that Sweden is a multicultural society.

These policy goals, especially the third one, have provided the legal basis for the establishment of migrant associations and collective organisation of immigrants. In terms of the organisational representation of immigrants, two basic qualities of the concept of ethnic pluralism introduced by the 'Immigrant and Minority Policy' were (i) the encouragement of the establishment of migrant associations and (ii) on the principal of ethnicity. It can be argued that these priorities have resulted in two basic consequences in terms of the development of migrant associations. First of all, the priority attached to ethnicity has led to ethnic identity becoming the main organising principle in the organised represen-tation of immigrants.Ålund and Schierup state in this regard that the immigration policy of the 1970s has established ethnicity as a collective ordering principle and thus ethnicity became the basic category that determines the membership of immigrants.[6] Within the framework of this membership model, immigrants have been classified according to their ethnic identity and each collective ethnic group has founded their own ethnic organisational network consisting of national federations and their local affiliates. And secondly, the promotion of ethnicity as the ordering principle has been largely internalised by immigrants themselves, 'to the extent that 'ethnic absolutism' became 'the minorities' own dominant ideological discourse'.[7]

Through its official policy for the collective organisation of immigrants, Sweden has turned into the European country with the highest level of organisation among immigrants.[8] Briefly stated, the founding of national immigrant federations dates to the late 1970s, when the Swedish state began to offer subsidies to immigrant organisations. By the second half of the 1980s, the number of national federations was more than 30 and local associations more than 1,500. Shipper records the number of national migrant associations by the 2000s as more than 131.[9] The number of national federations receiving financial support from the National Integration Bureau was 57 by the year 2005.[10] Moreover, it is not unusual for more than one national immigrant federation to claim to represent immigrant groups from the same ethnic identity and this naturally increases the number of organisations even more. Kurds, Iranians, Bosnians and Assyrians are among such examples. Founding a second national federation in 2003, Turks also joined these groups.

Swedish policy emphasis on migrant organisations, which is also demonstrated by these figures, can be evaluated with reference to the policy making model of the country. Although Swedish corporatism was eroded in the post-1980 period, the regulations adopted to ensure the political participation of immigrants were shaped under the influence of corporatism. An important characteristic of Swedish corporatism is the role of social organisations – first and foremost the workers' and employers' organisations, for sure – in the political decision making processes. They are viewed as the natural representatives of different social segments and have an important role in decision making processes as the 'formal partners' of the state. More specifically, they have a right to represent themselves in research commissions and advisory committees through participatory regulations of the state.[11] In accordance with this corporatist model of representation, migrant organisations were also considered as actors that would represent the interests of their own ethnic and national groups by exerting influence on decision making processes in line with the demands and interests of their particular groups. In order to achieve this, they have been given certain rights. One of the most important of these is that national federations have the right to represent their constituencies in the advisory committees affiliated to state bodies. Thus, they have *officially* become formal partners of the state, particularly in issues concerning immigrants.[12]

However, although they are officially formal partners of the state, it is rather contentious as to whether in practice they really function as such. To begin with, the official policy of the 1970s to turn migrant associations into corporatist negotiation partners did not completely come into effect and was finally abandoned in the 1990s with the fall of corporatism. In other words, corporatism has never become the main characteristic of the decision making process in the area of immigrant policy.[13] This is also confirmed by findings of research on migrant associations in Sweden. Accordingly, the local associations are preoccupied with sports and cultural activities, rather than political issues, and only a few national federations have been successful in functioning as 'pressure groups' by carrying the demands of language and education of their own ethnic groups onto the political agenda.[14] Issues such as preserving cultural identity and relations with language and motherland are given priority in the agenda of migrant associations.[15] In this sense, their role in the organisational life of Swedish society can be summarised through the formula of 'minority culture preservation'[16] and thus they can be better viewed as social clubs or ethnic foundations than pressure groups.[17]

Foundation and Differentiation

Turkish cultural associations

There were mainly four types of Turkish associations in Stockholm from the 1970s to the 1990s: Socio-cultural, Religious, Political associations and Sports clubs. Socio-cultural associations (or Turkish cultural associations) were the first type of association and formed the backbone of the organisational network within the Turkish community. They were born out of Turkish workers' need to have a place to come together without having to spend money. Leaving aside the first examples in the 1960s to be closed down due to lack of interest, Turkish cultural associations started to be founded in the first half of the 1970s, with the cooperation of Turkish migrants and some authorities in the local immigration service.[18] To illustrate, the first local association to be a member of the current national federation (The Federation of Turkish Workers' Associations, Turkiska Riksförbundet, TR from here on) was founded in 1973.[19]

Emphasis on ethnic identity in their names were explicit, they were usually named 'Turkish Cultural Association'. They were anticipated to function as cultural clubs, providing first generation migrant Turks, who had just arrived in Sweden and were lacking language and other skills, with a familiar setting in which to socialise. Accordingly, holiday celebrations, folk dances and meetings for information exchange were among the prevalent activities. Moreover, activities such as song festivals in which local artists participated, folkloric events and film screenings enabled the associations of those years, i.e. from the 1970s up until the 1990s, to play a relatively active role in the lives of Turkish migrants, while drama and painting classes for children and sports events for the youth, such as football and wrestling tournaments, broadened the participant profile beyond the usual adult male members. In this way, Turkish local associations eased a newcomer's first encounter with Swedish society and they soon turned into closed communities dominated by those from Kulu.[20] Meanwhile, it is worthy of note that the latter fact had also seemed to be the main reason that enabled Turkish associations in Sweden to stay together without being too affected by the divisions in Turkey's domestic politics, particularly those in the 1970s and 1980s.

As with many other migrant associations in Sweden, the gathering of Turkish associations under a federation took place at the end of the 1970s, when immigrant organisations received state support. First, two separate federations were founded in 1977 and then TR, which continues to exist today, came into being by the merging of these two federations in 1979. TR started publishing 'Yeni Birlik' by uniting 'Birlik' (Union) and 'Sıla' (Home-place), the publications that existed before the merge. Yeni Birlik has been publishing since 1979 without interruption and it is unique among Turkish migrant communities in Europe with regard to duration of publication. In 1985, TR, as a Stockholm-centred federa-tion, had 22 local associations and 7,884 members. Fifteen of the local associations were located in the areas of metropolitan Stockholm with a high density of Turkish population (three in central Stockholm, 12 in suburbs) and seven were in other cities. By 1988, TR, with 9,000 members in 27 local associations, had become the sixth biggest immigrant federation in Sweden. In 2016, it is still among the biggest national federations in Sweden in terms of the number of both members and local affiliates. Last but not least, it also seems crucial to mention that national federations in general, and TR in our case, can be influential in ethno-politics within Sweden as seen lately with Barbaros Leylani's case.[21]

Political and religious associations

In the 1970s and 1980s, there were several left-political associations in Stockholm founded by Turks who settled in Sweden after fleeing the military coups of 12 March 1971 and 12 September 1980. Among political associations, there were those founded by Social Democrat Turks as well as by the followers of the ultra-nationalist MHP (Nationalist Action Party). Turkish Grey Wolves (Bozkurtlar) can be given as an example of those ultra-nationalist groups which are still active, both in Sweden and in other parts of Europe. The most well-known among the left-political associations were the 'Union for Progressives of Turkey in Sweden' (İSTİB) founded by followers of the 'Turkish Communist Party' at the end of the 1970s and 'Stockholm Solidarity and Cultural Association for People of Turkey' which gathered around itself members of 'Dev-Yol' (Revolutionary Path, the biggest radical left political movement of the 1970s in Turkey). Unlike Turkish cultural and religious associations, left-political associations have been mostly named as 'Türkiyeliler' (people from Turkey), in order to avoid emphasis on ethnic identity. In their statutes, they defined themselves as a 'democratic mass organisation' of people from Turkey, identifying their main goal as to protect and improve the rights and cultures of immigrants from Turkey. Nevertheless, in practice, developments concerning Turkey have had an important place on their agendas, mostly to keep alive the expectation to return soon to the 'motherland', the vitality of political ties with Turkey, etc. However, as travel to Turkey became possible, as political bonds weakened and as the return myth lost its charm, this situation changed to some extent and the idea that activities of the association should also be towards Swedish society has become prevalent.

Religious associations, on the other hand, gained importance among Turks in the 1980s, when they still constituted a significant majority of the total Muslim population in the country (approximately one third of all the Muslims). They have been considered as the continuation of 'Turkish Cultural' associations and been named, with a few exceptions, as 'Turkish Islamic' associations. Although one could come across religious associations before the 1980s, it is only in the 1980s that they became fully active and, from the first half of the 1980s, religious services started to be given by imams sent out and paid for by the Turkish Directorate of Religious Affairs. By 2008 there were seven Turkish-Islamic associations of this kind in Stockholm. They are affiliated with the 'Sweden Muslim Federation' (Svenska Muslimska Förbundet, SMF), which was established in 1982 and is one of four officially recognised Islamic federations in Sweden. In the 1990s, two Islamic umbrella organisations together with women and youth local affiliates came into being. However, it was not until 2008 when the 'Swedish Muslims for Peace and Justice' (SMPJ) was founded by Mehmet Kaplan and Yasri Khan that the young generation as well as professionals engaged in and created a very active Islamic organisation. In addition to that, another very active association was established in 2013, namely the 'Union of Turkish Democrats, UETD', whose headquarters is based in Germany. UETD is known for its pro-Islamic activities and closeness to the 'Justice and Development Party' (Adalet ve Kalkınma Partisi, AKP), the ruling party in Turkey since 2002.

Women and youth associations

The emergence of women's activities in national federations through women's committees or sections dates back to the early 1980s[22] and the first immigrant women's federation in the country was established in 1984. Youth committees, in a similar manner, first came into being in the 1980s under the auspices of national federations and they later achieved autonomy as a separate federation. Moreover, it is also noteworthy that the emergence of both women and youth committees within federations was achieved with special encouragement from the Swedish state, particularly following the Equal Opportunities Act of 1980.[23]

Figure 7.1 The Prayer Room of a Religious Association

Although TR was established as early as 1979 and the Turkish women's associations were present at the local level, it took more than 20 years for the Turkish women's federation to emerge, till 2007, to be precise, when two separate women's federations were established. One of these is the 'İsveç Türk Kadınlar Federasyonu' (Turkiska Kvinnoförbundet Sverige-TKF), which was formed through the transformation of the women's committee of TR that had been active since 1985. The other is 'İsveç Türk Ulusal Kadın Federasyonu' (Svensk-Turkiska Kvinnors Nationella Riksförbund-STKNR). The conditions to become a federation, which requires one thousand members and the presence of women's associations in different cities, had led to an increase in the number of Turkish women's associations countrywide in a short time. Different from the multicultural women's organisations, TKF organises activities and studies aimed particularly at Turkish women in Sweden, whereas STKNR targets all Turkish-speaking immigrant women in the country (including Kurdish women as well). Both local women's associations and national federations point out that they have preferred separate organisations from men's because they could not voice their own demands in mixed organisations where men dominate administration and the clubhouses.

Organisations of youth, on the other hand, started when the youth committee within TR was established in 1983 with the active encouragement of the state. Separating from the TR, young people established their own federation in 1996. By 2008, İsveç Türk Gençlik Federasyonu (Turkiska Ungdomsförbundet-TUF) had 33 associations and 3,800 fee-paying members between the ages of seven and 25. TUF defines itself as a 'youth' federation of Sweden and states its main goal as 'not abiding by ethnic federation and activities but enabling

Turkish youth to turn their faces towards Swedish society'.[24] We will focus on the activities and future prospects of TUF in the last section.

Alevi associations and others

The level of differentiation among Turkish associations in Stockholm, in addition to the youth and women's associations, has increased even more with the emergence of 'Alevi Cultural Centre' (AKM), 'Association of Atatürkist Thought' (ADD) and several cultural associations such as football fan clubs, from the late 1990s on. The organising of Alevis (the second largest religious community in Turkey, after the Sunnis) in Sweden emerged partially as a reaction to the Sivas massacre (*Sivas Katliamı*) in 1993 in Turkey where 37 Alevi intellectuals were murdered by Islamist fundamentalists. AKM in Stockholm was founded two years after this incident, declaring its main goals as explaining and representing Alevism and Alevi culture in Sweden. AKM also established 'Sweden Alevi Federation' in 2008 by coming together with five other Alevi associations in Sweden. AKM indicates that it has an ethnically diverse member profile, with first and foremost Turks and Kurds and prefers the term 'Türkiyeli' (people from Turkey) to define its member base. The 'Association of Atatürkist Thought' was established in 2003, a year after the pro-Islamist Justice and Development Party (AKP) came to power in Turkey, although it had not succeeded in becoming an active organisation by the end of the 2000s. Developments in the home country had one more visible effect on Turkish associations in this period: As a consequence of the developments concerning the Kurdish Question in Turkey (repressive state policies, armed conflict, etc.), some of the Kurdish people who had come from central Anatolia and passed as Turks in daily life up to that time affirmed their ethnic identity and ceased to participate in Turkish associations from the early 1990s.

In conclusion, from the second half of the 2000s, there have been five types of Turkish associations in Stockholm: Socio-cultural, religious, political, women's and youth associations. It is difficult, however, to estimate the total number of Turkish associations and the distribution of different types. A number of reasons for this difficulty can be listed. First of all, exaggerating the number of associations and members has become a method for immigrants to receive larger financial aid since the 1970s when the process of organising started. Considering the cases we met during the field research, we can say that Turks are also faithful to this method. Similarly, the priority given to women and youth-related issues led many Turkish associations to establish their own women's and youth associations with the same aim. Although they are hardly active, executive boards composed of women and youth provide these newly-established associations with an official existence, which in turn results in a serious increase in the number of associations. In addition to these, the decline of organisational life in Sweden in the 1990s seemed to have blurred the very distinction itself between the 'active association' and the 'association on paper'. In order to receive financial aid, associations prepare projects in the areas given priority and realising these projects with a certain degree of participation counts as sufficient to be deemed an active organisation. However, as indicated above, limited participation of members and other prevalent cases also indicate the structural problems of Turkish associations which have existed since their foundation, such as 'disconnection between the leader and the grassroots', which will be addressed in sections below more closely.

Turkish Cultural Associations

Leaders and membership

It is known that the people taking initiatives for the establishment of migrant associations are usually those who have attained an above-average level of education.[25] With respect to educated migrant populations, one of the first occupational groups to come to mind is teachers. In Stockholm, Turkish teachers have played a significant role in the foundation of Turkish associations. For instance, the local association which was the first affiliate of the current federation was founded through the cooperation of Turkish teachers and the Swedish authorities. Later on, many teachers as well as people with higher education and academic degrees have been active in the executive board of the national federation. This may be seen as a conscious choice given that the TR regards itself as the representative of the Turkish people and needs well-educated persons in its relationships with the institutions of the Swedish state. The then (and current) president of the TR stated in our interviews that they valued the diversity in the executive board very highly and that they are happy to see people from different occupational groups such as academics, lawyers, businessmen, trade unionists and politicians as members of the board. Board members of the local associations, on the other hand, usually have an intermediate level of education and are either self-employed or employed in the public or private sectors. Therefore, they are closer to the average of the Turkish migrant community in terms of both educational level and occupational position. An exception to this is the fan clubs (e.g. 'Stockholm Association of Galatasaray Fans', 'Sweden Association of Beşiktaş Fans') and family associations (e.g. 'Stockholm Turkish Family Association') which emerged in the 1990s. Unlike Turkish cultural associations, it is possible to come across, on their executive boards, educated middle-class persons such as architects, businessmen and teachers.

On the basis of our findings about leadership, it can be added that many of the local associations depend on a few people who take on leadership tasks and other responsibilities. All the chairmen and executives of the cultural associations whom we interviewed were composed of first-generation male persons. The leadership is usually performed by the same people. We came across some directorate members who were performing the same duty for over 20 years. Moreover, such cases wherein one person performs more than one duty as chairman of an association along with executive board membership of the TR were not rare at all. Most of the chairmen among our respondents told us that they have difficulties in finding executives and candidates in the general assembly and that even unwillingly they continue their chairmanship, since otherwise associations would have to face the risk of closing down. They referred to the problems of leadership and administration through complaints and comments like 'if I leave this place today they will close it down tomorrow' or 'as the elections approach you can't find people to run for the directorate'. Some of the chairmen told us that even the directorate members themselves avoid taking up associational work and, hence, in practice, much of the association's work is left to them as chairmen alone. One of the participants, who said he agreed to become the chairman of the association to prevent it from closing down, remarked that this is the 'work procedure' of the Turkish associations:

Let me tell you about the Turkish association, how we do it. ... We are nine people, I am the chairman. All the activities, all the work is done by the chairman. I call my friends to a meeting, I explain them things; these other nine friends of mine listen to me, say okay or no. This is the work procedure of the Turkish associations. In the Swedish associations ... I am the only person who has the authority to sign. I have a secretary, a bookkeeper; I mean I have a lot of people working for me. ... They do all the work, they write down all the work they do and they attach a note to the attention of the director. They put it down on paper for the director to know and then they put the paper in my mailbox. Then they say, we will have a meeting on this and that issue. We go and have a meeting. ... We make a decision about it there ... This is the principle by which the Swedish people work. But, in our Turkish associations, not only in ours but in all of them, the chairman does everything. Now, what am I in the association? Am I the chairman, the bookkeeper, money register, a sports activity, a cultural activity!

Despite difficulties in finding leaders and executive board members, the number of associations' members is relatively high. TR informed us that it has over 13,000 members in around 40 affiliated local associations. The number of members of the local associations, on the other hand, varies generally between 250 and 750. However, the number of active members is very low in comparison to the total number; for example, members who pay membership fees in the majority of local associations are no more than between 100 and 200. The clubhouses of the associations are usually rented out as 'coffee houses' and the person who runs the place, in turn, covers part, or all, of the club's rent. In doing so, the associations have come up with a practical solution to the problem of collecting membership fees.

Goals and activities

Turkish associations' charters include a wide range of goals formulated in accordance with the main principles of Swedish immigrant policy (equality, freedom of choice and solidarity). One of the most basic and common goals is to perform necessary tasks to realise the main principles of Swedish immigrant policy in the district of the association. Another goal, which originates from the principle of solidarity, is to contribute to the development of cooperation and friendly relations between Turkish migrants and native Swedes, as well as other migrant groups in the district. The goal of organising activities that preserve and foster Turkish migrants' own cultural traditions, on the other hand, is based on the principle of freedom of choice. The associations also adopted the aim of helping Turkish workers find solutions to the problems they may have with local authorities and other institutions. Other objectives found in the associations' statutes are to deal with education-related problems of Turkish workers' children and to inform members – through conferences, panels and similar organisations – about the rights to which migrants are entitled under Swedish law and their duties. Regarding these objectives, it can be said that the Turkish cultural associations are oriented to Sweden rather than Turkey and that they aim to improve the status of Turkish migrants in Swedish society in compliance with the basic principles of Swedish immigration policy.

Despite this officially assumed representative or spokesperson role, nevertheless, most of the association executives informed us that in practice they do not play such roles. TR may be seen as an exception, in this respect, regarding which both former and present chairpersons and executives agreed that it seeks to act as a representative or pressure group particularly in issues concerning education and the mother tongue. In complete contrast to this, chairpersons of many local associations stated that they had no purpose and had not organised any activities at all in recent years, apart from striving to keep the club open. To give an example, a participant responded to our question 'What is the aim of your association?' by saying 'The association does not have any aims right now; it only has a symbolic objective!' There were also those, on the other hand, who think that local associations are still fulfilling a very significant and even 'therapeutic' task by enabling their members to get socialised in a familiar cultural setting. For example, one of these who is active on the TR's executive board said: 'Today associations function eighty per cent through therapy, while associational activities amount only to ten per cent.' This was in parallel with the idea of one another local chairman who said that the association's clubhouse is a 'health centre':

> In our association this is what we do: we will not close down our association, whatever the expense. ... Because our people need the association.... Association means for us in Sweden a Health Centre. I mean medicine. The association works like this: ... Our friend who has a problem comes to the association and pours his heart out. Say you have a problem, you want illumination on a subject, you come to the association, you talk to a few people. If there are people who know about the subject, you ask them, or you say, for example, I have a military issue or I have a bureaucratic problem there.... Somebody helps you. There are many friends of ours who went through the same stuff. At least they show you the way.... This is the thing about our association, the association, this is why I called it a health centre; it treats our people.

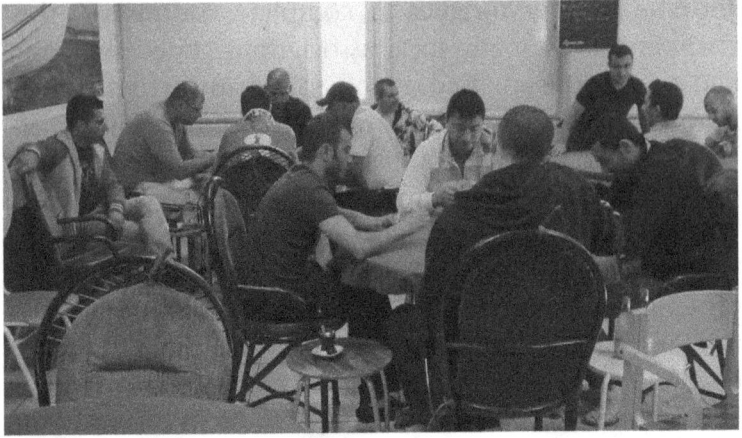

Figure 7.2 The Club-House of a Turkish Cultural Association

Not all views were so optimistic, as is to be expected. Rather, almost all respondents were disturbed in one way or another by the present form of the associations as coffee-houses, although not to the same extent as the chairperson of a family association who put forward the argument that the associations actually harm the Turkish community in Sweden by isolating them from society:

There are things and aspects in which the [Turkish associations] are successful, but there are also things in which they are unsuccessful, for example, considering they gather people together just to waste their energies. I don't know if the positive aspects are greater than the negative aspects though. Now, what are the positives? They have prevented our people from feeling lonely... But, apart from this, like I tried to explain before, you establish club houses, you collect people there. You know, we say that their actual goal is to make us mix with Swedish people, but we do the contrary. What do we do:

we take our people, put them into the clubhouse, in the clubhouse our friends are playing cards and rummikub, right, or they sit down talking about cars or other stuff. In this way, they don't even meet the people outside, their Swedish neighbours.... In fact [the associations] are places that have more negative aspects than positive aspects. I mean when you think about it this way, [they] really harm our community a lot.

Nearly all of the regular participants of the associations are adult men who meet in the clubhouses after work. There are almost no activities in the associations for children, young people and particularly women. In the interviews, we asked chairpersons to count the five most recent events organised by their associations. The answers suggest that the most common events are summertime picnics, celebrations of the national and religious holidays of the motherland, information dissemination meetings about work and retirement, and visits by politicians during election periods. Relatively more active associations also occasionally organise computer courses and supplementary classes for children to help them out with school. Young people come together at the clubhouses, usually at the week-ends, to watch football matches. However, it is clear that the category which has the weakest connection with the associations is women. Studies about migrant associations indicate that women are excluded from the power structures of the traditional migrant associations.[26] Actually, this is a correct but incomplete argument for Turkish associations in Stockholm, as the absence of women in them is valid not only for the power structures but also for the entire environment of the associations as such. Concerning women, there are either no activities, or they are limited to a few examples, such as women days and Turkish cuisine presentations, which are organised by the association executives from time to time and which, after all, reinforce their traditional roles. It is also possible to find female participation in summertime family picnics as well as in the celebrations of national and religious holidays of the motherland. However, apart from these activities, the associations function all together as gathering places for adult, or sometimes for younger, males. Some chairpersons stated that this, i.e. not having included women in associational works, is one of the worst features of the Turkish migrant community. According to one of them:

> In our society it is a handicap, it unfortunately is. We don't want to include our women within associational works. The ones that come, since they feel lonely for one reason or another, come to one or two activities only and then they don't come anymore either. This is something about our society. It is still the same today, there is still little that has changed. ... Our women enter the scene only when they organise an activity on their own.

Turkish associations and the issue of representation

As we mentioned earlier, migrant associations in Sweden are organisations founded not from below through migrants' own initiatives, but from above largely with government support. An immediate outcome of this has been the emergence of a clear gap between the leaders and the grassroots, which leads directly to the associations having only a limited organisational capacity. During our interviews, the executive board members pointed out that they had been unsuccessful in their attempts to overcome this distance and include the grassroots in associational work. Some participants even argued that this and similar problems present in the Turkish associations result from the weakness of democratic traditions in Turkey such as organising and seeking rights. The rural origin and low educational profile of the Kulu migrants is also a factor that reinforces this weakness. In any case, the lack of strong support from the grassroots was mentioned by the majority of the participants as one of the most important characteristics of the Turkish associations. As said by one participant who is active in the TR and in a local association, '(in Turkish associations) we could in no way activate the grassroots, this is our whole problem; the grassroots has not become active'.

The participants emphasised that, due to existing problems, the associations thus far had only carried out the task of representation formally and had not even been very effective in areas such as *immigrant policy*, where they are supposed to be. Furthermore, some chairpersons indicated that the state also had a certain responsibility for this situation. The inability to make use of the migrant associations as effective tools of participation and representation is not only due to a lack of strong grassroots dynamism, but also because of the state, which, contrary to the promises of its own immigration policy, has ignored associations in the decision making process. In this regard, a participant who came to Sweden as a political refugee and is thus more experienced in politics, commented on the issue as follows:

Because the problem is a political one in essence, I think there is nothing migrant organisations can do except to give voice to their problems. And I don't think that these are seriously debated and considered within society and decision making mechanisms as well as within political processes. ... Neither associations nor the federation could really have an influence on immigrant policy. They didn't listen to them, for example, they put limits on education in mother tongue, in spite of migrant associations' arguments. ... Our associations and the federation are performing their representation duties formally, but that's all. I really don't think they are influential or that they are being taken into account.

Despite a general bitterness about the situation, there were also chairpersons and executives who preserved their optimism about the potential of migrant associations in Sweden. They indicated that the associations can still turn into a powerful bargaining tool once active participation of the members is achieved. Let us finish this section with one of these optimistic views. A respondent, also an executive of the TR, answered our question 'Are the associations capable of solving the problems of migrants' as follows:

Of course they are. (For example, housing, education, discrimination in the workplace and so on.) They can help with many issues. For instance, we say that we have 750 members in our association. If we took the 750 signatures and went out as the Bredäng association, we could see whoever we want to see and we could talk about whatever problem we want to talk about. Say, we could go and bargain with an electricity firm. When I say to them, I have 750 members and if you sell us electricity for this price these 750 will make contracts with your firm and buy your electricity, then our members will definitely profit from that. This can also be done with a telephone firm, with a water firm, with a petrol station. ... Sweden is very advanced in this area, I mean in associations. Only if we want it, like I said, if the Bredäng association with 750 members becomes an active association we will make an appointment with the Swedish prime minister tomorrow, in only one day.

Turkish Migrant Women in Sweden

Erder argues that in the years when migration started from Turkey to Sweden, the term 'worker' referred to either 'sexless' persons or 'formal' workers, and also implied they were 'male' workers.[27] However, according to Swedish law, women who immigrated to the country by way of family reunification were also people legally holding individual rights to work and housing. Nevertheless, as documented by several studies, migrant women took up inferior jobs to be able to participate easily in the labour market and, by the end of the 1960s, they were not in the high income jobs as much as Swedish women, although they were at the top of the list regarding participation in the labour market.[28] The situation worsened following an increase in the unemployment rates in Sweden in the late 1970s, as migrant women were among the first groups to be laid off and began to experience unemployment intensively. In this respect, many scholars indicate that the Swedish social welfare system led to the marginalisation of migrant women, pushed them down the hierarchy of the labour market and thus increased their invisibility in society.[29]

Akpinar argues that working outside the home was a different experience, especially for women coming from the Kulu district of Konya.[30] Studying labour market participation with regard to the first and second-generation migrants, she states that the image of 'traditional, male-dependent women' has gradually changed. First-generation migrant men did not mind their wives working outside the home, even though they were not used to it. Sachs explains this phenomenon with the argument that men from Kulu perceived working life in the public area and private life at home as two different spheres regarding their own rules.[31] On the other hand, starting to work after arriving in Sweden has led to the strengthening of Kulu women's belief in gender equality.[32] Consequently, traditional gender relations peculiar to the life in Kulu has changed in Sweden to a certain extent, particularly after women's participation in the labour market. However, as Erder points out, this situation was perceived as a temporary 'extraordinary situation' by most of the Kulu men[33], while they regained dominance and excluded women from the decision making process in family matters. During the interviews, we observed that women experienced a similar exclusion while trying to organise themselves within associations, which will be addressed more closely in the next section.

Gender relations and women's organisations

Support from the Swedish state, firstly to women's committees within the organisational body of the national federation and, secondly, for the foundation of a separate women's federation, has undoubtedly been effective for the organising of women. It seems unlikely that women's demands would have been looked out for by the male-dominated executive boards of the national federation or of the local cultural associations, if there had not been state encouragement. Considering this, it is possible to say that the incentive policies of Sweden had positive effects on Turkish women's organising processes both in terms of women's associations and women's federations. Nevertheless, these effects should not be generalised excessively to the whole organising process of Turkish women, given that the establishment of some of the associations were based on their needs and resulted from their own initiative.

In this framework, apart from the women's federations at the national level, the development of local Turkish women's associations can be expressed in three steps. The 'Turkish Women's Association of Sweden' can be considered as the first step. It was established in the late 1970s by women who were urban and educated and used to be politically active in Turkey, unlike the women who came to Sweden by means of family reunification, mostly from Kulu. Women in this association wanted to maintain political activities, as they had done in Turkey, together with Turkish women in Sweden; hence, they tried to organise women from Kulu. However, we learn from Latife Fegan, who was involved in the association for ten years, that these efforts resulted in failure:

> In short, our efforts to formulise their demands [women from Kulu] on their behalf failed. We abandoned our [dining] culture nights. The number of our members rapidly decreased. The 12 September coup had already happened. We were the first and only association which explicitly took a stand against 12 September and husbands of our members forbade women to come to the association.[34]

As a result of abandoning these activities (such as cultural dining activities), the association lost its active structure over the years and ceased to function. The second step in the development of local women's organisations was the associations established after 1990 by Kulu women. These associations can be interpreted as the outcome of the unequal gender relations within the Turkish community, as illustrated by the male-dominated Turkish local associations where men hinder women from having a say. A woman, who wanted to come together with her friends, describes the difficulties they faced when they wanted to use Turkish cultural associations for this purpose:

> Normally we would meet at someone's home and then we said to ourselves, Turkish women need to have a place, then we tried with the associations but they didn't accept us. We found a clubhouse; they said, what will women do in social clubs? This is the way our Turkish men think .... They always think the worst. We could have turned that place into a family association, families would have come, it would have been open to everybody, and youngsters would have been helping each other there ... We as women couldn't use the associations, when I say we couldn't, I mean they didn't let us.

In our interviews with three of the longest serving presidents of the TR, we asked them why women participated less in both the national federation as well as the local Turkish cultural associations. One of the former presidents pointed to a patriarchal structure as the main problem behind the women's low participation:

> These associations are associations founded by men and for men, when this is the structure it can't be otherwise. We opened up that place [as men], it was all empty talk whether women came or didn't come. It is clear; we cannot be differentiated from Turkey. This is the first fact, the patriarchal structure continued in the associations as well. Let me also say another thing: This is not the same for other ethnic

groups, for example the Chileans. On the other hand, the thing we call the women's federation is not something that happened on its own, from below, with its own dynamics. It was the state that wanted it to happen.

The common elements of these associations are that they were established by Turkish women in order to provide solutions to their problems in Swedish society. Moreover, women from different nations also joined them and hence they started to work together following a multiculturalist policy. Most of the associations of this type perform activities basically in two areas. One of them is activities like handicrafts, knitting, trips (visit to the home country) and dining parties, which can be called 'cultural activities'. The second group of activities can be gathered under the title of 'integration-based work and counselling services'; such as language, computer, vocational education and informative courses in particular topics which are given in the associations to improve the integration of immigrant women into Swedish society. Counselling services are also provided for women to overcome problems in their private and business lives. Respondents especially noted unemployment, loneliness and lack of a social environment which push women into depression. In one of our interviews, a Kulu woman, who lives in the region of Tensta, mentioned the causes of immigrant women's depression as follows:

> There is no support for women, for instance women do not have a social environment, they don't have anybody and they don't have someone from their family. It is difficult to integrate into Swedish society, their culture is different from ours, languages and religions are different. There are so many women who

have health problems, especially psychologically. Even if they find a job, it is not the job that they want; so their psychological health is affected negatively. Women do not have adequate education; it was not enough to establish a women's association to deal with these issues. I mean the Swedish State should have handled these issues and started a bigger project.

The third step in the development of local women's associations were those organised by younger women (i.e. the second and the third generations) after 2000. The 'Turkish Women's Association of Jordbro' is one of them, the aim of which is to assist second and third-generation women to be more successful in education and business life, in other words, to assist them to integrate better into Swedish society. There are also other women's associations that were established after 2007, particularly to support the establishment of women's federations. However, as the years passed, only some of these federations managed to survive and this brings us to another important question, namely the future of women's organising.

The future of Turkish women's associations and federations

As we have mentioned above, although women's federations were established in 2007, there are also local women's associations which have been carrying out activities since the early 1990s. Those associations, which had 20 members in the beginning, reached the point of having approximately 400 members recently. So, one may ask to what extent Turkish women participate in them. How do the chairwomen of the local associations see the future of these organisations? Actually, it is not very hard to predict that the situation is not promising with them in terms of the issue of participation, given that many of the interviewees cited low participation of Turkish women both to local associations and national federations as a serious problem. According to the evaluation of the president of the 'Alby Women's Centre', the main reason behind this was related to cultural habits:

> Do you know that our Turkish women are very passive, I need at least 15 to 20 women to maintain this place; there are some women, but very few. Our women are always at home, they deal with their housework. They spend most of their leisure time at home with their family. They do not participate in education seminars and benefit from them. Our purpose is not to keep them in here for hours. [Showing other women] Look! All of them are foreigners; they are always in here in their leisure time. Our Turkish women should also come. We are very connected to home and children. If a Turkish woman wants, she can do everything.

On the other hand, women's interest in entertainment activities, which was underlined by many chairwomen as well as the presidents of the federations, is commented on by the same respondent as the result of a lack of social environment. In this regard, the newly established local associations together with the women's federations try to overcome the problem of women's low participation in association activities by organising meetings and entertainment facilities. Another major problem of the local women's associations is financial. The president of the 'Multicultural Women's Association of Tensta' stated that despite the increasing number of members, their financial problems had also increased since 1977 due to a decrease in the financial aid provided by the municipality:

In the beginning there were 20-25 members. We started with English language and sewing courses. Now there are 325 members, numbers have constantly increased. When it was established, the state was giving [financial] support, however the state changed its policy as from 2002 by saying that associations would make their own economy by writing projects. They made it very difficult, right now, they do not offer any financial help except projects. Projects last for a year. Now a Swedish volunteer helps us to write projects. It is not difficult to get the money but they ask to account for every penny of it.

Cutting down on the complimentary aid provided by the municipalities pushed both the women and other migrant associations into hardship so that many women's associations are not sure about how long they can maintain their existence in the long-term. To illustrate this, the chairwoman of the 'Women's Association of Alby' commented, saying: 'We cannot find any financial aid and we cannot afford the rent of the clubhouse. Maybe tomorrow we will need to shut the door and leave this place.' Another problem expressed by an executive board member of the women's federation was about the internalisation of a gender equality perspective. According to her, although there is a consensus on gender equality, it isn't always followed in practice:

I say yes to feminism, I am a feminist in a sense as well. However, as women, we should supervise ourselves first. For example, the other day we were sitting in the Turkish Women's Federation when a man walked in, and at this exact moment the atmosphere changed. Some women invited him to chair the session. Why is that? Why is a man asked to lead the women's federation meeting? This is a gender-related situation. A lady ought to be beautiful, smart, slim, sweet and experienced, but a man ought to be educated and that is the only necessary qualification. Men help each other but women never do!

Contrary to the example from the women's federation, gender sensitivity has been very strong in the local women's associations thanks to their close contact with women and their organisational experiences since the beginning of the 1990s. However, as mentioned above, local associations are facing financial problems and low participation of women. In this respect, the women's federations seem to have a more important role than before in the maintenance of the existence of women's local associations.[35]

Turkish Youth in Sweden and their Organising Process

Although international migration to Sweden has been under focus since the 1970s, studies on the second and third generation immigrants started mostly after the 1990s. Researchers note that the education of immigrant children has a key function in terms of their integration into society.[36] In Westin's text, in this respect, three problems which negatively influence the integration of Turkish youth are mentioned:[37] inadequate command of Turkish and Swedish, low degree of university education, and their employment in particular sectors of the labour market. As for employment, Ålund, in her study on second-generation immigrants, argues that children of those who came to Sweden via labour immigration have a much higher unemployment rate than their Swedish peers and discrimination against them can stem from different sources, such as social welfare policies and the media. Consequently, youngsters are pushed into sub-cultures as a result of the failure of integration.[38] In his study on second- generation Turkish migrants, Berg offers some arguments which are worth mentioning with regard to this sub-culture issue.[39] He argues that the 'youth' conception of the immigrants from Kulu is different from the Swedes' mainly for three reasons: a low degree of individualisation among Turks, a social situation where the discourse of 'we' instead of 'me' is stronger compared to Swedes as expressed by Narrowe[40] and the maintenance of a post-figurative position of Turkish culture that depends on age and sex and, finally, a high degree of social control. Therefore, according to Berg, second-generation Turks are being exposed to 'double normality' and thus try to fulfil both the Turkish culture that they experience at home and the Swedish culture in which they grow up.

Actually, one can argue that in the associations founded by Turkish youth, the reflections of what has been termed by Berg as double normality are salient and visible. Leaving below the task of addressing them, we can first outline the main steps of the organising process of Turkish youth. Actually, youth federations emerged in a similar way to the formation of women's and youth committees in the national federation in 1983 as a result of state incentives. Organisation of the youth committees as a separate federation – Turkiska Ungdoms-förbundet (TUF) – occurred in 1995. In 2008, TUF had 33 member associations in Sweden; 16 in Stockholm, eight in Gothenburg and three in Malmo. It is remarkable that many people in administrative roles in TUF continue their high education, have a good command of Swedish and make career plans for the future, although this is not the case with the executive cadres of local youth associations. As also mentioned above, the ratio of university education among second-generation Turkish youth is quite low and they generally work in manual-labour intensive sectors such as fast food, pizza shops (pizzeria), baby-sitting and supermarkets[41]. Considering such factors, it becomes easier to see why the executive cadres of TUF appear as a 'role-model' for the younger Turkish generations. Unlike most of the Turkish (or rather, many other migrant) associations, TUF find it important to use Swedish sources as much as possible in order to carry out joint activities with other Swedish organisations. Selçuk Ünlü, who was the president of the federation in 2008, identified their main aim as being not an 'ethnic federation' but a 'youth federation' of Turkish youngsters in Sweden and added: 'The aims of ethnic groups are different, they mostly try to solve the problems of the country they came from. They do not look at Sweden and it results in a problematic situation'.

TUF's activities are financially supported by the state more than other Turkish federations. While the national Turkish federation (TRF) received 566,000 SEK of aid, TUF received about 638,000 SEK in 2008. It is possible to classify activities of the federation under four main titles: *sports activities* such as the organisation of ski and football tournaments, publication of the half Turkish-half Swedish *Euro-Turk Magazine,* celebration of national days in Turkey such as 23 April and 19 May as *cultural activities* and finally *educational activities* such as seminars. The rate of participation in these activities is quite high. The president of TUF says that the trips and entertainment activities are the most popular, as in other Turkish associations and he notes that about 1,000 people participated in one dining party. Since youngsters do not have a good command of

Turkish, Swedish is used as the language of communication at most of the TUF's activities, although the executive board wants to carry out every activity in both Turkish and Swedish. It should be noted that the latter is an objective achieved at least in the bilingual *Euro Turk Magazine*, unlike those published by the TR mainly in Turkish.

Before concluding, it is also necessary to mention several of the local affiliates of the TUF which exhibit a remarkable profile in several respects. One of them is the 'Youth Association of Alby' which arranges activities for youngsters under 21 and won a prize from the Swedish state for its successful projects. These projects cover various topics such as discrimination, anti-drug campaigns, etc. Another interesting thing about this organisation is that girls and boys organise their activities separately and thus use the clubhouse at different times. This division might be explained with reference to various reasons, one of which is that members of the Youth Islam Federation are on the executive board. But it can certainly also be considered as one of the reflections of 'double normality' which has been referred to above. Another association displaying a different profile is the 'Association of Turkish Academics'. Board members have defined the main aims of the association as being to increase the rate of university education of Turks in Sweden and to assemble them under one roof. Habibe Erdis, the president, states that enrolment rates at the university level have increased among second and third-generation Turkish youngsters, especially in the last few years. She says that this, in a way, provides a response to the question as to what extent they, as an association, have (and will henceforth have) a part to play in this development. She explains how she succeeded in her work in the associational context with Turkish youngsters and the possible outcomes of this work:

In the beginning I was against the associations, I was criticising them; I was saying "Why do you [Turkish people] assemble under the same roof since you want to integrate. If you do not have a dialogue with Swedish people and if you group only among Turks how can you get yourself accepted by them or how can you accept them". But afterwards I realised that if we assembled together and the executive board was composed of reasonable people, we could orient people and do beneficial work. For example, it would be easier to encourage young people to continue their education rather than marrying young and to explain to them that marriage would be a later step ... and we saw that it worked!

Conclusion

As we have seen, the Turkish associational network in Stockholm does not maintain a considerable mobilisation of the Turkish community. Most of the chairpersons we interviewed considered the 1970s and 1980s as the 'golden age' of associations in terms of activities and participation. The associations were more active in those years in both political and cultural respects. While the period between the 1990s and the 2000s is distinguished as a period of decline in terms of activities; the 2000s, for many of the socio-cultural associations, refers to a stage where they cannot organise any activities except for their clubhouses which are being run as coffee-houses. Thus, particularly in the local cultural associations affiliated with the TR, the burden of management has often fallen onto the same shoulders throughout the years. Furthermore, local associations do not serve as spokesmen or pressure groups and their chairmen cannot be regarded as local political leaders of the Turkish community by any means. However, TR is closer to playing this role and acts more or less as an institutionalised voice of the Turkish community in Sweden.

Associations have no relations with other ethnic groups except religious associations where Muslims of different ethnic backgrounds participate in religious services. However, the tendency can be clearly recognised that most Turkish migrants prefer their own religious institutions to perform their religious practices. Local associations affiliated to TR bear the hallmark of 'first generation'. The participation of the second generation is characteristically low, except for some recreational activities such as watching football matches. Although there are different reasons for this, the most important one is certainly that local cultural associations lack any explicit agenda regarding the second generation. In this sense, one can assert that local associations have only a limited function in the maintenance of ethnic identity, or so-called minority culture preservation, which is referred to by some studies as one of the main roles migrant associations play in Swedish society.[42]

The historical development of the local Turkish women's associations can be divided into three stages: women's organisations established in the late 1970s by politically active Turkish women who came from the big cities of Turkey; local women's associations established mostly at the initiative of Kulu women after 1990; and those established after 2000 by younger (second and third) generations. However, many of these associations today face financial difficulties on account of the recent changes in state support. Our interviews also reveal that, although established as late as 2007, the emergence of the women's federations (TKF and STKNR) and the local associations undoubtedly corresponded to Turkish women's need to be organised separately due to their inferior positioning in the national federation (TR) in terms of decision making processes. Moreover, the case of the TKF, which organises activities for 'Turkish women and the Turkish community' in Sweden as its priority, also shows that when a migrant women's group organises themselves by targeting their own ethnic identity, they are very likely to lose the relationship and connection with other immigrant women, even though they may have similar problems. However, as indicated throughout the study, the loss of connection might also be the case even within a single migrant group. Neither male-dominated Turkish federations nor Turkish women's federations have significant organisational relations with the younger generations. It is clearly in this context that the youth federation (TUF) asserts itself as the rising organisation of the Turkish community in several respects, such as using Swedish sources as much as possible, organising activities both for Turks and Swedes and being a 'youth federation' of Sweden rather than an 'ethnic' federation. In this respect, the young people involved in the associational activities seem to be the most promising category that might develop strategies to find a way to ensure the maintenance of their organisations, especially in a political setting which is not as favourable as in the past. Furthermore, they are also the most likely to be the category among Turks in Sweden that engages in associations in order to turn them into places where people participate in activities towards integration. Let us finish by saying that, although this is a long-term process, any step in this direction will be counted as a contribution to the whole Turkish community in Sweden.

Notes

1. This research was conducted with the support of the Linnaeus Center for Integration Studies (SULCIS), Stockholm University in 2008 and the results were published in 2010 as a working paper

(ISSN 1654–1189). This book chapter is based on this research and updated with recent sources.

2. Ingrid Lundberg and Ingvar Svanberg, 'Turkish Associations in Metropolitan Stockholm', *Centre for Multiethnic Research* (Uppsala University, 1991), p. 15.

3. Charles Westin, 'Young People of Migrant Origin in Sweden', *The International Migration Review*, 37/4 (2003), p. 992. Since the Swedish census does not register either ethnicity, religion or language, it is not possible to know exact patterns.

4. Ibid, p. 993.

5. Gary Freeman, 'Immigrant Incorporation in Western Democracies', *The International Migration Review*, 38/3 (2004), p. 961.

6. Aleksandra Ålund and Carl-Ulrik Schierup, 'Prescribed Multiculturalism in Crisis', *Paradoxes of Multiculturalism: Essays on Swedish Society*, Avebury Publishers (Aldershot, 1991), p. 19.

7. Carl-Urlik Schierup, 'The ethnic tower of Babel: political marginality and beyond', in Aleksandra Ålund and Carl-Ulrik Schierup (eds), *Paradoxes of Multiculturalism: Essays on Swedish Society*, (Aldershot, 1991), p. 134.

8. Yasemin Soysal, *Limits of Citizenship: Towards a Post-national Membership in Europe*, University of Chicago Press (Chicago, 1994).

9. Apichai W. Shipper, 'Immigration Politics in Japan, Sweden, and the U.S.', Paper presented at the annual meeting of the American Political Science Association, (Chicago: 2007), p. 10.

10. Miguel Benito, 'Active Civic Participation of Immigrants in Sweden', Country Report prepared for the European research project POLITIS, Oldenburg (2005), see http://www.politis-europe. uni-oldenburg.de/ (accessed 20 April 2016), p. 33.

11. Jane Perry Clark Carey and Andrew Galbraith Carey, 'Swedish Politics in the Late Nineteen-Sixties: Dynamic Stability', *Political Science Quarterly*, 84/3 (1969), p. 472.

12. Pontus Odmalm, 'Civil society, migrant organisations and political parties: theoretical linkages and applications to the Swedish context', *Journal of Ethnic and Migration Studies*, 30/3 (2004), p. 475.

13. Johannes Lindvall and Joakim Sebring, 'Policy Reform and the Decline of Corporatism in Sweden', *West European Politics*, 28/5 (2005), p. 1067.

14. Maritta Soininen, 'The "Swedish model" as an Institutional framework for immigrant membership rights', *Journal of Ethnic and Migration Studies*, 25/4 (1999), p. 697.

15. Leonor Camauër, 'Ethnic Minorities and their Media in Sweden. An Overview of the Media Landscape and State Minority Media Policy', *Nordicom Review* (2003), p. 75.

16. Thomas Malm, 'The Impact of Immigration on Europe's Societies, Sweden', The European Migration Network, European Commission (2005), p. 28.
17. Odmalm, 'Civil society', p. 481.
18. Arslan Mengüç, a recently deceased journalist who lived in Sweden for a long time, described the need to organise in those years as follows: 'On weekends, Stockholm Train Station, T-Centralen, resembled a Turkish town. Everyone from those who had problems to those looking for jobs, from those who wanted to hear from hometown to translators, everyone came to T-Centralen. Those who did not have such reasons had another reason to come there. That was: to be a Turk!... Stockholm [Train Station], like in any other major European city, was filled with Turks every day, but especially on Saturdays and Sundays.... That is why we also met at T-Centralen, discussed Turkey's problems and exchanged newspapers and magazines. These meetings that took place on weekends started to become regular and an organisational basis was forming. We were sick and tired of meeting in cafeterias. We were looking for a place where we could drink our own tea and coffee and boil beans.... In the end, we decided to establish the *Turkish Workers' Union in Sweden*,' in Arslan Mengüç, *Sverige Jag Minns*, Daphne Publications (Istanbul, 2007), pp. 143–4.
19. Lundberg and Svanberg, 'Turkish Associations', p. 20. Furthermore, Assyrians and politically active Kurds were to found their own associations, while inactive Kurds from villages in Kulu district joined Turkish associations.
20. Ibid.
21. On 9 April 2016, Barbaros Leylani, then deputy head of TR, made a speech in the demonstration organised by the 'Coordination Center of Azerbaijani Associations in Sweden' in Sergelstorg in Stockholm as to the recent conflict in Nagorno-Karabakh. During his speech, Leylani called for 'Death to Armenian Dogs', which received strong criticism from different organisations as well as the Swedish authorities. TR issued a press release and announced soon afterwards that Leylani's speech reflected his individual ideas and not TR's while Leylani resigned as vice president of the TR. As expected, the reactions towards him didn't diminish and Leylani's relationship with Mehmet Kaplan, MP from the Green Party (who is also known for his ethno-nationalist and Islamist agendas), also came into question after photos of them at different events appeared in the Swedish media. Although Kaplan tried to ignore his relationship with Leylani and the extremist groups, in the end he couldn't

stand the pressure and handed in his resignation on 18 April 2016. For more information, see Bahar Başer, '"Death to Armenian Dogs": Turkish Ethno-politics causes Uproar in Sweden', Research Turkey (accessed 19 April 2016) http://researchturkey. org/death-to-armenian-dogs-turkish-ethno-politics-causes-uproar-in-sweden/.

22. Wuokko Knocke and Roxana Ng, 'Women's Organizing and Immigration: Comparing the Canadian and Swedish Experiences' in Linda Briskin and Mona Eliasson (eds), *Women's Organizing and Public Policy in Canada and Sweden*, QC, McGill-Queen's University Press (Montreal, 1999).

23. Ibid.

24. Interview with the former president of TUF, Selçuk Ünlü, (10 May 2008).

25. Magdalena Jaakkola, 'Informal Networks and Formal Associations of Finnish Immigrants in Sweden', in Rex John, Joly Daniele and Wilpert Czarina (eds), *Immigrant Associations in Europe* (Aldershot, 1987), p. 207.

26. See, for example, Marlou Schrover and Floris Vermeulen, 'Immigrant Organisations', *Journal of Ethnic and Migration Studies*, 31/5 (2005).

27. Sema Erder, *Refah Toplumunda Getto (A Ghetto in Welfare Society)*, Istanbul Bilgi University Publications (Istanbul, 2006), p. 301.

28. Knocke and Ng, 'Women's Organizing'.

29. Ibid.; Erder, *Refah Toplumunda;* Eskil Wadensjö, 'Renumeration of Migrant Workers in Sweden', *International Labour Review*, 112/1 (1975).

30. Aylin Akpinar, 'Immigrant Experiences in Different Sociopolitical Settings', Migration and Labour in Europe Conference: Views from Turkey and Sweden, MURCIR & NIWL (Istanbul, 2003), p. 206.

31. Lisbeth Sachs, *Evil Eye or Bacteria: Turkish Migrant Women and Swedish Health Care*, Stockholm Studies in Social Anthropology, University of Stockholm, (1983), p. 128.

32. Aylin Akpinar, 'Challenged Family and Kinship Ideals: Family Crisis and Social Networks Among Turkish Immigrants', *Swedish Institute for Social Research Working Papers, 10*, Stockholm University (Stockholm, 1988).

33. Erder, *Refah Toplumunda*, p. 316.

34. Latife Fegan, '10 Yıllık Deneyimin Düşündürdükleri', in Yeni Birlik, No. 5 (1988), p. 9.

35. Nevertheless, in 2016, no new information could be found about those local women's associations such as the ones in Tensta and Alby. Besides, although two different women's federations were

established in 2007, as TKF and STKNR, no records about the latter could be reached either for the period after 2010, except its registered address in the Swedish system.
36. Aleksandra Ålund, 'Pathways of Social Exclusion; Youth in Multicultural Sweden', in *Perspectives of Multiculturalism – Western and Transnational Countries*, Unesco (Milan, 2004).
37. Westin, 'Young people of Migrant Origin'.
38. Ålund, 'Pathways of Social Exclusion'.
39. Magnus Berg, 'Double normality: Reflections on style and Turkish second generation immigrants', *Young*, 1/39 (1993).
40. Judith Narrowe, *Under One Roof: On Becoming a Turk in Sweden*, Stockholm Studies in Social Anthropology, University of Stockholm, (1998).
41. Berg, 'Double normality', p. 43.
42. Malm, 'The Impact of Immigration'.

References

Akpinar, A. 'Challenged Family and Kinship Ideals: Family Crisis and Social Networks Among Turkish Immigrants', *Swedish Institute for Social Research Working Papers*, 10, Stockholm University (Stockholm, 1988).

———, 'Immigrant Experiences in Different Sociopolitical Settings', *Migration and Labour in Europe. Views from Turkey and Sweden*, MURCIR & NIWL (Istanbul, 2003) pp. 197–214.

Ålund, A. and Schierup, C.U., 'Prescribed Multiculturalism in Crisis', in Ålund, Aleksandra and Schierup, Carl-Ulrik (eds), *Paradoxes of Multiculturalism: Essays on Swedish Society*, Avebury Publishing (Aldershot, 1991).

———, 'Pathways of Social Exclusion; Youth in Multicultural Sweden', in *Perspectives of Multiculturalism – Western and Transnational Countries*, Unesco (Milan, 2004).

Başer, B., '"Death to Armenian Dogs": Turkish Ethno-politics causes Uproar in Sweden', Research Turkey http://researchturkey.org/death-to-armenian-dogs-turkish-ethno-politics-causes-uproar-in-sweden/ (accessed 19 April 2016).

Benito, M., *Active Civic Participation of Immigrants in Sweden*, Country Report prepared for the European research project POLITIS, Oldenburg (2005), Available at http://www.politis-europe.uni-oldenburg.de/ (accessed 20 April 2016).

Berg, M., 'Double normality: Reflections on style and Turkish second generation immigrants', *Young*, 1/39 (1993), pp. 39–50.

Camauër, L., 'Ethnic Minorities and their Media in Sweden. An Overview of the Media Landscape and State Minority Media Policy', *Nordicom Review* (2003).

Carey, J.P.C. and Carey, A.G., 'Swedish Politics in the Late Nineteen-Sixties: Dynamic Stability', *Political Science Quarterly*, 84/3 (1969), pp. 461–85.

Erder, S., *Refah Toplumunda Getto (A Ghetto in Welfare Society)*, Istanbul Bilgi University Publications (Istanbul, 2006).

Fegan, L., '10 Yıllık Deneyimin Düşündürdükleri', in *Yeni Birlik*, No. 5 (1988), pp. 8–10.

Freeman, G.P., 'Immigrant Incorporation in Western Democracies', *The International Migration Review*, 38/3 (2004), pp. 945–69.

Jaakkola, M., 'Informal Networks and Formal Associations of Finnish Immigrants in Sweden', in Rex John, Joly Daniele and Wilpert Czarina (eds), *Immigrant Associations in Europe*, Gower Publishing (Aldershot, 1987).

Knocke, W. and Ng, R., 'Women's Organizing and Immigration: Comparing the Canadian and Swedish Experiences' in Linda Briskin and Mona Eliasson (eds), *Women's Organizing and Public Policy in Canada and Sweden*, QC, McGill-Queen's University Press (Montreal, 1999), pp. 87–116.

Lindvall, J. and Sebring, J., 'Policy Reform and the Decline of Corporatism in Sweden', *West European Politics*, 28/5 (2005), pp. 1057–74.

Lundberg, I. and Svanberg, I., *Turkish Associations in Metropolitan Stockholm*, Centre for Multiethnic Research, Uppsala University (1991).

Malm, T., *'The Impact of Immigration on Europe's Societies, Sweden'*, Final Version, The European Migration Network, European Commission (2005).

Mengüç, A., *Sverige Jag Minns*, Daphne Publications (Istanbul, 2007).

Narrowe, J., *Under One Roof: On Becoming a Turk in Sweden*, Stockholm Studies in Social Anthropology, University of Stockholm, (1998).

Odmalm, P., 'Civil society, migrant organisations and political parties: theoretical linkages and applications to the Swedish context', *Journal of Ethnic and Migration Studies*, 30/3 (2004), pp. 471–89.

Sachs, L., *Evil Eye or Bacteria: Turkish Migrant Women and Swedish Health Care*, Stockholm Studies in Social Anthropology, University of Stockholm, (1983).

Schierup, C.U., 'The ethnic tower of Babel: political marginality and beyond', in Ålund, Aleksandra and Schierup, Carl-Ulrik (eds) *Paradoxes of Multiculturalism: Essays on Swedish Society* (Aldershot, 1991).

Schrover, M. and Vermeulen, F., 'Immigrant Organisations', *Journal of Ethnic and Migration Studies*, 31/5 (2005), pp. 823–32.

Shipper, A.W., 'Immigration Politics in Japan, Sweden, and the U.S.', *Paper presented at the annual meeting of the American Political Science Association*, (Chicago, 2007).

Soininen, M., 'The 'Swedish model' as an Institutional framework for immigrant membership rights', *Journal of Ethnic and Migration Studies*, 25/4 (1999), pp. 685–702.

Soysal, Y., *Limits of Citizenship: Towards a Post-national Membership in Europe*, University of Chicago Press (Chicago, 1994).

Wadensjö, E., 'Renumeration of Migrant Workers in Sweden', *International Labour Review*, 112/1 (1975).

Westin, C., 'Young People of Migrant Origin in Sweden', *The International Migration Review*, 37/4 (2003), pp. 987–1010.

CHAPTER 8

THE TRANSNATIONAL ACTIVISM OF THE KURDISH DIASPORA AND THE SWEDISH APPROACH TO THE KURDISH QUESTION

Bahar Başer, Idris Ahmedi and Mari Toivanen

Introduction

In this chapter, our aim is to scrutinise the Kurdish diaspora and the transnational activism and advocacy in which it engages in Sweden. Due to the scope of this book, our focus is specifically on Kurds from Turkey. At the same time, we want to emphasise that diaspora Kurds, especially in Sweden, have overcome the typical fragmentation that is characteristic of Kurdish identity and politics in the sending country and that the diaspora has managed to unite Kurdish communities from different parts of the Middle East.[1] This is, for instance, visible among second-generation Kurds in Sweden. Young Kurds imagine the unofficial Kurdistan divided between four states as a single homeland and refer to its various parts in terms of 'South Kurdistan' (Iraq), 'North Kurdistan' (Turkey), 'East Kurdistan' (Iran) and 'West Kurdistan' (Syria), respectively.[2]

Thus, in some situations Kurds can identify and act as one single nation in the diasporic space, regardless of the fact that Kurdish activism contains great diversity in terms of cultural and political constellations. Yet, given the geopolitical realities in the Middle East, the activism of Kurds from Turkey is mostly directed towards Turkey, albeit at times it is supported by Kurds from Iran, Iraq and Syria. The same observation applies to diaspora Kurds from other countries.

We find it particularly important to focus on the situation of Kurds in Sweden and to pay attention to their relatively distinct mobilisation patterns for a number of reasons. Firstly, it can be said that migration research from Turkey is very much focused on the Turkish community and this research literature rarely makes a differentiation between these two groups or their varied experience in Sweden. The Kurdish diaspora mobilises differently, manages different dynamics and constitutes a community with different interests to Turks in Sweden. While the Turkish diaspora very much continues to act as a state-linked diaspora that has organic links to the Turkish state, the Kurdish diaspora acts as a stateless diaspora while making borders of the Middle East fluid with its transnational connections to other Kurds from different regions of the Middle East and challenges the sovereignties of many Middle Eastern states at the same time. Theoretical frameworks and empirical evidence regarding the Turkish community in Sweden is not enough to explain the diasporic behaviour of the Kurdish community. Therefore, while analysing migration from Turkey, this fact needs to be underlined. Secondly, diaspora Kurds from Turkey have established a strong relationship with Sweden and Swedish politicians that has no equivalent in other European countries. For instance, Sweden became the first country to give material and non-material support to the diasporic activities of the Kurds, thus providing favourable conditions for linguistic and cultural development in the diaspora.[3] In comparison to Kurdish diaspora communities in other Western countries, the one in Sweden has been exceptionally vocal and assertive in the political sphere. This surely deserves more attention, especially when we compare the diaspora's situation with that in other countries such as Germany, where Kurdish activism is largely criminalised to the extent of being perceived as a security threat.[4]

Our aim is to contribute to this bourgeoning literature on migrant communities from Turkey and their diversity by focusing on the peculiarities of the Kurdish diaspora. Therefore, we strive not only to contribute to knowledge about the political and social situation of migrants from Turkey, but also to the literature on the Kurdish diaspora in a more general manner. The chapter proceeds as follows. We give a brief account of Kurdish migration from Turkey to Sweden. We will then focus on political mobilisation and cultural production by Kurdish diaspora members before finally discussing how the Kurdish cause has become accommodated in Swedish politics since the 1970s. We argue that political opportunities pertaining to prevalent ideas and material conditions, such as Sweden's commitment to international solidarity and generous funding of immigrant associations, account for the specificities of the Kurdish diaspora community in Sweden.

The Kurdish Diaspora in Sweden

In the 1970s a number of Kurdish migrants from Turkey, specifically from the Konya region, came to Sweden as labour migrants with the first waves of migration.

Particularly after the 1971 coup in Turkey, the number of Kurdish immigrants from Turkey rose significantly. Furthermore, several Kurds were accepted by the country with a refugee status and this increased after the 1980 Turkish coup d'état. During this period, the Kurds fled the chaotic atmosphere of oppression, non-recognition and persecution that they were facing in Turkey.[5] After their settlement, they became mobilised, yet differently in comparison to the Turkish community, due to their initial motivations for migration. Indeed, they managed to raise the profile of the Kurdish community in Sweden by becoming visible not only in political circles but also in the media and on other civil society platforms.

Given that Sweden has traditionally pursued a generous refugee policy, it has been relatively easier for Kurds than for Turks to enter the country. For this reason, Sweden has always been a favourable destination for Kurds. Compared to other European countries, Sweden has the highest percentage of political refugees compared to labour migrants. Today, the Kurdish population in Sweden is mainly concentrated in the cities of Stockholm and Uppsala. There are also a significant number of Kurds who live in Malmö, Gothenburg, Örebro, Linköping and Västerås.[6] It is challenging to cite accurate figures with respect to the number of Kurds from Turkey in Sweden; however, according to some estimates there are between 50,000 and 60,000 Kurds in the country, with diverse historical and geographical backgrounds.[7]

During the 1980s and 1990s, there was a systematic oppression of Kurdish activists in Turkey, which, in some cases, was combined with torture and extrajudicial killings. The PKK (Kurdistan Workers' Party) launched an armed struggle against the Turkish state in 1984 and after this date the Kurdish movement gradually transformed itself into a social movement that now enjoys great support both in the homeland and in the diaspora. The intensification of the conflict between Turkey and the PKK led to a mobilisation among many Kurds, who had not previously been active in politics. In countries such as Germany or France, this meant a significant awareness-gaining process in terms of politicised identity[8]; however in countries such as Sweden, which predominantly accepted asylum seekers, who were already politically active, the intensification of the conflict changed the power dynamics among different groups more than anything else.

In comparison to other diaspora groups, the Kurdish one is often portrayed as a highly political one, and not least in Sweden, where the country's political realities and developments have opened up new possibilities for political engagement and cultural production. There are several important Kurdish figures who have produced a great deal of information and material, thus raising the awareness of the Swedish public to the events taking place in Turkey. From 1974 until the 1990s, the late Mahmut Baksi and his Swedish wife, Elin Clason, played an important role in that regard. In 1974 Baksi authored a book entitled *Den kurdiska frågan* [the Kurdish Issue], and later, Baksi's nephews, Kurdo Baksi and Nalin Pekgul, played significant roles as public figures and politicians. In his capacity as a journalist, Kurdo Baksi wrote on the Kurdish issue in the Swedish press, whereas Nalin Pekgul became the first member of the Swedish parliament of Kurdish origin, where he served from 1994 till 2002. In recent years, new generations have played important roles in shaping public opinion in favour of the Kurdish issue. Among them are the celebrated author and journalist Mustafa Can, the pop singer Diba Demirbag, the columnist Sakine Madon, the Member of Parliament Gulan Avci, and the stand-up comedian Özz Nujen, who constantly bring up the Kurdish issue in their political/ journalistic or artistic production.

Kurds have managed to preserve their positive image in Sweden for a lengthy period of time. However, some issues have cast a shadow over the public image of the Kurdish community in the country. Many researchers, including Khalid Khayati[9], mention cases of honour killings and the assassination of Olof Palme as the definitive reasons for the emergence of negative perceptions of Kurds in Sweden. Firstly, the image of the Kurds suffered serious damage with the assassination of the former Prime Minister, Olof Palme.[10] Hans Holmér, Chief of the special investigation unit working on Palme's case, suspected that the PKK had been involved in the assassination. Its members in Sweden were interrogated, while some were put under surveillance and even suffered harassment at the hands of the police.[11] Since the assassination remains unsolved, no apology has been issued to the Kurds, despite the fact that many Kurdish activists have demanded an official apology for their unfair treatment. Secondly, the death of Fadime Sahindal, who was killed by her father, sparked a debate about the issue of honour killings. Given the brutal nature of the killing and the fact that Fadime Sahindal, prior to her death, had spoken openly about her situation to the Swedish media, her murder became something of a watershed in how Kurds were perceived in the country. Prior to Fadime's murder, the Kurds' public image was largely based on their situation as an oppressed people, one fighting for its rights in repressive states such as Iran, Iraq, Turkey and Syria. After the murder, Kurds were portrayed as being primitive, with the Kurdish culture condoning honour killings. While honour-related violence had traditionally been associated with migrant communities of Turkish, Persian and

Arab origins, in the aftermath of this incident it became exclusively associated with Kurdish culture. In one piece in the Swedish daily *Dagens Nyheter* in 2002, the headline, alluding to Uppsala, read: 'Mordet på Fadime: Ett Kurdistan i miniatyr' (*The Murder of Fadime: A Kurdistan in Miniature*).[12] Other newspaper articles also suggested that the negative image engendered by the honour killing cases still lingers.[13] In addition, Khayati[14] observes that mainstream Swedish political parties have a tendency to relate crime to the perpetrator's ethnic background, thus making it even harder for Kurds to contest the association of honour killings with Kurdish culture, and to ameliorate their public image in Sweden. However, it seems that this brand of stereotyping has not influenced the way the 'Kurdish Question' is approached in Sweden on a political level. Neither has it hindered the Kurds from gaining political support for the Kurdish cause despite the fact that some misgivings remain.[15]

The situation of Kurds in Sweden does not differ from that of other immigrant groups when it comes to assessing challenges related to integration and discrimination. Although their public visibility largely alludes to the observation that they are fully integrated into Swedish society, research has shown that they still face difficulties concerning integration. The majority of Kurds in Sweden live in segregated housing areas or suburbs that are usually populated by other ethnic groups than Swedes. Although there are several examples of Kurds successfully entering Swedish politics, business and other spheres of society, integration problems related to discrimination continue to persist. A prominent study conducted by Minoo Alinia[16] demonstrates that Kurds are satisfied with the political and social opportunities that they have in Sweden, although they still suffer from everyday racism and segregation in the labour market.

Furthermore, in their encounters with some Turks, Persians and Arabs, Kurds also face social attitudes prevalent in Turkey, Iran, Syria and Iraq, which involve either subtle or overt practices of hostility toward and stigmatisation of the Kurds as 'primitive' to outright denial of Kurdish identity. While it is true that the diaspora provides a breathing space or a safe haven for Kurds to express their identity without fear, relations of power and subtle practices of stigmatisation and belittlement of the Kurds nevertheless persist in the diaspora. It is noteworthy that Kurdish youth born and raised in Sweden experience this in their interactions with their peers of Persian, Turkish and Arab origin in various social settings.[17]

Kurdish Political Mobilisation and Cultural Production in Sweden

Similar to many other stateless diaspora groups such as Tamils or Palestinians, Kurds have been highly active in terms of establishing associations and being vocal in the political sphere. While these political and cultural efforts have ensured the preservation of the Kurdish identity and traditions in diaspora, they have also enabled their transmission to second-generation Kurds. Sweden has also adopted rather supportive policies that have enabled the cultivation of the Kurdish identity via supporting civil society organisations and other similar migrant associations. For instance, as early as the 1980s, an umbrella organisation for all Kurdish organisations – the Federation of Kurdish Associations in Sweden (*Kurdiska Riksförbundet*, KRF, more on this organisation below) – was formed and subsequently officially recognised by the Swedish government.

In the 1970s, Sweden mostly welcomed Kurdish intellectuals, who were already politically active and belonged to Kurdish political movements other than the PKK. For instance, the first arrivals did not initially sympathise with the PKK, and some even tried to keep it at a distance. Indeed, most of the Kurdish political organisations in Sweden had a clear political orientation and (albeit unofficially) had pre-established links to political movements in Kurdistan. Hence, it is impossible to conclude that the conditions in Sweden would have suddenly homogenised the Kurdish community. Furthermore, although some members of the Kurdish community changed their perceptions in later years, they still constituted a separate stratum of the Kurdish movement, known as the 'Swedish School' (İsveç Ekolü), which placed a strong emphasis on the cultivation of the Kurdish culture and language besides political activities. On the other hand, the diaspora members who sympathised with the PKK founded their own associations, which gradually grew larger as a result of time and energy invested in the recruitment process.

Regarding the transnational activities of Kurdish immigrants, Sweden is an interesting case as its profile of Kurdish diaspora differs from that of other European countries. Comparatively speaking, the country hosts a highly educated Kurdish intelligentsia consisting of journalists, authors, academics, artists and directors.[18] In addition, Sweden became a safe haven for Kurds fleeing state oppression in the Middle East, thus granting them an opportunity to engage politically, but also to cultivate their culture through the preservation of their traditions and their mother tongue, the use of which was highly criminalised in Turkey. Van Bruinessen[19] emphasises that Kurdish writers found Sweden 'a much more stimulating environment for developing Kurdish into a modern literary language than they would have found back in Turkey, even if the language had not been banned there'. He has also pointed out that it was in Sweden that 'A true revival of Kurmanji [one of the two main dialects in Kurdish, spoken predominantly by Kurds in Turkey] literature' took place. In the first comprehensive study on Kurdish literature in Sweden by Tayfun[20] it is argued that the significance of this development for Kurdish literature becomes even more apparent if one compares the number of books published in Turkey and Sweden. Between the period from 1925 to 1980, only 20 books in Kurdish were published in Turkey. From 1971 until 1997, 109 books in Kurdish were published in Turkey. During the same period, that is 1971–97, 402 books in Kurdish were published in Sweden. One of the most prominent Kurdish authors, Mehmet Uzun's[21] words about Sweden are also very telling. In an interview he stated that the Kurdish diaspora is different in character in Sweden because it has the capacity to bring all Kurds from different parts together. He also underlined the importance of the Kurdish language, how it has flourished in Sweden and how he has witnessed support and empathy for his work in the country.[22] As these experiences of prominent figures in the diaspora show, Sweden was perceived as a positive environment for expressions of Kurdish identity and the related cultural production. In 1998, Tayfun[23] also noted that 'the number of books in Kurdish published in Sweden had surpassed the number of books published in Turkey and other European countries.'

The opportunities that the diaspora found in Sweden were also conducive for enhancing visual media capabilities. Today, Kurdish television channels and a number of radio stations broadcast from Sweden, which is also home to three main Kurdish umbrella organisations with international and transnational networks, and several publishing houses that promote Kurdish culture and ideas.[24] The Swedish government has also financed the publication of books in Kurdish since the early 1980s, being the only country to have offered such opportunities for Kurdish cultural production at that time. The government sponsored the Kurdish library in Stockholm and several Kurdish publishers in Sweden have together published thousands of books and journals, thus drawing attention to the Kurdish cause and its cultural and linguistic dimensions. For instance, the children's book *Zaroken Ihsan* (*Ihsans barn*, Ihsan's child), by Mahmut Baksi, was the first Kurdish-language children's book published in Europe, back in 1978. Since 1981, Kurdish children have been granted the right to receive education in their mother tongue (called 'hemspråksundervisning' in Swedish) for a few hours a week after regular school time. Children's books were translated from Swedish to Kurdish to that end. However, when the first Kurdish day-care with Kurdish staff was established in Tensta, a Stockholm suburb, in 1985, Turkish officials reacted irritably by reminding their Swedish counterparts that in the constitution of Turkey, it is stated that the country only has one language.[25] Several children's books were subsequently published in Kurdish and smuggled to Turkey.[26] In 2007, a controversy broke out when a Kurdish translation of one of the most well-known Swedish children's books by Astrid Lindgren, *Pippi Långstrump*, was seized by the Turkish customs authorities. Eventually, a ministry-level involvement in Sweden resolved the issue.[27] This example demonstrates how intertwined Kurdish cultural production and politics is, even in diaspora.

As we have seen, Kurdish activism in Sweden has traditionally focused more on linguistic and cultural issues from a nationalist perspective. Among the Kurdish migrants in Sweden, there were influential figures – authors, singers, and public intellectuals – who placed importance on the promotion of Kurdish cultural and linguistic production and its visibility in the public sphere. Hence, Kurdish activism took the form of literary publications that aimed for language standardisation and emphasised the distinctiveness of Kurdish culture with regards to Turkish, Persian, or Arab influences.[28] Language, however, was, and continues to be, a major area of struggle in determining minority-majority relations in the Kurdish diaspora.[29] Tayfun writes that a state's 'cultural policy can serve the goal of either extinguishing or vitalizing a particular culture,' implying that the two strategies have been pursued by Turkey and Sweden, respectively, towards Kurdish culture.[30] Irrespective of whether this has been a deliberate policy on the part of the Swedish state, Tayfun's research on state funding for publications in the languages of immigrant groups demonstrates that 'Kurdish authors and publishing houses have been more lucky compared to other immigrant groups in Sweden in receiving a greater share of the funding in support for literature in the languages of immigrant groups and minorities.'[31]

Besides cultural production, political activism associated with an awareness of the situation that the Kurdish minority faces in the homeland was also transmitted to the next generations. The second generation is more integrated into Swedish society than their parents, but at the same time they express interest and dedication to the Kurdish cause, making them interested simultaneously in both homeland and hostland politics. The younger Kurdish generations in Sweden have developed a 'hybrid' identity in that they view themselves as Swedes and Kurds. However, political developments in the various parts of Kurdistan resonate with the collective memory of oppression and resistance, thus resulting in a highly politicised identity among Kurdish youth in Sweden. Many express a desire to raise awareness concerning the oppression of the Kurdish people as well as to shape Swedish public opinion in favour of the Kurdish cause.[32]

Main Kurdish diaspora organisations

The main Kurdish umbrella associations in Sweden include: The Federation of Kurdish Associations in Sweden (*Kurdiska Riksförbundet*, KRF), the Council of Kurdish Associations in Sweden (*Kurdiska Rådet*), and KOMKAR-Swed (*Svensk-Kurdiska Arbetarföreningen*). Created in 1981, the KRF has around 42 affiliated associations. It is one of the oldest and probably the largest Kurdish organisation in the country, and describes itself as religiously and politically independent. Their mains aims include the organisation of integration-related activities, providing more information on Kurds and Kurdistan as well as fighting against discrimination.[33] It has between 8,500 and 9,000 members[34] with independent women's and youth organisations.[35] Focusing on language, identity and cultural policies related to Kurds, they emphasise that they are the only Kurdish organisation in the world that brings together Kurds from all parts of Kurdistan.

The Council of Kurdish Associations in Sweden is aligned with the PKK and is a member of the European-wide umbrella organisation called KONKURD. Founded in 1994, it has more than 20 affiliated organisations.[36] The Council frequently organises demonstrations and seminars that focus on raising awareness of the on-going situation of Kurds in Turkey.[37] Recently, these activities have focused on the on-going violent conflict that is taking place in south-east Turkey.

In 1976, KOMKAR-Swed was established with organic links to the Kurdish socialist party founded by Kemal

Burkay.[38] It focuses mostly on integration-related issues and cultural events and activities, including activities for youth and children.[39] As the youth branch of KOMKAR, Komciwan (Kurdish Children and Youth Association) organises youth events and formulates projects that aim to both facilitate integration into Swedish society and to cherish the Kurdish identity. Komciwan was founded in 1998 in Stockholm and has since presented itself as Sweden's principal organisation, providing information on and promoting Kurdish culture. It initially offered folk dance lessons but, due to high demand, it expanded its activities to sports and the arts taught by professional instructors.

The most active Kurdish youth organisations in Sweden are the Federation of Young Kurds (*Riksförbundet UngKurd Sverige*) and the Association for Kurdish Students and Academics (*Kurdiska Student- och Akademikerföreningen*, KSAF). Politically the most active youth group, the Federation of Young Kurds, is a second and third-generation Kurdish organisation that aims to organise and mobilise Kurdish youth in Sweden. It is a platform that works to solve issues of integration, equality, solidarity and education. The union currently has five member organisations in Sweden: Stockholm, Uppsala, Gothenburg, Örebro and Borlänge. In 2007, the first local association was formed in Stockholm; by 2009 they had founded a Congress of Young Kurds that encompasses different associations across Sweden.[40]

The Association for Kurdish Students and Academics was founded in Stockholm in 2002, and several umbrella organisations were founded in 2009. Their website claims that the association and its branches are politically and religiously independent. As stated by its members, their goal is to bring together Kurdish and Kurdistan-interested persons through various activities, such as cultural activities that focus on Kurds and Kurdistan. In addition, members are committed to attract attention on the Kurdish issue. Its activities are mostly academic and cultural, targeting the younger generation of those with a Kurdish background in Sweden, but they have also worked in cooperation with the Social Democratic Students of Sweden (*Svenska socialdemokratiska student förbundet*, SSF).[41] Today, local associations are present in almost all university cities in Sweden, including Linköping, Örebro, Stockholm, Uppsala, Väst and Scania. WeKurd, an organisation founded by second generation Kurds, was mainly active between 2004 and 2008.[42] The organisation compiled a ballot paper including all the Kurdish candidates who stood at the 2006 local, regional and national elections. They also sent out questionnaires to the main Swedish political parties to shed more light on their views on the Kurdish Question.[43]

The Swedish public space created a conducive environment for members of the Kurdish diaspora to express themselves free from oppression and restrictions. The Swedish context undoubtedly provided a positive environment to a migrant from Turkey seeking a better life within this welfare state. However, the situation of the Kurds differs immensely when it comes to political and cultural opportunities. Many authors have argued that opportunity structures in the host country determine diaspora groups' mode of actions.[44] As Odmalm pointed out: 'The modes of migrant organisational action is facilitated or constrained by the incorporation pattern that the host country chooses, the opportunity structures that it grants to the migrant community and the institutional form that the host state has in terms of making immigrants formal partners in the decision making mechanisms'.[45] Therefore, the *political opportunity structures* are of particular importance in terms of diaspora mobilisation and claims-making in a receiving country. Different host countries provide different opportunities for diasporas that come from the same homeland, and host countries might also provide different opportunities for different diaspora groups. The Kurdish diaspora, similarly to the Assyrian diaspora, found an environment to further their language and culture without fear. This situation was combined with freedom of speech and association, which enabled the Kurdish community to recover their self-confidence as a nation and to embrace Sweden and Swedish political culture more than other groups that did not establish such a strong connection with the host state and its society. Kurdish groups found a transnational space where they were able to get together with each other without the interference of borders and foster their multiple identities, which also include Swedishness. To conclude, we can say that the diaspora space has provided all Kurdish groups with a platform, not only to overcome the political fragmentation, but also one for undoing the effects assimilation measures had had on Kurdish populations. Sweden meant a new page for many, the beginning of a new life.

The Swedish Approach to the Kurdish Question in Sweden

The Swedish approach to the Kurdish Question has oscillated with the changing political landscape in Sweden. Olof Palme, who was the long-standing leader of the Swedish Social Democratic Party, made a considerable impact on how the Swedish state, as well as the public, perceived international conflicts. He became known as a defender of the third world as he explicitly distanced himself from major political actors by supporting liberation movements. He was indeed characterised by many as a true internationalist. Palme's foreign policy priorities were centred on sustaining peace in the world, and he spent his life supporting movements in different global regions, ranging from Cuba to South Africa. As Johansson and Norman[46] have argued, he 'set his stamp' on Swedish foreign policy, and his perspective is evident in the Social Democratic Party's (*Socialdemokraterna*) programme from 1975 onwards. Under the heading: 'All People's Freedom, the Whole World's Peace', the Social Democratic Party declared its support for 'self-determination for every nation' in the pursuit of a just world order.[47] Palme believed that Sweden had a special mission to support liberation movements in the third world, help the 'oppressed' and spread the message of international solidarity – not for reasons of self-interest for Sweden but for the sake of humanity.[48]

The former president of the Kurdish association (*Federasyona Komaleyen Kurdistan Li Swede*), Keya Izol, stated in an interview with Bahar Başer[49] that he believed Palme followed the Kurdish mobilisation in Sweden with utmost interest and sympathy. According to him, Palme visited their associations and demonstrations after 1980 and gave his full support to events organised in Sweden. Similar to this testimony, in another interview with Başer[50] the president of the Kurdish Women's Association, Seyran Duran, also acknowledged Palme's legacy and stated that both Palme and the former Foreign Minister Anna Lindh[51] made the Kurdish diaspora in Sweden feel more self-confident and secure in its status. For example, Lindh supported the establishment of the Kurdish library in Stockholm, which was inaugurated by the Minister of Culture Marita Ulvskog on October 10, 1997.[52] Exactly four years later Lindh herself visited the library and gave a speech where she discussed developments in the Middle

East and the Kurdish issue.[53] During an EU-summit in Cologne in 1999, when other EU foreign ministers wanted to grant Turkey candidate status, Lindh opposed the proposal and succeeded in persuading the other foreign ministers to postpone the issue. This prompted the *Financial Times* to declare Lindh 'Turkey's public enemy number 1', which was also picked up by the Swedish media.[54] Sweden was one of the most vocal supporters for Turkey becoming a member of the EU. However, Lindh believed that Turkish membership of the EU should be contingent on its respect for human rights. As Niklas Orrenius of the Swedish daily *Dagens Nyheter* summarised ten years after her death:

Turkey represents a clear-cut case of Anna Lindh's courage and advocacy for human rights. No one can claim that she was soft on Turkey. She supported the Kurds' struggle and demanded that they should be allowed to speak their own language. She irritated the Turkish political establishment by having lunch with Kurdish mayors in Ankara. ('Sexismen kom som en käftsmäll för Anna Lindh', *Dagens Nyheter*, January 1, 2014).[55]

Kurdish activists benefitted from this positive Swedish approach towards their cause and got involved in projects related to the Kurdish situation in the Middle East. Certain Kurdish activists saw these political opportunity structures in Sweden as a chance to muster Kurds from Iran, Iraq, Syria, and Turkey and started mobilising in diaspora spaces. However, other activists lent their support to the PKK, which followed a different strategy through a more radical approach that they considered as the only viable path to a definitive solution of the Kurdish Question. The PKK organised fundraising

Kurds and Turks erupted in Stockholm in 2015 as a result of resumed hostilities between the Turkish army and the PKK in the summer of 2015.[65] On February 13, 2016 a Kurdish man was severely wounded during a Kurdish demonstration in Stockholm after having been shot at by unknown persons. Swedish police believe the attack was politically motivated. Analysts voiced their concern that the ongoing conflict in Turkey could have spill-over effects on Sweden.[66]

Secondly, the Swedish perception of liberation movements, human rights and linguistic rights in general has been a factor determining the degree of support for the Kurdish movement. Kurdish activists benefitted from this approach and took advantage of the opportunities enabled by Swedish policies. Integration into Swedish society was prioritised through entering different sectors of the society, for instance spheres related to media, art, cinema, literature, and academia. Therefore, in the public sphere, the Kurdish movement does not have criminal connotations, but relies rather on a successful image construction. For instance, it is quite common to see Swedish participants at Kurdish festivals, gatherings, or political meetings. Also representatives from all Swedish political parties attend the yearly event on the anniversary of the Republic of Kurdistan established in Iranian Kurdistan on 22 January 1946. Indeed, the Kurdish cause has met with varying support across the entire Swedish political landscape from left to right since the 1970s.[67]

The Kurdish Question in Swedish politics

By the 1970s, Turkey's Kurdish Question had already become an issue in parliamentary discussions, even before the PKK-affiliated associations were established in Sweden. At times, Swedish parliamentarians debated the

Kurds and Turks erupted in Stockholm in 2015 as a result of resumed hostilities between the Turkish army and the PKK in the summer of 2015.[65] On February 13, 2016 a Kurdish man was severely wounded during a Kurdish demonstration in Stockholm after having been shot at by unknown persons. Swedish police believe the attack was politically motivated. Analysts voiced their concern that the ongoing conflict in Turkey could have spill-over effects on Sweden.[66]

Secondly, the Swedish perception of liberation movements, human rights and linguistic rights in general has been a factor determining the degree of support for the Kurdish movement. Kurdish activists benefitted from this approach and took advantage of the opportunities enabled by Swedish policies. Integration into Swedish society was prioritised through entering different sectors of the society, for instance spheres related to media, art, cinema, literature, and academia. Therefore, in the public sphere, the Kurdish movement does not have criminal connotations, but relies rather on a successful image construction. For instance, it is quite common to see Swedish participants at Kurdish festivals, gatherings, or political meetings. Also representatives from all Swedish political parties attend the yearly event on the anniversary of the Republic of Kurdistan established in Iranian Kurdistan on 22 January 1946. Indeed, the Kurdish cause has met with varying support across the entire Swedish political landscape from left to right since the 1970s.[67]

The Kurdish question in Swedish politics

By the 1970s, Turkey's Kurdish Question had already become an issue in parliamentary discussions, even before the PKK-affiliated associations were established in Sweden. At times, Swedish parliamentarians debated the

Kurdish situation in Swedish society by underlining that Sweden should condemn the repression and assimilation policies towards the Kurds in Turkey.[68] In a parliamentary speech in 1979, Oswald Söderqvist, the foreign spokesman of the Communist Party (*Vänsterpartiet Kommunisterna*, today's Left Party), addressed the conflict from a leftist perspective and highlighted that the Kurdish nation's statelessness is closely linked to the oppressive measures that the Kurdish minorities face in their respective countries.[69] Several Swedish politicians also considered that the Kurds had experienced historical injustice, since the borders of the Middle East had been drawn without taking them into consideration. Politicians frequently followed the news from the Middle East and supported Kurdish activists, either by taking their concerns to parliament, giving political support, or facilitating asylum applications. Parliamentary discussions touched upon the issues related to political prisoners throughout Turkey and the oppression of the Kurdish identity. Various politicians demanded that the Swedish government adopt a strong stance concerning these issues.[70] For instance, the matter concerning the state of emergency in the Kurdish regions of Turkey provoked left-wing Swedish politicians to condemn Turkey on several occasions. A number of Swedish politicians also tried to draw the UN authorities' attention to the Kurdish Question.

In the 1980s, the decision to label the PKK as a terrorist organisation sparked a heated debate in parliament, with numerous parliamentarians being against the decision.[71] Although the strategies employed by the PKK were not condoned, the motivations behind their acts were interpreted in the context of the Turkish oppression of the Kurdish population and the harsh measures the Turkish military had used after the 1980 coup d'état. Several of them addressed parliament in efforts to draw attention to the forced displacement of Kurds from their villages by the Turkish government and demanded the Swedish parliament take a strong political stance condemning Turkey for its behaviour.[72]

At the end of the 1980s and during the 1990s, the intensification of the conflict in Turkey echoed into the diaspora spaces. Sweden harshly criticised Turkey in the context of the EU membership negotiations. Turkey's application to join the EU, the Copenhagen criteria, and minority rights were frequently brought up in parliamentary discussions in Sweden whenever Turkey and its aspirations to join the EU became the topic of discussion.[73] For instance, the Social Democrats brought up human rights abuses committed by Turkey with a motion they presented in the Swedish parliament in 1996, drawing attention to the forced evacuation of villages by the army as well as to documented torture cases in Turkish prisons. They also gave the examples of South Africa, Northern Ireland and Chechnya, stating that peaceful negotiations were needed to solve such problems.[74] In fact, Sweden became one of the leading countries to criticise human rights abuses in Turkey.

In the early 2000s, Sweden became one of the strongest supporters of Turkish accession to the EU, and many Swedish politicians made speeches about the benefits of Turkey's membership. The underlying motivation for this was the belief that membership would contribute to Turkey's democratisation processes, particularly concerning minority rights.[75] On the other hand, Turkish–Swedish relations were in their golden era, with greater cooperation, and several trade agreements were signed between the two countries. There have also been many diplomatic meetings between Sweden and Turkey, especially since the AKP came to power. In the first decade of the millennium, better diplomatic relations were cemented by visits to Turkey by the former Swedish Prime Minister Göran Persson in 2004, Swedish King Carl XVI Gustaf and Queen Silvia in 2006, followed by the Swedish Prime Minister in 2009. Simultaneously, the main Kurdish political party in Turkey (at that time the BDP) had strong relations with leftist parties in Sweden. Aside from the Social Democratic Party (*Socialdemokraterna*), which has been a supporter of Kurdish rights for decades, the Left Party (*Vänsterpartiet*), in particular, became known as the most Kurdish-friendly political party in Sweden. For instance, the Left Party MP, Jacob Johnson, visited Turkey in the summer of 2010 and declared that the PKK should be taken off the US and EU list of terrorist organisations. He also organised a press conference in Diyarbakir to discuss the current situation of the Kurds in Turkey.[76]

In terms of the Turkish approach to Kurdish mobilisation in Sweden, Turkey has, unsurprisingly, been less than pleased by Swedish support for the Kurdish cause. Turkish politicians have made various appeals to the Swedish authorities to curb the PKK's activities on Swedish soil. To Turkey's relief, Sweden was obliged to outlaw the PKK due to EU policies, and Sweden's official recognition of the PKK as a terrorist organisation followed the 2002 decision by the EU Council to place the organisation on its list of terrorist groups. Over the last couple of years, frustrated by a perceived lack of action, several Turkish politicians have declared that Sweden should be more aware of PKK mobilisation in Sweden and highlighted the fact that the PKK is still on the EU terrorist list.[77]

Nearly all political parties in Sweden have expressed criticism of the Turkish state's treatment of its Kurdish population; however, their level of support shifts, depending on the position of parties on the right-left spectrum and their engagement with Kurdish groups on a voter basis. In recent years, centre-right political parties have attracted Kurdish voters and some Kurds have become members of these parties. This may in part reflect the emergence of a Kurdish middle class in Sweden as well as the fact that the Kurds have become a significant constituency, thus catching the attention of the liberal and conservative parties. The liberal party, *Folkpartiet* (which has changed its name to *Liberalerna* in 2015), has had two members of parliament of Kurdish origin, Gulan Avci until 2010, and Ismail Kamil until 2014. Liberalerna's former spokesperson on foreign policy, Fredrik Malm, is well-known for his prolific writing on the Kurdish issue in the press as well as for the motions he has put down in parliament. For example, Malm pioneered the creation of a leaflet 'Demands of the Liberal Party Regarding Kurdistan and the Kurdish Question' that was distributed to native Kurdish voters before the elections in September 2010. The leaflet condemned Turkey's failure to improve Kurdish rights in the country. It also demanded that investigations be carried out in Turkey regarding the use of chemical weapons against PKK fighters.[78] Together with the former Integration Minister, Erik Ullenhag, Malm also took the initiative as an individual politician and signed a bill calling for a coordinated Swedish policy towards Kurdistan to protect Kurdish rights in the region. It states: 'The people of Kurdistan have the right to self-determination – in the form of federalism, autonomy or local self-government'.[79]

The conservative Moderate Party (*Moderaterna*) strongly supports Turkish membership of the EU, yet it frequently makes remarks on minority rights issues in Turkey, reminding the Turkish authorities about the Copenhagen criteria. They also strongly criticise the PKK for its violent acts. They have good relations with the AKP government and gave support to AKP's 'Kurdish opening'. Their 'good relations' with Turkey means the Kurdish diaspora has distanced itself from the *Moderaterna*. When Carl Bildt from *Moderaterna* was the country's foreign minister, there was almost no sign of support for the Kurds. This changed when Margot Wallström, from the Social Democrats, became the foreign minister. Wallström not only received the de facto foreign minister of the Kurdistan regional government, Falah Mustafa Bakir, on January 12, 2015,[80] but also the leader of the pro-Kurdish HDP party, Selahattin Demirtas, in mid-August 2015,[81] as an acknowledgement of Kurds as a significant political actor that has the potential to contribute towards democratic developments in Turkey.[82]

In April 2015, Sweden joined the international coalition against the Islamic State (IS) by sending troops specifically to train the Peshmerga in Iraqi Kurdistan. 'We have responded to the Iraqi government's request and we want to contribute through training and advice primarily to the Peshmerga-units', Wallström stated to the press.[83] When clashes between the Turkish military and PKK erupted in the summer of 2015, Wallström was one of the first European leaders to call for a ceasefire and the resumption of the peace process.[84] When the offices of the HDP party were attacked in Turkey prior to the 2015 elections, Wallström called Demirtaş, to express her concern over the deteriorating security situation.[85] In recent years, the Kurds' pivotal role in the fight against Islamic State (IS) has resulted in Swedish support for the Pershmerga and positive coverage in the Swedish media of the Syrian-Kurdish Peoples Protection Units, YPG, and their female fighters.[86] Recent events in Turkey have further mobilised the Kurdish diaspora as well as Swedish politicians who have called for an end to the curfew imposed in South-Eastern Turkey as well as for a resumption of peace negotiations.[87]

Conclusion

By focusing on Kurdish immigrants from Turkish Kurdistan or Turkey, this chapter discussed the cultural and political participation of the Kurdish diaspora as well as its mobilisation in Sweden. We wish to highlight four intertwined factors that have played a role in this regard. Firstly, structural opportunities, ideational as well as material, in the host country enable the diaspora groups to mobilise for political gains as well as for cultural production. There has been a strong emphasis on international solidarity in Swedish foreign policy and support for oppressed peoples; there have also existed political parties that have been willing to consider the political dimension of the Kurdish issue, initially the Left Party (*Vänsterpartiet*) and later the Liberal Party (*Liberalerna*), while central political figures such as former Foreign Minister, Anna Lindh of the Social Democratic Party (*Socialdemokraterna*), played a pivotal role in putting violations of the human rights of Kurds in Turkey on the political agenda. The Swedish state has also provided generous funding to immigrant associations, which they have used for the mobilisation of their community members. A number of Kurdish associations, such as the Federation of Kurdish Associations in Sweden (*Kurdiska Riksförbudent*), capitalised on this opportunity, while Swedish funding for Kurdish literature and culture have been of great significance. Secondly, while Kurds from Turkey originally came as labour immigrants, many politically active Kurds fled to Sweden following the coup in 1980, thus bringing with them the skills and determination to mobilise their fellow Kurds in Sweden. Thirdly, the Kurdish movement in Turkey became stronger after 1984 when the insurgency started, in effect leading to a politicisation of Kurdish diaspora communities, including the one in Sweden. Finally, evaluating the sending country's internal dynamic and political situation is essential to better understand the diasporic mobilisation and how the political developments back home become reflected in such mobilisation processes. In particular, the shifting political situation in Turkey, specifically concerning the Kurdish issue, has throughout recent decades been reflected in the ways the Kurdish diaspora in Sweden organises and mobilises politically.

Until recently, there had been no violent mass encounters between Turks and Kurds in Sweden, and pro-Kurdish demonstrations have generally been conducted in a peaceful manner without ending in interventions by the police. However, this seems to have changed, as clashes between Kurds and Turks have erupted in Sweden as a result of resumed hostilities between the Turkish army and the PKK in the summer of 2015. Therefore, as long as the conflict in Turkey continues or further deteriorates, there is no guarantee that it will not have a spill-over effect in Sweden. Over the years, calls supporting the Kurds' quest for human rights, including basic cultural and linguistic rights, in Turkey have increased in Sweden. Given the sizable number of Turks and Kurds in Sweden and the possible effects of the conflict, Sweden might find itself to have yet another incentive to be engaged in the Kurdish Question.

Notes

1. Abbas Vali, 'The Kurds and their Others: Fragmented Identity and Fragmented Politics', *Comparative Studies of South Asia, Africa and the Middle East.* 18/2, *(1998).* Bahar Başer, *Diasporas and Homeland Conflicts: A Comparative Perspective*, Ashgate Publishers, (Farnham, 2015).
2. Idris Ahmedi, 'Identitetens olika skepnader: Kurdiska ungdomar, "identitetspolitik" och globalisering', in Maria Borgström and

Katrin Goldstein-Kyaga (eds), *Gränsöverskridande i globaliseringens tid*, Huddinge, Södertörns högskola, (2006).

3. Martin Van Bruinessen, 'Shifting national and ethnic identities: the Kurds in Turkey and the European diaspora', *Journal of Muslim Minority Affairs*, 18/1 (1998), pp. 39–52. Ann-Cathrin Emanuelsson, 'Transnational Dynamics of Return and The Potential Role of the Kürdish Diaspora in Developing the Kürdistan Region', Defence Academy of the United Kingdom, (2008). Lisa Pelling, Post-Remittances? On Transnational Ties and Migration Between the Kurdistan Region in Iraq and Sweden. PhD Thesis, University of Vienna, (Vienna, 2013).

4. Bahar Başer, 'Tailoring Strategies According to Ever-Changing Dynamics: The Altering Image of the Kurdish Diaspora in Germany', *Terrorism and Political Violence*, (2015), DOI: 10.1080/09546553.2015.1060226.

5. Charles Westin, 'Young people of migrant origin in Sweden', *The International Migration Review*, 37/4 (2003), p. 992.

6. Khalid Khayati, Diasporian Kurds in Sweden as transnational citizens. World Congress of Kurdish Studies, Erbil, 6–9 September, (2006).

7. Hamit Bozarslan, 'Kemalism, Westernization and Anti-Liberalism', in H.-L. Kieser (ed.), *Turkey Beyond Nationalism: Towards Post-Nationalist Identities*, I.B.Tauris, (London, 2006), pp. 27–34.

8. Başer, 'Tailoring Strategies'.

9. Khalid Khayati, *From Victim Diaspora to Transborder Citizenship? Diaspora Formation and Transnational Relations among Kurds in France and Sweden*. (Doctoral dissertation). University of Linköping, (Linköping, 2008).

10. For more information on this investigation see: http://citeseerx.ist. psu.edu/viewdoc/download?doi=10.1.1.471.7241&rep=rep1& type=pdf. (accessed 20 November 2016).

11. See more also on the Ebbe Carlsson Affair: http://articles.chicagotri bune.com/1988-08-30/news/8801260630_1_ebbe-carlsson-prime-minister-olof-palme-social-democrats (accessed 20 November 2016).

12. See: http://www.dn.se/arkiv/nyheter/mordet-pa-fadime-ett-kurdistan-i-miniatyr (accessed 20 November 2016).

13. See http://rudaw.net/turkish/world/020720154 (accessed 20 November 2016)

14. Khayati, 'From Victim Diaspora', pp. 224–6.

15. Başer, 'Diasporas and Homeland Conflicts'; Pelling, 'Post-Remittances?'

16. Minoo Alinia, 'Spaces of diasporas: Kurdish identities, experiences of otherness and politics of belonging', *Studies in Sociology 22*, Department of Sociology, Göteborg University, (Göteborg, 2004).

17. Ahmedi, 'Identitetens olika skepnader'.
18. Khalid Khayati, 'Behind the line of disintegration. Practices of transborder citizenship among diasporan Kurds in Sweden', in Erica Righard, Magnus Johansson and Tapio Salonen (eds), *Social Transformations in Scandinavian Cities: Nordic Perspectives on Urban Marginalisation and Social Sustainability*, 265–80, Nordic Academic Press (Sweden, 2015).
19. Martin van Bruinessen, The Kurds in movement: Migrations, mobilisations, communications and the globalisation of the Kurdish Question. Working paper no. 14, Islamic Area Studies Project, (Tokyo, 1999).
20. Mehmet Tayfun, *Kurdiskt författarskap och kurdisk bokutgivning: Bakgrund, villkor, betydelse*, Apec Förlag, (Stockholm, 1998), p. 42.
21. Mehmet Uzun, *Bir Dil Yaratmak*, İthaki Yayınları, (Istanbul, 2012), p. 254.
22. For further information, see another interview with Uzun: http://www.dn.se/arkiv/nyheter/sondagsintervjumehmed-uzun-rosten-turkiet-vill-tysta (accessed 20 November 2016).
23. Tayfun, '*Kurdiskt författarska*, p. 42.
24. Martin Bak Jorgensen, National and transnational identities: Turkish identity in Denmark, Sweden and Germany. Unpublished PhD Thesis, Spirit series no. 19, (2009), p. 223.
25. Tayfun, '*Kurdiskt författarska*, p. 44.
26. See: http://wwwc.aftonbladet.se/kultur/0005/08/landet.html (access 20 November 2016)
27. See: http://www.svd.se/turkiska-tullen-slappte-pippi-bocker (access 20 November 2016).
28. Tayfun, '*Kurdiskt författarska*'.
29. Nesrin Ucarlar, *Between majority power and minority resistance: Kurdish linguistic rights in Turkey*, Unpublished PhD thesis, Lund University, (2009).
30. Tayfun, '*Kurdiskt författarska*', p. 60.
31. Ibid.
32. Ahmedi, 'Identitetens olika skepnader'.
33. For more info see: http://www.fkks.se/default.aspx?lang=2 (access 20 November 2016).
34. Khayati, 'Victim Diaspora', p. 232.
35. Jorgensen, 'National and Transnational Identities'.
36. Khayati, 'Victim Diaspora'; Jorgensen, 'National and Transnational Identities'.
37. See: http://www.kurdiskaradet.se/ (accessed 20 November 2016).
38. See: http://www.komkar.se/filer/haluk_intervu.htm (accessed 20 November 2016).

39. See: http://www.komkar.se/index_s.htm (accessed 20 November 2016).
40. Başer, 'Diasporas and Homeland Conflicts'.
41. Khayati, 'Behind the line of disintegration', p. 274.
42. Ibid.
43. Ibid.
44. Yasemin Soysal, *Limits of citizenship: Migrants and postnational membership in Europe*, University of Chicago Press (Chicago, 1994). Pontus Odmalm, 'Turkish organisations in Europe: How national contexts provide different avenues for participation', *Turkish Studies* 10/2, (2009), pp. 149–63.
45. Pontus Odmalm, 'Civil society, migrant organisations and political parties: Theoretical linkages and applications to the Swedish context', *Journal of Ethnic and migration studies*, 30/3, (2004), p. 475.
46. Alf W. Johansson and Torbjorn Norman, 'Sweden's Security and World Peace', in *Creating Social Democracy*, eds Klaus Misgeld, Karl Molin, Klas Amark. Penn State University, (USA, 1992), p. 365.
47. Ibid.
48. Johansson and Norman, 'Sweden's Security', p. 366.
49. Başer, 'Diasporas and Homeland Conflicts'.
50. Ibid.
51. Anna Lindh was a prominent figure in the Social Democrat Party. In her youth, she was the chairman of the Social Democratic Youth League from 1984 to 1990, a member of parliament from 1982 to 1985 and Foreign Minister of Sweden from 1998 to 2003. She was murdered in 2003.
52. See: http://kurdlib.org/history/ (access 20 November 2016).
53. See: http://sverigesradio.se/sida/artikel.aspx?programid=2200& artikel=588595; citation from her speech (accessed 20 November 2016).
54. For more info see: http://www.aftonbladet.se/ledare/sondagsrosten/ emineonatli/article10487626.ab (accessed 20 November 2016).
55. 'Sexismen kom som en käftsmäll för Anna Lindh', *Dagens Nyheter*, 1 January 2014, http://www.dn.se/nyheter/politik/sexismen-kom-som-en-kaftsmall-for-anna-lindh/ (accessed 1 August 2017).
56. Aliza Marcus, *Blood and belief: The PKK and the Kurdish fight for independence*, New York University Press, (New York, 2007).
57. Ibid, pp. 89–95.
58. See: http://www.dn.se/arkiv/kultur/mannen-som-trotsar-pkk-jag-ville-inte-bli-medbrottsling and http://www.aftonbladet.se/ nyheter/fralagen/article12029649.ab (accessed 20 November 2016).
59. Jan Bondeson, *Blood on the Snow: The Killing of Olof Palme*, Cornell University Press, (USA, 2005).

60. See: http://www.nytimes.com/1987/06/14/world/feuds-of-turkish-kurds-spilling-over-into-europe.html?pagewanted=all (accessed 20 November 2016).
61. According to Bondeson, the reason for such a decision was the possibility of torture and prosecution in case they were delivered to the Turkish authorities, regardless of the cooperation between Turkish and Swedish intelligence services regarding PKK activities in Sweden (Bondeson, *Blood on the Snow* 2005) p. 89.
62. Michael Gunter, 'Transnational sources of support for the Kurdish insurgency in Turkey', *Conflict Quarterly*, 11, (1991), pp. 7–29.
63. See: http://www.dn.se/arkiv/nyheter/rattegangen-mot-ocalan-vaxande-stod-for-pkk-i-sverige-i (access 20 November 2016).
64. Bahar Başer, 'Diasporas and Imported-Conflicts: The case of Turkish and Kurdish Second Generation in Sweden', *Journal of Conflict Transformation and Security*, Vol. 3, No. 2, (2013), pp. 105–25.
65. See: http://www.dn.se/nyheter/sverige/polisen-utreder-samband-mellan-attentat-mot-turkiska-och-kurdiska-lokaler/ (accessed 20 November 2016).
66. See: http://www.svd.se/finns-risk-att-konflikten-trappas-upp (accessed 20 November 2016).
67. See: https://www.riksdagen.se/sv/Dokument-Lagar/Forslag/Motioner/om-stod-at-det-kurdiska-folket_GB02U521/?text=true (accessed 20 November 2016) Swedish MPs create a parliamentary network for Kurdistan, KRG, 25.3.2006: http://cabinet.gov.krd/a/d.aspx?r=95&l=12&a=10058&s=&s=010000 (accessed 20 November 2016).
68. Riksdagens protokoll 1979–80: 66.
69. Ibid.: 47.
70. Ibid.: 159.
71. Riksdagens protokoll 1989–90: 90.
72. Ibid.: 85.
73. Motion 2003/04: U286; Motion 2007/08: U307; Motion 2015/16: 1497.
74. Motion 1996/97: U634.
75. Fredrik Langdal, 'The Swedish debate on Turkey's prospects for EU membership, in Turkey, Sweden and the European Union', Experiences and Expectations, SIEPS, (Stockholm, 2006), p. 20.
76. 'Johnson'dan çözüm önerisi', *Yüksekova Haber*, 2 July 2010. Available at http://www.yuksekovahaber.com/haber/johnsondan-cozum-onerisi-33244.htm (accessed 10 June 2016).
77. 'Turkey Expects More from Sweden to Counter PKK', *Hurriyet Daily News*, (accessed 12 June 2012). http://www.hurriyetdaily news.com/default.aspx?pageid=438andn=turkey-expects-more-from-sweden-to-counter-pkk-2011-05-23.

78. Başer, 'Diasporas and Homeland Conflicts'.
79. Ibid.
80. See: http://www.regeringen.se/artiklar/2015/01/wallstrom-tog-emot-utrikesrepresentanten-for-krg/ (accessed 20 November 2016).
81. See: http://www.regeringen.se/artiklar/2015/08/margot-wallstrom-tog-emot-selahattin-demirta/. (accessed 20 November 2016).
82. See: http://www.hurriyetdailynews.com/Default.aspx?pageID=238&nid=88338, (accessed 20 November 2016).
83. See: http://www.aftonbladet.se/nyheter/article20597905.ab. (accessed 20 November 2016).
84. See: http://www.svd.se/sverige-uppmanar-turkiet-att-varna-vapenvi lan/om/kriget-i-syrien. (accessed 20 November 2016).
85. See: http://www.hurriyetdailynews.com/Default.aspx?pageID=238&nid=88338. (accessed 20 November 2016).
86. For more information see: http://www.svd.se/kvinnornas-krig-tar-aldrig-slut-7v4M, (accessed 20 November 2016).
87. Motion 2015/16: 1497.

References

Ahmedi, I., 'Identitetens olika skepnader: Kurdiska ungdomar, "identitetspolitik" och globalisering', in Gränsöverskridande i globaliseringens tid, Maria Borgström and Katrin Goldstein-Kyaga. Huddinge, Södertörns högskola, (eds), (Sweden, 2006).

Alinia, M., 'Spaces of diasporas: Kurdish identities, experiences of otherness and politics of belonging', Studies in Sociology 22, Department of Sociology, Göteborg University, (Göterborg, 2004).

Başer, B., 'Diasporas and Imported-Conflicts: The case of Turkish and Kurdish Second Generation in Sweden', Journal of Conflict Transformation and Security, 3/2 (2013), pp. 105–25.

———, Diasporas and Homeland Conflicts: A Comparative Perspective, Ashgate Publishers (Franham, 2015).

———, 'Tailoring Strategies According to Ever-Changing Dynamics: The Altering Image of the Kurdish Diaspora in Germany', Terrorism and Political Violence, (2015) DOI: 10.1080/09546553.2015.1060226.

Bondeson, J., Blood on the Snow: The Killing of Olof Palme, Cornell University Press, (USA, 2005).

Gunter, M.M., 'Transnational sources of support for the Kurdish insurgency in Turkey', Conflict Quarterly, 11 (1991), pp. 7–29.

Johansson, A.W., and Norman, T., 'Sweden's Security and World Peace', in Creating Social Democracy, Klaus Misgeld, Karl Molin and Klas Amark (eds), Penn State University, (USA, 1992).

Jorgensen, M.B., National and transnational identities: Turkish identity in Denmark, Sweden and Germany, Unpublished PhD Thesis, Spirit series no. 19, (2009).

Khayati, K., 'Behind the line of disintegration. Practices of transborder citizenship among diasporan Kurds in Sweden', in *Social Transformations in Scandinavian Cities: Nordic Perspectives on Urban Marginalisation and Social Sustainability*, Erica Righard, Magnus Johansson, Tapio Salonen, (eds), Nordic Academic Press, (Lund, Sweden, 2005), pp. 265–80.

——, Diasporian Kurds in Sweden as transnational citizens. Presentation at the World Congress of Kurdish Studies, Irbil, (6–9 September, 2006).

Langdal, F., The Swedish debate on Turkey's prospects for EU membership, in Turkey, Sweden and the European Union. Experiences and Expectations, SIEPS, (Stockholm, 2006).

Odmalm, P., 'Turkish organisations in Europe: How national contexts provide different avenues for participation', *Turkish Studies*, 10/2 (2009), pp. 149–63.

——, 'Civil society, migrant organisations and political parties: Theoretical linkages and applications to the Swedish context,' *Journal of Ethnic and migration studies*, 30/3 (2004), pp. 471–89.

Pelling, L., Post-Remittances? On Transnational Ties and Migration Between the Kurdistan Region in Iraq and Sweden. PhD Thesis, University of Vienna, (Vienna, 2013).

Soysal, Y.N., *Limits of citizenship: Migrants and postnational membership in Europe*, University of Chicago Press, (Chicago, 1994).

Tayfun, M., *Kurdiskt författarskap och kurdisk bokutgivning: Bakgrund, villkor, betydelse*, Apec Förlag, (Stockholm, 1998).

Uzun, M., *Bir Dil Yaratmak*, İthaki Yayınları, (Istanbul, 2012).

Van Bruinessen, M, The Kurds in movement: Migrations, mobilisations, communications and the globalisation of the Kurdish question. Working paper no. 14, Islamic Area Studies Project, (Tokyo, Japan, 1999).

——, Transnational aspects of the Kurdish question. Working paper, Robert Schuman Centre for Advanced Studies, European University Institute, (Florence, 1999).

——, 'Shifting national and ethnic identities: the Kurds in Turkey and the European diaspora', *Journal of Muslim Minority Affairs*, 18/1 (1998), pp. 39–52.

Westin, C., The effectiveness of settlement and integration policies towards immigrants and their descendants in Sweden. Migration branch, ILO, Geneva. International migration papers 34, (2000).

——, Young people of migrant origin in Sweden, *The International Migration Review*, 37/4 (2003), pp. 987–1010.

CHAPTER 9

IN SEARCH OF A NEW HOME: THE ASSYRIAN DIASPORA IN SWEDEN

Aryo Makko

Introduction

The majority of the people that established the Assyrian diaspora in Sweden in the late 1960s and early 1970s were labour migrants and political refugees from the Tur Abdin region in south-east Turkey.[1] Over the course of the recent decade or so, the community has attracted considerable scholarly and public interest beyond Sweden's borders.[2] A recent cause for this interest is its growth resulting from the influx of war refugees from Iraq and Syria. In 2008, international media reported with bafflement that the Swedish city of Södertälje, located about 35 kilometres south of Stockholm, sheltered more refugees than the United States.[3] This earned the city's major, Anders Lago, an invitation to speak before the Congress in Washington DC, where he also visited Barack Obama and shared his experiences and opinions with US officials. This was, however, not the first time that Sweden's Assyrian community made headlines abroad. The reasons for this are manifold and more diverse: in certain areas, the community has helped to realise the multicultural vision held in high esteem by many Swedish (and other European) politicians since the 1970s through exceptional achievements in politics, sports and business life. Two of its football clubs, Assyriska FF and Syrianska FC, have played in the *Allsvenskan*, the first tier of Sweden's football league system and the country's equivalent to the German *Bundesliga* or the English Premier League. In 2003, Assyriska were only one win away from reaching the UEFA Cup Qualifiers when they lost the Swedish Cup Final to Elfsborg IF.[4] Since 2010, there has been a record high of six members of parliament of Assyrian background from four different political parties. The most prominent politician is Social Democrat Ibrahim Baylan, who was a member of the Persson and Löfven administrations as Minister for Schools (2004–6) and has been the acting Minister for Energy since 2014. The community is also overrepresented on regional (*län*) and local (*kommunal*) levels. In 2006, a total of 140 Assyrian candidates ran for 174 political posts in Sweden.[5] Four years later, in March 2010, the Swedish parliament voted in favour of acknowledging the incidents that occurred in the Ottoman Empire during the World War I as genocide. To a large extent, this was the result of the political lobby work carried out by the local Assyrian community.[6] Assyrians are also widely acknowledged as successful entrepreneurs, mostly (but not exclusively) in the restaurant and service sectors.[7] At the same time, Assyrians have become equally known for gang violence and organised crime. One of the first organised Swedish street gangs involved in public shootings and murders in the early 1990s, 'Original Gangsters' (commonly known as 'OG') from Gothenburg, was established by Assyrian immigrant Denho Acar, who acted as leader until he was forced to escape the Swedish legal authorities and flee to Turkey. OG is still active, using the Assyrian flag as its logotype, which members have to wear as a tattoo. In 2010, the Swedish authorities launched a combined effort by the police, law enforcement and tax authorities, the so-called *'Operation Tore 2'*, to break up the *Södertäljenätverk* (Södertälje Network), a criminal organisation engaged in the abuse of welfare services, illegal banking services and money laundering, illegal gambling, match-fixing, the sale of illegally acquired goods as well as protection rackets and extortion rackets.[8] Experts have compared the network to the Italian mafia and Swedish police travelled to Italy to attempt to learn from the experiences of the Italian authorities.[9] The Swedish authorities' efforts have resulted in the most expensive criminal investigation in Swedish legal history resulting in 50 court cases and 65 persons being sentenced to a total of 166 years and 10 months of jail.[10] There are no reliable statistics but it is estimated that more than 120,000 Assyrians live in Sweden today, which makes them one of the largest immigrant communities in the country.

The aim of this chapter is to give an overview of the history of the Assyrian diaspora in Sweden and offer an explanation for the reasons for its successes and failures. Based on primary sources and the literature, and departing from a theoretical framework on the various dimensions of integration, the chapter will argue that the rather heterogeneous character of the community results from the fact that its social and emotional integration remains flawed. Despite the fact that they constitute a large part of the diaspora from Turkey in Sweden and elsewhere, they are usually overlooked in Turkish studies in general, and in studies of the Turkish diaspora in particular.[11]

Drawing on the work of Emilé Durkheim, Max Weber and David Lockwood, German sociologist Hartmut Esser

Table 9.1 Integration (*Sozialintegration*) according to Esser

Acculturation	Placement	Interaction	Identification
Acquisition of knowledge and cultural skills, including the language	Occupation of (professional or societal) positions and the provision of rights (citizenship, electoral rights etc.)	Establishment of social relations in daily life	Emotional devotion towards a social system or society (e.g. 'We-feeling', national pride etc.)
Cultural integration	**Structural integration**	**Social integration** (*Soziale integration*)	**Emotional integration**

explains integration (*Sozial integration*) as a process comprising of four elements: *acculturation, placement, interaction* and *identification*. Acculturation is defined as the acquisition of knowledge and skills such as the language of the receiving country or social skills allowing immigrants to integrate culturally. Successful acculturation paves the way for immigrants to place themselves in society, for example by taking up certain positions in the labour market, the housing market or the marriage market. Applying the human capital gained through successful acculturation and placement, interaction on a daily basis may result in social integration (*soziale integration*) and, through identification with the receiving society, even in emotional integration.[12]

Much of the existing research has focused on the first two aspects mentioned above, acculturation and placement, whereas interaction and particularly identification remain under researched issues.[13] At the same time, it is well known that lack of interaction and identification with the receiving society; often resulting from racially motivated spatial segregation, lie behind failing integration.[14] Therefore, this author argues that in order to understand the successes and failures of the Assyrian diaspora in Sweden, we need to integrate interaction and identification in our analysis.

The Early Years: Alienation and the Revival of Nationalism

The first group of Assyrian immigrants came to Sweden from Lebanon in 1967. It consisted of 205 individuals, which had been granted asylum by the Swedish government upon a request from the World Council of Churches and the UNHCR (United Nations High Commissioner for Refugees) the year before. The majority of the members of that group had roots in the Mardin and Sirnak provinces in south-eastern Turkey; others came originally from Syria and Iraq. Between 1972 and 1976, another 50 Assyrians migrated to Sweden as part of the abovementioned decision. The community grew twenty-fold during the second half of the 1970s, numbering about 9,000 by the end of the decade. The growth resulted from a combination of political refugees from Turkey and *Gastarbeiter* from West Germany who chose Sweden as their destination in search of security and improved socio-economic conditions and often entered the country with the help of organised traffickers. Sweden's generous welfare benefits, its tolerant integration policies and its image as a humanitarian country were the major pull factors complementing push factors such as the harsh working conditions in West German factories and rising tension in Turkey following the 1971 military coup and the 1974 Cyprus crisis. The immigration wave sparked off a fierce public debate in which conservative critics warned about the dangers of an 'Assyrian invasion'. The Swedish government did not consider the Assyrians met the criteria defined in the 1951 Refugee Convention, but nevertheless passed new legislation in November 1976, which granted collective amnesty and permanent residence permission to everyone who had made it to Sweden and established new visa requirements in order to reduce the influx of refugees.[15] More than 4,000 Assyrians settled in Södertälje by the early 1980s, transforming the hometown of famed tennis player Björn Borg into an important centre of the Assyrian diaspora.[16] Today, after several migrant waves following the outbreak of war in Iraq and Syria, the number of Assyrians in Sweden is estimated between 100,000 and 120,000. There are no reliable statistics available due to the fact that the Swedish authorities register the citizenship of immigrants rather than their ethnicity.[17]

The 1960s and 1970s were a period of unrest among Assyrian migrants from Turkey. After decades of oppression during the Republican era, nationalist ideas adopted by Assyrian intellectuals in the Ottoman Empire prior to the World War I regained momentum in diaspora. This resulted both from the freedoms granted in the West and the meeting with Assyrians from countries who had allowed a greater level of social and cultural activities such as Syria and Iraq. As a result of this resurgence, sociocultural institutions promoting nationalist ideas and political goals were established all over Sweden through the course of the 1970s. In addition to Södertälje and other municipalities near Stockholm, cities like Gothenburg, Jönköping and Norrköping became home to newly arrived Assyrians. This resulted in the foundation of umbrella organisations such as the Assyrian Federation of Sweden (*Assyriska Riksförbundet i Sverige*, ARS) in 1977.[18] Today, ARS represents some ten thousand members organised in more than 30 local associations.[19] Between 1978 and 2006, ARS published *Hujådå magazine* in four languages: Swedish, Assyrian (Syriac), Turkish and Arabic.[20] It contained various materials such as leading articles dealing with political, economic and sociocultural issues, activity reports from local Assyrian associations, but also letters and poetry from readers. The publication reflects both the identity and ideology of the community, and how they have changed over time, but has not been studied thoroughly by historians.

The Assyrian identity established in Sweden comprised of three elements: traditional (Eastern) Christianity, a newly recovered sense of ethnicity and a feeling of belonging to the international labour movement. The first issue of *Hujådå* nicely illustrates the way in which the first generation immigrants viewed their identity. The editorial team's first lead article explained that 1 May

(1978) had been chosen as the publication date because it combined Labour Day with the Easter celebration of the Syriac Orthodox Church. It stated that the ARS 'congratulates our people and the Swedish people in honour of these occasions' and encouraged Assyrian workers to express solidarity with the Swedish working class and contribute to Sweden's political and economic well-being. It was the aim of the new magazine, wrote the editors, to enlighten the Assyrians about Swedish society in order to help them with this task.[21] The issue also contained the first part of a longer article series entitled 'We are Assyrians historically, geographically, linguistically and culturally' written by well-known writer and poet Yuhanon Qashisho (1918–2001), the magazine's original editor-in-chief.[22] The article described the history of the Assyrian people as a continuity from ancient times to modernity in a popular scientific fashion and criticised the (Syriac Orthodox) church for its usage of Arabic, Turkish and Kurdish.[23] Although none of this was new, as mentioned earlier, these were revolutionary statements provoking fierce reactions from various directions. Middle Eastern regimes disliked the revival of ethnic nationalism, even if it declared that its goals were social and cultural rather than political, as it reminded them about the territorial claims presented to the Paris Peace Conference in 1919 by Assyrian delegations.[24] When the Republic of Turkey came into existence in 1923, Patriarch Ignatius Elias III (Shaker) and the leadership of the Syriac Orthodox Church quickly adapted to the minority politics of Ankara in order to avoid renewed oppression.[25] The clergy felt vindicated by the expulsion of Apostolic (Nestorian) and Chaldean Assyrians from Hakkari in 1924–5 by the new Turkish government and by the Simele massacre of August 1933. It tightened measures and ordered its followers to abandon all notions of ethnic identity and Assyrian heritage in the following decades.[26] This resulted in conflicts between the patriarchate and the early diaspora communities of the United States where the Assyrian name had been in use for both people and church since the 1890s.[27]

In the early Swedish diaspora of the 1970s, nationalism and the identification with ancient forefathers was not limited to elite groups, as some have suggested.[28] In terms of identity, the gap was not between educated and illiterate or rich and poor but rather between young and old Assyrians. While the former reconstructed their identity upon arrival in diaspora, the latter stuck with their traditional self-perception based on religion and kinship. This fact also expressed itself in various readers' letters to *Hujådå*. In one poem entitled 'Who am I?' and published in one of the early issues in 1978, an anonymous refugee took a metaphoric approach, comparing his own situation to the state of the nation which, the poem read, had been 'befallen by darkness since the fall of Nineveh' (the capital of ancient Assyria).[29]

Assyrian identity was also openly viewed as opposed to Turkey and Turkishness. There were two main reasons for this: firstly, the Assyrian perception of a recent past dominated by genocide, discrimination and exclusion, and secondly, the view of some nationalist groups that the Assyrian area of settlement was occupied by Turks. This expressed itself repeatedly. In October 1978, the Assyrian association of Södertälje boycotted the *Temadagarna* (Theme days), a multicultural festival organised by Södertälje municipality because the official poster of the event had used a Turkish flag to represent the town's Assyrian population. In its statement on the boycott, the Assyrians referred to the fact that their members weren't exclusively from Turkey but also from Iraq, Syria and Lebanon, adding that:

Assyrians are forced into flight by the oppression and persecution they are subjected to in Turkey. Therefore, the municipality should have shown greater understanding for the absence of the Assyrian association because everything related to the country that has oppressed people and forced them to flee can be very sensitive to individuals. *Södertälje kommun* should neither have missed the fact that although the Assyrians do not have a country of their own, they possess a flag of their own of which they are very proud.[30]

The boycott of the festival occurred shortly after the Turkish government had ordered the closure of two Assyrian monastic schools in the Mardin region that were accused of cooperating with Armenian and Greek nationalists.[31] Together with the increasing political violence in Turkey, such negative events deepened the rift between the Assyrian diaspora and its old country.

When Turkish Prime Minister Bülent Ecevit visited Stockholm in December 1978, he disappointed the local Assyrian immigrants further by claiming publicly that they had left his country for economic reasons, because the development programme of his party hadn't yet reached their area of settlement and in order to liberate themselves from the feudalism that dominated their community.[32] This wasn't the first time Ecevit turned out to be a disappointment in the eyes of the Assyrians. For obvious reasons, the Assyrians sympathised with leftist ideologies and Ecevit and his Republican People's Party (*Cumhuriyet Halk Partisi*, CHP) had become bearers of hope when they adopted social democracy in 1960. Eventually, however, the CHP's attempt to combine social democracy with Kemalism proved of little significance to the country's minorities.[33] To many

Assyrians, the murder of Andreas Demir Lahdik, the mayor of Kerboran/Dargeçit, in 1979 and the 1980 coup d'état were the final nail in the coffin crushing any hopes for progress. When a delegation from the Swedish (social democratic) youth organisation *Unga örnar* (Young Eagles) visited Assyrian areas of Turkey in March 1979, it concluded that 'hostility is everywhere in Turkey. ... there is real horror, especially among the Assyrians, but also in the country at large. The Assyrian population lives outlawed in Mardin and is easy prey to anyone.'[34] As a result, the Assyrians turned away from Turkey and Turkish politics and focused on the challenges posed by daily life in the Swedish diaspora.

Assyrian ethnic identity was also defined as part of the international labour movement and its struggle towards the liberation of oppressed peoples and viewed as opposition, and as a reaction, against Turkish and Arab nationalism. Its socialist element expressed itself in various ways, such as the use of Marxist history and rhetoric. Catchwords such as 'solidarity' and 'production goods' were popular and so was the issuing of resolutions and declarations of socialist character. The Assyrians also sought cooperation with similar groups. One example is their participation in a demonstration, held on 12 August 1978 in Stockholm, which requested asylum for political refugees and was carried out together with the local Committee for Chile (*Chilekommittén i Stockholm*), the Swedish-Kurdish Workers Association, the Colombia Committee, the Iranian Leftist Students Association, the Association Peru Bulletin and the Cultural Association Simon Bolivar.[35] An editorial published as a commemoration of the centennial jubilee of the Labour Day compared the victims of the Haymarket affair in Chicago to the martyrs of the Assyrian people and ended full of pathos with the words 'long live the unity between the working class and the oppressed peoples and their common struggle!'.[36] Drawing from this ideological background, nationalism was described as a 'humanitarian feeling' aiming at the survival of peoples living under oppression and which had to be separated from fascism.[37]

Attempting to (re)develop the own identity between Assyrian nationalism and Swedish internationalism had ambivalent effects on the integration of the immigrants in Swedish society. In theory, Sweden was a country of equality and justice *par excellence* and thus a perfect fit. Everyday life with ethnic Swedes, however, didn't meet the high expectations raised by that kind of idealised image. The large numbers of Assyrian refugees and the fact that many of them had travelled to Sweden illegally or resisted expulsion orders attracted heavy criticism from conservative and anti-immigrant circles. The Assyrians felt that the media had portrayed them as a group of illegal immigrants and criminals. This hampered the adjustment of the group to the new country.[38] Although Assyrian organisations responded with a combination of calling on their members to abide by the law and condemning discrimination against refugees and immigrants by the authorities, the debate continued for several years.[39] Some Assyrians went further in their criticism of Swedish racism. One reader of *Hujådå* claimed in a letter published in 1980 that 'in our home countries, we weren't fully accepted citizens. In Sweden, we aren't even fully accepted as human beings'.[40] These feelings were in conflict with the official picture drawn in the report of the Discrimination Commission (*Diskrimineringsutredningen*) in 1982, which asserted that the Swedish attitude towards immigrants and immigration was increasingly positive.[41]

During the early years, institutions like the ARS lobbied in favour of refugees whose expulsion had been ordered.

They drafted public statements and organised demonstrations in support of the refugees, gaining the support of some Swedish politicians and officials in the process.[42] Ethnic Swedes helped in addressing the asylum issue publically, such as Allan Björck, a former social affairs inspector, who wrote open letters to Foreign Minister Karin Söder (Centre Party) in which he described the authorities' deportation measures as a brutal and unjust manhunt, comparing them to dark episodes that had occurred during the 1930s.[43] In January 1980, Per Gahrton, a member of parliament, initially for the Liberals and later for the Greens, wrote an article in *Hujådå* in which he described Turkey as a country in crisis where Assyrians suffered from violence, lawlessness, economic crisis, Muslim resurgence and Kurdish nationalism. As a conclusion, Gahrton urged the Swedish government to accept as many as 10,000 Assyrian refugees.[44]

The Assyrians were thankful for this kind of support and the opportunities Sweden offered to them both as individuals and as a group. On many occasions, their organisations publically promised that the Assyrians would contribute to the well-being of Swedish society.[45] But there were limits as well: encounters with ethnic Swedes were not always friendly and the multicultural policies of the Swedish state were used in order to develop a strong Assyrian identity rather than tight bonds with Swedes and the Swedish nation, which could be linked to Esser's definition of emotional integration as 'emotional devotion towards a social system or society (e.g. 'We-feeling', national pride etc.)'. Ironically, at the time, Assyrians protested the fact that the authorities and public housing associations opposed segregation out of fear of ghettoisation. Referring to freedom of choice, equality and cooperation, the three goals defined in the government's principal declaration on migration policy and unanimously accepted in parliament in 1975,[46] ARS representative Besim Soysal (Aho) argued that this was a continuation of earlier assimilation policies.[47]

Another Swedish social worker, Gunilla Roxström, concluded that many Assyrians were heading in the wrong direction and argued that it was necessary to 'break the isolation'.[48] Controversy and segregation set boundaries for the integration of the Assyrians early on. The majority among them succeeded in terms of acculturation and placement but faced problems with regard to daily interaction and emotional integration. As expressed in the statement on the Assyrian boycott of the festival mentioned above, emotions were invested in the vitalisation of the ethnic identity instead, something the Assyrians had been prevented from doing in Turkey and their countries of origin:

> We Assyrians are refugees. We hide our faces, yet no one is without fail. Only one is infallible, he who lives and never dies. We, the young people, have to focus. Together we shall fight. We shall lead our people, in the struggle for our culture, for an Assyrian tradition.[49]

This turn away from complete integration into Swedish society and towards internal issues and the development of an Assyrian identity occurred in 1982–3 and was a result of the many critical voices raised against Assyrian immigrants by political parties, of media reports who portrayed them as criminals, and of political profiles such as diplomat Ingmar Karlsson who described them as economic refugees. Instead of the earlier emphasis on bonds between Assyrians and Swedes, the discourse shifted clearly towards narratives of isolation, otherness and frustration.[50] Many community members were absorbed by Assyrian activities such as annual summer camps, mother-tongue teaching and the increasingly intense conflict between the different fractions (the so-called *namnkonflikten* between *assyrier* and *syrianer*).[51]

This introspective thinking and the widening gap between successful acculturation and placement and less successful social integration and emotional integration expressed itself in various ways during the second half of the 1980s. When the younger members of the Assyrian Associations of Sweden elected a committee that would take up the task of founding a separate youth federation, none of the goals laid out for the future organisation was related to life in Swedish society.[52]

The ARS and its local member associations were initially of great benefit to the success of the early wave of Assyrian migrants to Sweden. They lobbied for political asylum, helped their members with administrative services such as applications for residence permits and social housing and offered a feeling of belonging through their social and cultural activities. They also helped to introduce the migrants to Swedish customs, laws and the country's labour market and entrepreneurial opportunities through publications and public seminars. In the 1970s and 1980s, *Hujådå* published official announcements by authorities such as the immigration agency (*Statens invandrarverk*, SIV) or Stockholm City Council (*Stockholms läns landsting*), which offered information about government benefits or free vaccination.[53] With this kind of work, ethnic organisations helped the migrants' integration in terms of acculturation and placement. Drawing up a generally positive picture of Sweden, sometimes in contrast to Turkey, they also laid a potentially fertile ground for the immigrants' identification with the new country and thus what Esser defines as emotional integration. This was, however, confronted by negative everyday encounters with ethnic Swedes and a rather critical public discourse which together with the Assyrians' victim mentality created a gap between the theory and reality of life in Sweden.

Successes and Failures of Multiculturalism: Assyrians from Sweden, Swedish Assyrians or Swedes with Assyrian Roots?

It is fairly correct to say that much of the more recent successes and failures of the Assyrian diaspora in Sweden are the result of the developments that occurred in the late 1980s and during the 1990s. During that period, the dissonance between successful acculturation and placement and less successful social and emotional integration became more obvious when expressed by the first Sweden-born generation. Naturally, the community faced new challenges such as alcohol and drug abuse, changing family structures, interethnic marriage, a decreasing interest in the seminars and camps arranged by Assyrian organisations and fears of the Swedish language replacing the own mother tongue. Politically, the Assyrians went through an identity crisis when social democratic hegemony finally came to an end in 1991. The identification with the Swedish and international labour movement decreased further and was replaced by a more introvert nationalism, a process symbolised by the murder of Olof Palme in February 1986. Palme had been the symbol of a different Sweden, the moral superpower that had offered the Assyrians shelter. Therefore, Palme's violent death shocked the community profoundly.[54] The enthusiasm of the first years of immigration, resulting from what many in the 1970s viewed as a promising future in one of the world's model societies, gave way to a more sober attitude once limits to the perceived opportunities made their presence felt.

The ARS described the growing struggle against younger Assyrians' alcohol consumption and drug abuse as a result of the 'emigration from a backward agricultural society to advanced industrialised societies in Europe, the United States and Australia'.[55] As a countermeasure, aiming to 'enlighten our youth, families and organisations about the importance of this problem', the Federation launched its first major campaign against narcotics abuse in 1987.[56] It became apparent that in the search for identity, the children of the immigrants looked in directions their parents hadn't anticipated. In an attempt to capture these changes, young university student Fuat Deniz, whose deep interest in these issues would result in his authoritative 1999 doctoral thesis in sociology, asked rhetorically 'where are we heading ...?'.[57] Deniz discussed the problems that the younger generation was facing, but also lauded the fact that life in diaspora had democratised family relations with communication, dialogue and the youth daring to criticise instead of the earlier attitude of absolute obedience towards the elderly. He also warned his readers that material things couldn't replace happiness, love and companionship and suggested that the community was 'in greater trouble than ever before. We feel lost in Swedish society, Swedishised (*försvenskade*) and insulted'.[58] Deniz and his generation, youngsters born or raised in Sweden, were stunned by the increasingly openly expressed racism of the early 1990s. One 17-year-old girl, born in Germany and raised in Sweden, reacted to the fact that her local newspaper published openly racist letters, and lamented the fact that many Swedes seemed to react negatively to the fact that immigrants were working their way up and gaining access to higher education and better jobs:

> Sweden is a democratic country so we cannot forbid them to say whatever they want but I mean ... how

disgusting can you be claiming that we immigrants are worse than animals!! ... They also complain about us coming here causing trouble, stealing and taking their apartments and jobs. ... Another thing that irritates me is that as long as immigrants have the worst jobs, they [the Swedes] say nothing but as soon as a foreigner gets an education and aims higher they go nuts (like animals) and backbite. ... Finally, I want to say that I'm proud to be Assyrian and immigrant and I don't care what the world's racists think. I am and remain an immigrant.[59]

Most of the enthusiasm for Sweden had vanished by the early 1990s, but there was no alternative to the Assyrians from Turkey as the situation in the old country worsened. Reports published in 1989 by visitors to the area expressed little hope for improvement and suggested that the exodus from Turkey to the West would continue due to the deteriorating security situation in the shadow of the war between the State and the PKK.[60] A series of murders perpetrated against the remaining Assyrians in south-eastern Turkey between 1990 and 1994 proved that the scepticism had been more than fearmongering.[61] The chairman of ARS blamed the Turkish authorities for failing to protect the remaining Assyrians of the region, or to at least carry out proper murder inquiries as the identity of the murderers and their motives remained unknown.[62] Interestingly, this didn't result in any kind of tension with the Kulu Turks of Sweden and the Turkish Federation of Sweden (*Turkiska Riksförbundet* or *İsveç Türk İşçi Dernekleri Federasyonu* in Turkish), with which the Assyrians maintained relatively friendly relations, partly as a result of cooperation within SIOS, the Cooperation Group for Ethnic Associations in Sweden (*Samarbetsorgan för etniska organisationer i Sverige).* This relationship deteriorated only when the genocide debate appeared a few years later.

The Assyrian response to the recurring violence and murder in Turkey and to discrimination in Sweden was a continuously introverted nationalism, communicated at social gatherings, weekend courses and summer camps that prioritised the teaching of Assyrian history and culture over dealing with issues related to integration into Swedish society.[63] An editorial, published in December 1996, described the decreasing interest in the promotion of Assyrian culture observed in many of the local associations around Sweden as 'national treachery'.[64]

The community also saw itself confronted with changing social structures being confronted with issues related to love, sex, relationships and intermarriage.[65] The Assyrians adapted ideas of gender equality rather quickly; partly in response to accusations of sharing the so-called 'honour culture' identified in the Kurdish and Yazidi communities in Sweden.[66] This resulted in some progress and the election of the first female presidents of a local association and the Federation in 1997 and 2001 respectively.[67] Eventually, the Assyrian Women's Federation (*Assyriska Kvinnoförbundet*, AKF) was founded as a separate organisation. In recent years, however, this process has somewhat stagnated with male actors dominating most Assyrian issues once again.

The second half of the 1990s witnessed a breakthrough in terms of placement that complemented the earlier success in the food service industry. Members of the Assyrian community took up the chairmanship of SIOS and *The Migrant's Federation* (*Migranternas Förbund*).[68] In 1998, social democrat Yilmaz Kerimo, originally from Midyat and a leading figure within the younger generation of the community, became the first ethnic

Assyrian member of the Swedish parliament.[69] Assyriska FF from Södertälje continued its rise through the country's football system and was only one goal away from promotion to the first tier in 1999. Andreas Arsalan, acting chairman of ARS, pointed out that this success was about much more than just football, an argument which most Assyrians were in agreement with at the time:

The successes of Assyriska, even if they are maybe unplanned and spontaneous, are proof of the capability of our people to achieve great things, if allowed to work in liberty and a goal oriented way. It is a fact that our people are still alive, although we've been without power and a state for 2,500 years, despite all mass murders, ethnic cleansings, forced conversions and the deprivation of its identity, among others. We have been able to establish ourselves better than any other immigrant group in this country socially, economically and in terms of education during the roughly 30 years that we've spent in Sweden.[70]

'The Winds of Change Blow Harder'

The new millennium has been an era of rapid change and polarisation for the Assyrian diaspora in Sweden. It has witnessed a fresh but more fragmented discourse on identity, changing perceptions of the political situation in Turkey and its other Middle Eastern countries of origin, as well as both the deterioration of traditional social structures and continued economic and political success. These developments have confirmed the earlier success in terms of acculturation and placement. They have also resulted in improved social integration but emotional integration still seems to be stagnating.

For the first three decades, the public debate among Swedish Assyrians in general and their discourse on identity in particular was the result of rather rigid socioeconomic structures allowing (individuals from) influential families to play important roles in associations and churches. This changed in the late 1990s and early 2000s when a new generation of educated individuals born or raised in Sweden challenged the dominance of those traditional elites. These circles consisted of journalists, university students, (future) politicians, artists and early career researchers. These groups took the successes of the first generation even further but seemed nevertheless to keep struggling with social integration, to varying degrees, and emotional integration in particular.

At an evaluation meeting of the establishment of an adult education centre (*Folkhögskola*) for the community in 1999, Denho Özmen, a schoolteacher and one of the leading figures behind the initiative, declared that 'we will take roots in Sweden, fresh roots'.[71] Özmen argued that integration and education were tied together and that it was imperative that the Assyrian community would not only be influenced by Swedish society but rather attempt to develop and work towards reciprocity in order to take part in shaping society as well.[72] A year later, Zeki Yalcin, a university student in political science and history who completed a doctoral degree in 2010, argued that much of the controversy between *assyrier* and *syrianer* resulted from the fact that the occidental type of nationalism based on ethnicity was not adaptable to an oriental community whose centre of gravity had been religion for more than two millenia.[73] Yalcin argued that Western-style nationalism had neither liberated the people from religious shackles nor unified them but rather created further division, hampering the younger generation's quest for identity in diaspora.[74] The earlier hegemony of churches and organisations like the ARS was not only challenged by individuals. On an organisational level, the emergence of a diasporic civil society contributed further to the change. Examples are lobby groups formed by a small number of active individuals, such as the *Assyrian Chaldean Syriac Association* (ACSA), or public and professional organisations such as the *Syrianska Assyriska Akademiker i Sverige* (SAAIS, Syriac Assyrian Academics in Sweden). This development created a more diverse and complex public discourse with the younger generation discussing current issues on online platforms such as the privately-owned *Turabdin Community* and consuming news provided by ACSA's TV show *Renyo hiro* (Free Thought) or independent news agencies like ESNA (Eastern Star News Agency).[75]

A 2003 lead article in *Hujådå* highlighted the fact that 'the winds of change are blowing harder', referring to an increasing number of active youth, the success of Assyrian teams and athletes in sports and the growing number of young adults choosing education over taking on their parents' businesses in the food service industry.[76] This description was limited to the activities of the Assyrian organisations, but it very much captures the general situation of the early 2000s. It also included, among others, gender equality expressing itself both in a growing number of women pursuing higher education, often in other cities which meant they would break an earlier taboo and leave the family home, and in the gradual acceptance of intermarriage.

Turkey and the Assyrian Diaspora since the 1990s

The relationship between the Swedish Assyrians and Turkey has been on a rollercoaster for more than a decade. After collapsing as a result of the violence of the early and mid-1990s, described above, it was revitalised mainly by two issues: the European Council's acknowledgement of Turkey as a candidate country for full EU membership at its December 1999 meeting in Helsinki and an intense debate about whether the massacres of 1915 constituted genocide following the public denial of local school teacher Jonas Linderholm from Södertälje.[77] The possibility of Turkey joining the EU raised high hopes among the members of the Assyrian diaspora communities. These hopes stretched from the mere recognition of an Assyrian presence in Turkey by Ankara to the possibility of returning to the native land. Initially, the prosecution of Yusuf Akbulut, a priest at the St. Mary's Church in Diyarbakir (the *Meryem Ana Kilisesi*), cast shadows on Turkey's reform path. Akbulut had spoken of 1915 as genocide in an interview with the Turkish newspaper *Hürriyet* in October 2000 and was charged with the incitement of religious or ethnic enmity according to paragraph 312 of the Turkish Penal Code.[78] Assyrian organisations in the Western diaspora made strenuous efforts, lobbying in their respective countries and attending the trial together with European members of parliament. They considered it a success of their own political efforts as well as a sign of progress in Turkey when Akbulut was cleared of all charges six months later.[79] By late 2001, Assyrians in Sweden started expressing renewed faith in the improvements occurring in Turkey.[80] This even resulted in a new wave of returnees from various European countries to the Turabdin area starting in 2005–6.[81] There were mixed voices with regard to the AKP's early years in government. Critics argued that Turkey was far from a being a liberal democracy that could be allowed to enter the EU.[82] Simon Barmano, the chairman of ARS, however, voiced a more positive opinion in October 2004:

Although the Turkish Prime Minister Recep Tayyip Erdogan is leading a conservative pro-Islamic party, he is trying to keep the distinction between religion and politics in order to lead Turkey into the EU. There are many other strong conservative and fanatic forces within Turkey's borders that want to turn this political course into a different direction. ... We from the Assyrian Federation praise the work of the government and admit that the Erdogan administration actually has achieved major progress through many changes. Currently, not all criteria have been met yet but the government is on the right track. ... We are worried what might happen to the Assyrians and other minorities if Brussels doesn't take a positive decision in December.[83]

A year later, he retreated from this positive stand because progress in Turkey fell short of its pledge as Boğaziçi University had been forced to cancel a conference on the 1915 genocide and reports appeared about new cases of confiscation of Assyrian property and attacks against Assyrian visitors.[84] The court case against the Mor Gabriel Monastery near Midyat in 2009–10 and the recognition of the genocide of the Christian population of the Ottoman Empire by the Swedish parliament in March 2010 have since created renewed tension. But in contrast to earlier periods, Assyrian organisations have been able to maintain formal contacts with the Turkish government and Kaya Türkmen, the Turkish ambassador to Sweden, visited the ARS for informal talks as late as 24 March 2016.[85]

Much empiric research remains to be carried out before definite conclusions can be made but it seems that the many successes of the Assyrians in the Swedish diaspora have still not allowed them to overcome the emotional barrier described in the earlier parts of this chapter. This was nicely illustrated in a number of recent articles written by Nisha Besara, a well-known social democrat and earlier chief editor of the social democratic web journal *Dagens Arena*. Besara is the current CEO of the *Unga Klara* theatre in Stockholm and was one of the candidates for the position of Minister of Culture in the Löfven administration.[86] She is married to an ethnic Swede.[87] In one of her articles published in *Expressen*, one of the country's major tabloids, in June 2015, she describes how she is seen as a stranger in her own country and summarised her narrative as follows: 'You can decide what you want to be in Sweden – but at the same time, the environment pins you down to your name and the colour of your hair'.[88]

Conclusion

The Assyrian diaspora has attracted public and scholarly interest for its remarkable successes – and more recently even for its failures. It has produced well-known politicians, entrepreneurs and football stars but also a substantial number of frustrated youth entering gang criminality and what has been described as Sweden's first fully-fledged mafia structure. This chapter has argued that Esser's four dimensions of integration can help us to understand the reason behind this ambivalence. In comparison to other ethnic groups, Assyrians have succeeded well in terms of acculturation and placement, allowing them to achieve remarkable goals. At the same time, they have shared the struggle of other groups in integrating into Swedish society on a daily basis and in terms of emotional identification, leaving some of them outside of the success path paved early on by the first generation of immigrants.

Appendix 1: Members of the Swedish parliament with Assyrian background

Edip Noyan (m), 2011–2013
Metin Ataseven (m), 2010–2014
Ibrahim Baylan (s), 2004–present
Yilmaz Kerimo (s), 1998–present
Roger Haddad (fp/l), 2010–present
Robert Halef (kd), 2010–present
Robert Hanna (fp/l), 2014–present
Emanuel Öz (s), 2014–present

Notes

1. The Tur Abdin ('mountain of the servants (of God)') area consists of the eastern part of Mardin province and part of Şırnak province west of the Tigris river, bordered by the Karaca Dağ in the west, Hasankeyf in the north and the Syrian border in the south.

2. See, for example, Naures Atto, *Hostages in the homeland, orphans in the diaspora: identity discourses among the Assyrian/Syriac elites in the European diaspora*, Leiden University Press, (Amsterdam, 2011); Anders Ackfeldt and Dan-Erik Andersson, *Assyrier och Syrianer i Sverige: en forskningsöversikt med bibliografi*, Center for Middle Eastern Studies, Lund University, (Lund, 2012); Svante Lundgren, *Hundra år av tveksamhet: osmanska folkmordet på kristna och Sveriges reaction*, Tigris Press, (Sodertalje, 2015); David Gaunt, 'Identity conflicts among Oriental Christians in Sweden', *Sens public*, 4 October 2010. http://www.sens-public.org/article767.html? lang=fr (accessed 5 February 2016); Önver A. Cetrez, *Meaning-making variations in acculturation and ritualization: a multi-generational study of Suroyo migrants in Sweden*, Acta Universitatis Upsaliensis (Uppsala, 2005); Verde Kucukkaplan and Marianne Freyne-Lindhagen, *Syrianska kvinnobilder*, Örebro University Press (Örebro, 2003); Fuat Deniz, *En minoritets odyssé: det assyriska exemplet*, Örebro University Press (Örebro, 1999).

3. See, for example, Christopher Harress, 'Syrian and Iraqi refugees are half the population of this Swedish city', *International Business Times*, 3 July 2014. http://www.ibtimes.com/syrian-iraqi-refugees-are-half-population-swedish-city-1619232 and Richard Milne, 'Sweden immigration: don't look back', *Financial Times*, 5 October 2015. http://www.ft.com/intl/cms/s/0/a8573532-65bf-11e5-97e9-7f0bf5e7177b.html#slide0 (both accessed 16 February 2016).

So far, very few studies have been published on the matter. For ongoing research on the topic, see Önver A. Cetrez and Valerie de Marinis, 'Gilgamesh: Mental health, meaning-seeking, and adaptation in the acculturation process among Iraqi immigrants in Sweden', Presentation at the International Association for the Psychology of Religion. University of Lausanne, 27–30 August 2013. The presentation is part of a large ongoing project funded by the Swedish Research Council entitled 'Mental health and religio-cultural resources and problems in the acculturation process among Iraqi refugees in Södertälje and Uppsala'.

4. Robert Erickson, *Det assyrisk-syrianska fotbollsundret*, GML (Stockholm, 2010).

5. Afram Barryakoub, 'Valet-06: Rekordmånga assyrier kandiderar i valet', *Hujådå*, 8 September 2006. http://www.hujada.com/old/gallery/nyheter/assyrierivalet.pdf (accessed 4 February 2016).

6. Peter Vinthagen Simpson, 'Sweden to recognize Armenian genocide', *The Local*, 11 March 2010. http://www.thelocal.se/20100311/25468 (accessed 5 February 2016). For the reaction of the local (ethnic) Turkish community, see Bahar Başer, 'Swedish parliament's recognition of the "Genocide Resolution" and its impact on the Turkish community in Sweden', *Diaspora Studies* 3/2 (2010), pp. 187–206.

7. Oscar Pripp, *Företagande i minoritet: om etnicitet, strategier och resurser bland assyrier och syrianer i Södertälje*, Mångkulturellt centrum (Tumba, 2001). For the broader context, see Nima Sanandaji, *Att skapa egna möjligheter: hur bättre villkor för företagare kan lyfta integrationen*, Fores (Stockholm, 2015) and Anders Johnson, *Invandrarna som byggde Sverige*, 2nd edn, Centrum för näringslivshistoria (Bromma, 2015).

8. Amir Rostami and Carina Gunnarson, 'Organized Crime in Sweden: an analysis of "the Syriac mafia" in the city of Södertälje', Unpublished paper presented at the Old and New Forms of Organised and Serious Crime between the Local and the Global Conference in Naples, 11–12 December 2015. https://ecprsgoc. files.wordpress.com/2015/12/gunnarson-and-rostami-the-syriac-mafia.pdf (accessed 3 February 2016).

9. Torbjörn Granström, 'Vi jobbar oss uppåt i pyramiden', *Länstidningen Södertälje*, 5 July 2014. http://lt.se/nyheter/sodertalje/1.2550990--vi-jobbar-oss-uppat-i-pyramiden- (accessed 23 February 2016).

10. Torbjörn Granström, 'Snart åtal i kyrkohärvan', *Länstidningen Södertälje*, 19 October July 2015. http://lt.se/nyheter/sodertalje/1.3208995-snart-atal-i-kyrkoharvan (accessed 25 February 2016).

11. In contrast to the Armenians and other minorities, they are hardly mentioned at all in standard references like Jan-Erik Zürcher, *Turkey: A Modern History*, 3rd edn, I.B.Tauris (London, New York, 2004) or Feroz Ahmad, *The Making of Modern Turkey*, Routledge (London, 1993) and neither are they dealt with properly in leading specialist journals such as *Turkish Studies* or *European Journal of Turkish Studies*.

12. Hartmut Esser, *Integration und ethnische Schichtung*, Mannheimer Zentrum für europäische Sozialforschung (Mannheim, 2001), pp. 8–16.

13. The most extensive works remain Cetrez, *Meaning-making variations*, and Deniz, *En minoritets odyssé*.

14. Paulina de los Reyes, Irene Molina & Diana Mulinari (eds), *Maktens (o)lika förklädnader: kön, klass & etnicitet i det postkoloniala Sverige*, Atlas (Stockholm, 2012); Susanne Alm, Olof Bäckman, Anna Gavanas and Anders Nilsson (eds), *Utanförskap*, Dialogos (Stockholm, 2011); Lena Magnusson Turner (ed.), *Den delade staden*, Borea (Umeå, 2008); Allan Pred, *Even in Sweden: racisms, racialized spaces, and the popular geographical imagination*, University of California Press (Berkeley and Los Angeles, 2000). Experts have studied the phenomenon continously since the 1970s, see for example Irene Molina, *Stadens rasifiering. Etnisk boendesegregation i folkhemmet*, Acta Universitatis Upsaliensis, (Uppsala, 1997); Anna-Lisa Lindén and Göran Lindberg, 'Immigrant housing patterns in Sweden', in Elizabeth D. Huttman (ed.), *Urban housing segregation of minorities in Western Europe and the United States*, Duke University Press (Durham, 1991), pp. 92–115; Göran Arnman & Ingrid Jönsson, *Segregation och svensk skola: en studie av utbildning, klass och boende*, Arkiv (Lund, Sweden, 1983); On the consequences of segregation for the Swedish education system, see Ove Sernhede and Ingegerd Tallberg Broman (eds), *Segregation, utbildning och ovanliga lärprocesser*, Liber (Stockholm, 2014).

15. Deniz, *En minoritets odyssé*, p. 235. See also Editorial, 'Emigrationen till Sverige', *Hujådå* 1/3 (1978), pp. 1–2.

16. Stefan Andersson, *Assyrierna. En bok om präster och lekmän, om politik och diplomati kring den assyriska invandringen till Sverige*, Tiden (Stockholm, 1983), p. 7.

17. Anders Q. Björkman, 'De var alla kristna och skulle därför dö', *Svenska Dagbladet*, 10 April 2015. http://www.svd.se/de-var-alla-kristna-och-skulle-darfor-do (accessed 27 March 2016).

18. The organisation was founded as *Assyriska föreningarnas riksförbund i Sverige*, AFRS. It met resistance from conservative circles who founded a Syriac counter organisation in 1978.

19. See the website of ARS at http://www.assyriskariksforbundet.se/#!
om/cee5 (accessed 5 March 2016).

20. After 31 years and a total of 368 issues, the printed magazine was replaced by an online journal. In 2015, ARS relaunched *Hujådå* as a quarterly journal in print.

21. Editorial, 'Hujådå.', *Hujådå* 1/1 (1978), p. 1.

22. Yuhanon Qashisho, 'Vi är assyrier historiskt, geografiskt, språkligt och kulturellt', *Hujådå* 1/1 (1978), p. 1.

23. Ibid., p. 2.

24. For a detailed account of Assyrian political claims, see Raid Gharib, *Priester, Paläste und Politik: zur Entstehung und Entwicklung des Nationalbewusstseins bei den syrischen Christen seit dem 19. Jahrhundert bis in die Gegenwart* Verlag Dr. Kovač (Hamburg, 2012), pp. 150–69.

25. Much has recently been published on the matter, see for example Augin Kurt Haninke, *Patriark Shakers arvtagare*, Tigris Press (Södertälje, 2015) and Jan Beṯ-Ṣawoce, *Den assyro-kaldeiska aktionen I–III*, Nsibin (Södertälje, 2011–15).

26. Racho Donef, *Massacres and deportation of Assyrians in Northern Mesopotamia: ethnic cleansing by Turkey 1924–25*, Nsibin (Stockholm, 2009).

27. See Sargon Donabed and Shamiran Mako, 'Ethno-Cultural and Religious Identity of Syrian Orthodox Christians', *Chronos* 19 (2009), pp. 71–113 and Aryo Makko, 'The Historical Roots of Contemporary Controversies: National Revival and the Assyrian "Concept of Unity"', *Journal of Assyrian Academic Studies* 24/1 (2010), pp. 59–86.

28. Atto, *Hostages in the homeland*, pp. 8–20.

29. Anonymous, 'Vem är jag?', *Hujådå* 1/2 (1978), p. 3.

30. Editorial, 'Södertälje kommun's temadagar', *Hujådå* 1/7 (1978), p. 3.

31. Editorial, 'Assyriska klosterskolor stängs', *Hujådå* 1/7 (1978), p. 3.

32. Editorial, 'Ecevit gömde sanningen om minoriteterna i Turkiet', *Hujådå* ii/x (1979), p. 2.

33. Sinan Ciddi, *Kemalism in Turkish Politics: The Republican People's Party, Secularism and Nationalism*, Routledge (London, 2009), pp. 47–65.

34. Unga Örnar Södertälje, 'Intryck från Syrien och Turkiet', *Hujådå* ii/17 (1979), p. 1; *Hujådå* 2/18 (1979), p. 3; *Hujådå* 2/19 (1979), p. 3 and *Hujådå* 2/20 (1979), p. 2.

35. Editorial, 'Asyl åt politiska flyktingar', *Hujådå* 1/5 (1978), p. 4.

36. Editorial, 'Arbetarnas dag fyller 100 år', *Hujådå* 9/9 (1986), p. 3.

37. Editorial, 'Assyriska folkets samhörighetskänsla', *Hujådå* 1/4 (1978), p. 1.

38. Editorial, 'Förpassade assyrier misshandlas', *Hujådå* 1/8 (1978), p. 2.

39. Editorial, 'Respektera landets lagar', *Hujådå* 3/11 (1980), p. 1; Aziz Tezel, 'Våra skyldigheter mot samhället och kommande generationer', *Hujådå* 3/11 (1980), p. 2 and Editorial, 'Hetspropaganda mot invandrare', *Hujådå* 4/1 (1981), pp. 1–2.

40. Editorial, 'Skamligt gjort', *Hujådå* 3/11 (1980), p. 3.

41. Diskrimineringsutredningen, *Invandrarna i svenskarnas ögon: egna föreställningar och andras eller opinionen som syntes* (Stockholm: Liber/Allmänna förl., 1982) cited in 'Invandrare i svenskarnas ögon. Egna föreställningar och andras eller opinionen som syntes', *Hujådå* 5/50 (1982), pp. 8–9.

42. See for example Editorial, 'Erkänn assyrierna som politiska flyktingar', *Hujådå* 1/7 (1978), pp. 1–2.

43. Allan Björck, 'Assyriefrågan', *Hujådå* i/6 (1978), pp. 2–3.

44. Per Gahrton, 'Turkiet – ett krisdrabbat land', *Hujådå* iii/21 (1980), pp. 2–3.

45. Editorial, 'I samhällets utveckling', *Hujådå* iv/37(1981), pp. 1–2.

46. Sveriges Riksdag, 'Regeringens proposition om riktlinjer för invandrar- och minoritetspolitiken m. m. (1975:26)', 1975, 1975:26 http://www.riksdagen.se/sv/Dokument-Lagar/Forslag/Propositioner-och-skrivelser/Regeringens-proposition-om-rik_ FY0326/?text=true (accessed 5 March 2016).

47. Besim Soysal, 'Invandrarnas bostadssituation', *Hujådå* 2/18 (1979), p. 3.

48. Gunilla Roxström, 'Assyrierna i Sverige – har dom någon framtid?', *Hujådå* i/8(1978), p. 3.

49. Editorial, 'Södertälje kommun's temadagar', *Hujådå* 1/7 (1978), p. 3.

50. See, for example, Augin Kurt, 'Offer för kulturkollision', *Hujådå* 4/43 (1981), p. 2 and 'Familjen Kavakcioglu. I början fick vi bra behandling i Sverige!', *Hujådå* v/45 (1982), pp. 6, 7 and 9.

51. See, for example, Augin Kurt, 'Hemspråksundervisningen symbolisk', *Hujådå* v/50 (1982), pp. 4, 5 and 11; Aziz Bozkurt, 'Sommarlägret och dess betydelse', *Hujådå* 5/55 (1982), p. 7; Anonymous, 'Varför går jag till Assyriska föreningen', *Hujådå* 6/6 (1983), p. 10 and Stefan Andersson, 'Invandrarverkets chef besökte Syrien: "Kyrkan är inte demokratisk"', *Länstidningen Södertälje*, 9 June 1982.

52. See 'mål' in Yilmaz Duzgunoglu, 'Ungdomsverksamheten blomstrar återigen', *Hujådå* 9/93 (1986), p. 10.

53. SIV, 'SIV informerar: tips om olika bidragsregler', *Hujådå* 5/45 (1982), pp. 8 and 11.

54. See *Hujådå* 9/95 (1986).

55. Editorial, 'Missbruket och dess följder', *Hujådå* 10/105 (1987), p. 4.

56. Ibid. See also Yilmaz Dusgunoglu, 'Kamp mot alkohol- och narkotikamissbruket', *Hujådå* 10/105 (1987), pp. 8–9.

57. Fuat Deniz, 'Vart är vi på väg', *Hujådå* x/105 (1987), pp. 10–12.
58. Ibid, pp. 10–11.
59. Belgin Barkarmo, 'Utlänningar sämre än djur', *Hujådå* 14/157–8 (1991), p. 17.
60. See, for example, Zeki Onuk, 'Vart är vi på väg', *Hujådå* xii/127 (1988), pp. 8–9 and *Hujådå* xii/128 (1989), pp. 10–12; Sadik Duzgun, 'Assyrierna i Turkiet förtrycks politiskt och religiöst', *Hujådå* 12/134–5 (1989), p. 15.
61. ADO, ARS and ZAVD, 'Stoppa det tilltagande våldet mot assyrierna i sydöstra Turkiet', *Hujådå* 13/145 (1990), p. 7.
62. Maravgi Ciftcioglu, 'Ytterligare en assyrisk familj mördad i sydöstra Turkiet', *Hujådå* 13/146–7 (1990), p. 7.
63. See for example Sonya Duzgun, 'Veckoslutskurs i Bockaberga', *Hujådå* 19/211 (1996), p. 16.
64. Editorial, 'Ett nationellt förräderi att bagatellisera kulturens roll', *Hujådå* 19/222 (1996), p. 3.
65. See for example Viktoria Soma, '..om ett äktenskap i kris', *Hujådå* 21/241–2 (1998), pp. 30–31 and Gabriella Barhanna, 'Falsk oskuld', *Hujådå* 21/246 (1998), p. 21.
66. See for example Konstantin Sabo, 'Baksis uttalande i tv-programmet Debatt upprör assyrier', *Hujådå* 24/274 (2001), p. 9.
67. Demir Aho, 'Maria Dikmen – första kvinnliga ordförande', *Hujådå* 20/228 (1997), pp. 10–11 and Augin Kurt, 'Första kvinnan som ARS-ordförande', *Hujådå* xxiv/273 (2001), pp. 6–7.
68. Demir Aho, 'Sait Yildiz vald till ny ordförande i SIOS', *Hujådå* 29/219 (1996), p. 7 and 'Grattis till hedersuppdraget, Orhan', *Hujådå* 29/219 (1996), p. 15.
69. Kerimo appeared on the cover of *Hujådå* along with the title 'The first Assyrian in the Swedish parliament', *Hujådå* 21/243 (1998).
70. Andreas Arsalan, 'Assyriska FF:s framgång det assyriska folkets framgång', *Hujådå* xxii/257 (1999), p. 3.
71. Patrick Lundström, 'Vi ska slå rötter i Sverige, friska rötter', *Hujådå* 22/255(1999), pp. 11–12.
72. Ibid.
73. Zeki Yalcin, 'Orientalisk eller västerländsk nationalism?', *Hujådå* 22/257 (2000), pp. 11–12.
74. Zeki Yalcin, 'Fel att anamma västerländsk modell för ett orientaliskt folk', *Hujådå* 23/259–60 (2000), pp. 6–7.
75. Most of these independent platforms have been forced to give way to larger social media networks like Facebook or the (online) TV Channels owned or initiated by federations and political parties in recent years.
76. Editorial, 'Förändringens vind tilltar', *Hujådå* 26/297 (2003), p. 3.

77. Editorial, 'Intensiv debatt om historieläraren i Södertälje', *Hujådå* 23/262 (2000), p. 15 and Abraham Staifo, 'Turkiet in i EU?', *Hujådå* 23/258 (2000), p. 6.
78. Se the various articles, press releases and statements of members of parliaments published in *Hujådå* xxiii/269 (2000), pp. 9–12.
79. See, among others, Simon Barmano, 'Stort internationellt stöd för fader Yusuf', *Hujådå* 24/271 (2001), pp. 6–8 and 'Fader Akbuluts andra rättegång drog till sig ännu större utländsk uppmärksamhet', *Hujådå* 24/273 (2001), pp. 8–10; Afamia Maraha, 'Fader Yusuf Akbulut är äntligen frikänd', *Hujådå* 24/274 (2001), pp. 10–11.
80. See for example Augin Kurt, 'Hoppet har återvänt till Turabdin', *Hujådå* 24/280 (2001), pp. 9–12.
81. See for example Sadik Düzgün, 'Är Turabdin en trygg plats?', *Hujådå* 28/326 (2005), pp. 4–5.
82. Dikran Ego, 'En militärdiktatur platsar inte i ett demokratiskt EU', *Hujådå* 27/309 (2004), pp. 6–7.
83. Simon Barmano, 'Turkiets EU fråga avgörs i december', *Hujådå* 27/314 (2004), p. 3.
84. Simon Barmano, 'Är Turkiet ett tryggt land för återvändande assyrier?', *Hujådå* 27/326 (2005), p. 3.
85. 'Turkish ambassador visits Assyrian federation of Sweden', *Assyria TV*, 25 March 2016. http://www.assyriatv.org/2016/03/turkish-ambassador-visits-assyrian-federation-of-sweden/ (accessed 29 March 2016).
86. Hedvig Weibull, 'En av dem kan bli kulturminister', *Sveriges Television*, 2 October 2014. http://www.svt.se/kultur/de-kan-bli-kulturministrar-i-morgon (accessed 15 March 2016).
87. 'Om Nisha Besara', *diverse*. https://divblog.wordpress.com/om-nisha-besara/ (accessed 21 March 2016).
88. Nisha Besara, 'Varför ses jag som en främling i Sverige?', *Sveriges Television*, 25 June 2015. http://www.expressen.se/kultur/varfor-vill-inte-mitt-sverige-slappa-in-mig/. See also Besara's chapter in Lejla Hastor & Nivin Yosef (eds), *Sverige: en (o)besvarad kärlekshistoria*, Wahlström&Widstrand (Stockholm, 2016).

References

Ackfeldt, A. and Dan-Erik A., *Assyrier och Syrianer i Sverige: en forskningsöversikt med bibliografi*, Center for Middle Eastern Studies (Lund, 2012).
Ahmad, F., *The Making of Modern Turkey*, Routeledge (London, 1993).
Alm, S., Bäckman, O., Gavanas, A., and Nilsson, A., (eds), *Utanförskap* (Stockholm, 2011).

Andersson, S., *Assyrierna. En bok om präster och lekmän, om politik och diplomati kring den assyriska invandringen till Sverige* (Stockholm, 1983).

———, 'Invandrarverkets chef besökte Syrien: "Kyrkan är inte demokratisk"', *Länstidningen Södertälje*, 9 June 1982.

Arnman, G., and Ingrid J., *Segregation och svensk skola: en studie av utbildning, klass och boende* (Lund, 1983).

Atto, N., *Hostages in the homeland, orphans in the diaspora: identity discourses among the Assyrian/Syriac elites in the European diaspora* (Amsterdam, 2011).

Barryakoub, A., 'Valet-06: Rekordmånga assyrier kandiderar i valet', *Hujådå*, 8 September 2006.

Başer, B., 'Swedish parliament's recognition of the "Genocide Resolution" and its impact on the Turkish community in Sweden', *Diaspora Studies* 3/2 (2010), pp. 187–206.

Besara, N., 'Varför ses jag som en främling i Sverige?', *Sveriges Television*, 25 June 2015.

Beṯ-Şawoce, Jan, *Den assyro-kaldeiska aktionen I* (Södertälje, 2011).

———, *Den assyro-kaldeiska aktionen II* (Södertälje, 2012).

———, *Den assyro-kaldeiska aktionen III* (Södertälje, 2015).

Björkman, A.Q., 'De var alla kristna och skulle därför dö', *Svenska Dagbladet*, 10 April 2015.

Cetrez, Ö.A., *Meaning-making variations in acculturation and ritualization: a multi-generational study of Suroyo migrants in Sweden*, Uppsala University Press (Uppsala, 2005).

Ciddi, S., *Kemalism in Turkish Politics: The Republican People's Party, Secularism and Nationalism*, Routledge (London, 2009).

De los Reyes, P., Irene, M., and Mulinari, D., (eds), *Maktens (o)lika förklädnader: kön, klass & etnicitet i det postkoloniala Sverige*, Atlas (Stockholm, 2012).

Deniz, F., *En minoritets odyssé: det assyriska exemplet*, Örebro University Press (Örebro, 1999).

Donabed, S., and Mako, S., 'Ethno-Cultural and Religious Identity of Syrian Orthodox Christians', *Chronos* 19 (2009), pp. 71–113.

Donef, R., *Massacres and deportation of Assyrians in Northern Mesopotamia: ethnic cleansing by Turkey 1924–25*, Nsibin (Stockholm, 2009).

Erickson, R., *Det assyrisk-syrianska fotbollsundret*, GML (Stockholm, 2010).

Esser, H., *Integration und ethnische Schichtung*, Mannheimer Zentrum für europäische Sozialforschung (Mannheim, 2001).

Gaunt, D., 'Identity conflicts among Oriental Christians in Sweden', *Sens public*, 4 October 2010.

Gharib, R., *Priester, Paläste und Politik: zur Entstehung und Entwicklung des Nationalbewusstseins bei den syrischen Christen seit dem 19. Jahrhundert bis in die Gegenwart*, Verlag Dr. Kovač, (Hamburg, 2012).

Granström, T., 'Vi jobbar oss uppåt i pyramiden', *Länstidningen Södertälje*, 5 July 2014.

———, 'Snart åtal i kyrkohärvan', *Länstidningen Södertälje*, 19 October July 2015.

Harress, C.S., 'Syrian and Iraqi refugees are half the population of this Swedish city', *International Business Times*, 3 July 2014.

Hastor, L. and Yosef, N., (eds), *Sverige: en (o)besvarad kärlekshistoria*, Wahlstrom&Widstrand (Stockholm, 2016).

Hujådå magazine

Johnson, A., *Invandrarna som byggde Sverige*, 2nd edn, Centrum för näringslivshistoria (Bromma, 2015).

Kucukkaplan, V., and Freyne-Lindhagen, M. *Syrianska kvinnobilder*, Orebro University Press (Örebro, 2003).

Lindén, A.L., and Lindberg, G. 'Immigrant housing patterns in Sweden', in Elizabeth D. Huttman (ed.), *Urban housing segregation of minorities in Western Europe and the United States*, Duke University Press (Durham, 1991), pp. 92–115.

Lundgren, S., *Hundra år av tveksamhet: osmanska folkmordet på kristna och Sveriges reaktion*, Tigris Press (Södertälje, 2015).

Magnusson Turner, L. (ed.), *Den delade staden*, Borea (Umeå, 2008).

Makko, A., 'The Historical Roots of Contemporary Controversies: National Revival and the Assyrian "Concept of Unity"', *Journal of Assyrian Academic Studies* 24/1 (2010), pp. 59–86.

Milne, R., 'Sweden immigration: don't look back', *Financial Times*, 5 October 2015.

Molina, I., *Stadens rasifiering. Etnisk boendesegregation i folkhemmet*, Uppsala University Press (Uppsala, 1997).

Pred, A., *Even in Sweden: racisms, racialized spaces, and the popular geographical imagination*, University of California Press (Berkeley and Los Angeles, 2000).

Pripp, O., *Företagande i minoritet: om etnicitet, strategier och resurser bland assyrier och syrianer i Södertälje*, Mångkulturellt centrum (Tumba, 2001).

Rostami, A. and Gunnarson, C., 'Organized Crime in Sweden: an analysis of "the Syriac mafia" in the city of Södertälje', Unpublished paper presented at the Old and New Forms of Organised and Serious Crime between the Local and the Global Conference in Naples, 11–12 December 2015.

Sanandaji, N., *Att skapa egna möjligheter: hur bättre villkor för företagare kan lyfta integrationen*, Fores (Stockholm, 2015).

Sernhede, O., and Tallberg Broman, I., (eds), *Segregation, utbildning och ovanliga lärprocesser*, Liber (Stockholm, 2014).

Simpson, P. Vinthagen, 'Sweden to recognize Armenian genocide', *The Local*, 11 March 2010.

Weibull, H., 'En av dem kan bli kulturminister', *Sveriges Television*, 2 October 2014.

Zürcher, J.E., *Turkey: A Modern History*, 3rd edn, I.B.Tauris (London, New York, 2004).

INDEX

www.ingramcontent.com/pod-product-compliance
Lightning Source LLC
Chambersburg PA
CBHW060146280326
41932CB00012B/1658